THE COMPLETE
BACKYARD PLANNER

L. DONALD MEYERS

CHARLES SCRIBNER'S SONS · NEW YORK

Copyright © L. Donald Meyers 1985

Library of Congress Cataloging in Publication Data

Meyers, L. Donald, 1929–
    The complete backyard planner.

    Includes index.
    1. Dwelling–Maintenance and repair. 2. Garden
structures–Design and construction. 3. Grounds
maintenance. I. Title.
TH4817.M49   1984   643'.55   84–14147
ISBN 0–684–18117–7

1 3 5 7 9 11 13 15 17 19   H/C   20 18 16 14 12 10 8 6 4 2

Printed in the United States of America.

THE COMPLETE BACKYARD PLANNER

Contents

THE COMPLETE BACKYARD PLANNER

A pleasant setting for your home shows it off to best advantage.

Drawing Up a Plan 1

Over the years I've observed an interesting fact about homeowners. Although they put a great deal of effort into making the insides of their homes as personal and individual as they can, they often do their best to make the outsides look just like every other house on the block. There is nothing intrinsically wrong with this, of course—if that's what you want. But do you *really* want a huge expanse of lawn that takes half the weekend to mow? Before you load up with grass seed and fertilizer, it's a good idea to ask yourself if you are ready to become an entry in the Kentucky bluegrass derby. Surely, you want some lawn. But lawn and only lawn? What purpose will it serve?

And now we get to the real question: What *is* the purpose of all that open area around your home? Obviously, you wanted the land for a reason, or you wouldn't have considered buying a home set in a lot or open area.

Your reasons for buying a home may have been the basic ones— a little space, fresh air, and greenery. But now that you actually own the home, it's time to make both the inside and outside reflect your own family's individual tastes and needs, giving the outside as much thought as you gave the inside. The aim of this book is to help you carefully plan how you want to use and enjoy your grounds and show you how to realize your plan. After all, your home is probably your major asset, and its setting should do everything it can to set it off and give you the greatest use and pleasure indoors and outdoors.

ESTABLISH A GOAL

If possible, you should establish goals for your home long before you buy it. If you want a view, for example, look for a home in a scenic area. If you want a big backyard for entertaining, look for a spacious lot.

There will, of course, always be compromises when you're buying a home. Most of us can't afford the house of our dreams, so we do the best we can with the money we have. The most important point is to think about your goals in buying a house, pondering them carefully. A family discussion is a good way to establish your goals, for each member of the family may have different, and sometimes conflicting, ideas.

The family should discuss tastes, habits, and activities. Is privacy important? Do you entertain a lot and therefore want room for an outdoor barbecue? Do you love trees, flowers, shrubs? What sports do you like? Do you want a pool someday? If so, what kind, and should you reserve space for it? Is your version of suburban bliss relaxing in the shade in a lounge chair with a bottle of beer and soft music? And yes, maybe you even want nothing other than the huge expanse of lawn you don't mind mowing.

This family discussion should be a real brainstorming session. At this point, ignore such limitations as finances, geography, and the existing landscape. There will be conflicts, but don't worry about them either. They can be resolved later. The idea is to list all of the things that everyone would *like* to have in the backyard (and front yard).

Air your dislikes, too. If anyone doesn't like grass cutting, leaf raking, thorns, bugs, dirt, or concrete, this is the time to say so. Physical condition should be discussed, too. Most outdoor work involves digging, bending, lifting, and other hard physical effort. A bad back or a weak heart should be taken into consideration right from the start.

Whether pertinent, crazy, or impossible, the family likes and dislikes should be listed. When they are all written down, there will be some immediate weeding out. If finances rule out a built-in pool, either now or in the future, cross it out (but consider aboveground pools). If one of the kids wants a shooting gallery in the yard and the laws forbid it, cross that out too. For now, leave in questionable items such as a basketball court on a sloping lot. You *might* be able to level some land, even though it's unlikely you'll want to bother.

CONSIDER THE LIMITATIONS

So far, your list may be more fantasy than reality. Sooner or later, common sense must be reckoned with, and it may as well be sooner. Much as you might want a cactus garden, geography limits them to a small part of the southwestern United States. By the same geographic logic, lush, rolling lawns are almost impossible in the arid regions where the cacti flourish.

Like geography, climate plays an important part in realistic planning. At first, they may seem the same, but they aren't. For example, the states of Washington, Minnesota, and Maine are at approximately the same latitude. The climates are quite different, however, with Washington having relatively warm, rainy winters, and Minnesota having frigid, snowy winters. Maine is somewhere in between. Even within states, climates can differ radically. The Cascades of Washington are much colder year-round than the coastal areas around Seattle. Long Island, New York, is considerably warmer and has less snow than Buffalo or Watertown in the same state.

Geography and climate make a crucial difference in the types of trees, shrubs, and other vegetation that can be grown successfully. Certain types of flora are more winter-hardy than others. Annual rainfall is a decisive factor for other plants. Some plants need more sunshine than others. Others do not like "wet feet" (although soil type may be the most important factor in controlling that problem).

Sometimes the water table plays an important role. In the coastal areas of the Carolinas, for example, it is virtually impossible to build a home with a basement or to plan any outdoor project that involves digging deep into the soil. The land is so low and the water table so high that anything dug too deep will soon fill with groundwater.

Another limitation closely allied with geography and climate is the soil itself. Certain parts of the country tend to have certain types of soil, in part because of geography and climate, and in part because of history and geology. Some areas have limestone soil, deposited thousands of years ago. The soil there will be "sweet," or alkaline. In areas that were on the leading edge of the glaciers, the soil will be sandy and "sour," or acid.

So your soil may be nice and rich or sandy; rocky or clayey; acid or alkaline or perhaps right in the middle (neutral). Since your choice of plantings and outdoor facilities may depend heavily on the condition and pH (acidity or alkalinity) of your soil, your county or state agricultural agent should be consulted. Most agencies provide free soil analysis. Also look at the test borings on your plot survey. They will give you a good idea how much topsoil is on the property and other valuable information, such as how far down you can go before you hit bedrock. (A neighbor of mine once contracted for a built-in pool without checking his soil. The contractor hit bedrock 2 feet down and charged him several thousand extra dollars for blasting out the rock.) If you don't have test borings already, have them done, or do some exploratory digging on your own.

THE PLOT

No matter what the general topography or geographic conditions of your region as a whole are, your plot is another matter entirely. The region can be flat, while your particular piece of property is on an isolated hill. There can be variations, even on your own land. The house can be built on an elevation while the backyard receives the runoff from the rest of the block and is a virtual marsh.

Natural features can be assets as well as liabilities. A sloping bank, which can mean difficulties for grass growing and mowing, can be turned into an attractive terraced planting. An outcropping of rock is easily transformed into a rock garden centerpiece. That depressed marshy area can be lined to make a garden pool for water plants.

Obviously the size of the lot is an influential factor. When you have a small section of a city acre, the choices are extremely narrow. You can have a rose garden *or* a patio—rarely both. And there may be little room for a kiddie pool, much less a larger one. Zoning restrictions also should be studied carefully before considering decks, patios, pools, or other outdoor structures. Many towns have a 10-foot setback ordinance, which means that you cannot build on the first 10 feet inside the property line. You may have a 2-acre plot, but if the house is built into a corner of the lot, any addition may extend into the forbidden 10-foot area next to your property line.

Orientation of your home is another important factor to consider. The relation of your house to the sun is vital to many outdoor additions, such as a deck or patio. The sun travels in one pattern in the summer and another in the winter. Plot the sun's location at various times of the year and different times of the day, and make your own chart as shown.

Wind direction should play a part in outdoor planning, too. In most of the United States and Canada, the prevailing winds are from

A garden pool transforms this corner of the backyard into a pleasant sight.

Clever planning, including an attractive privacy fence, makes the most of every square inch of this small plot.

the west. But these wind patterns can vary, and the colder winds of winter are usually from the northwest, while warmer winds, in all seasons, may be from the southwest. Coastal areas or mountainous regions may have different wind patterns because of local geography. If weather conditions are unfamiliar to you, check with the local weather service for assistance.

Plantings can modify wind and other weather effects in both summer and winter. Properly placed shade trees can reduce the summer temperature of a frame house in an arid climate by as much as 20 degrees. Evergreen trees and shrubs are highly effective as wind screens in cold weather and help cut down on heat lost by infiltration.

If your landscape is already in place, take a good hard look at it. Ask the purpose of every tree and bush. Many times, a planting is just plopped in haphazardly, with little rhyme or reason and no thought about its effect on the overall design. As discussed in the following chapters, smaller plantings can be moved for better effect. Overgrown shrubs can often be cut back. Very often, foundation plantings

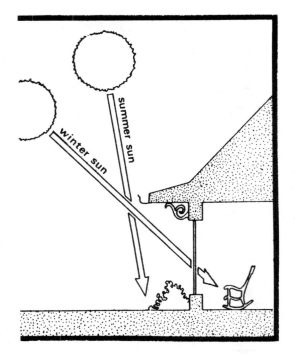

When planning, remember that at the same time of day the sun is much higher in the sky in the summer than in the winter. The overhang in this enclosed patio screens out the sun when it's hot and lets it in when the weather is cold.

start off small and grow unchecked so that they detract from, rather than enhance, the appearance of your home. Most of the time, such shrubbery will have to be pulled out and discarded. Both evergreen and deciduous trees are often planted on a whim, providing shade in the wrong places at the wrong times and poking their roots into drainage systems, walks, driveways, and even the foundations of homes. That willow tree may have looked nice when it was small, but now it may be unsightly, block out needed sun, and cover the children with aphid droppings in summer. Consider chopping it down.

The lay of the land also should be documented carefully in your ledger of limitations. You don't have to hire a surveyor, but make a map of the topography and a scale model—out of modeling clay, the

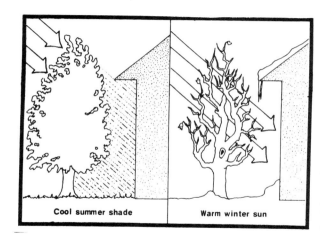

Cool summer shade   Warm winter sun

By planting deciduous trees on the sunny side of the house, you can provide cooling shade in the summer and take advantage of the sun's heat after the leaves fall.

A grove of evergreens acts as a windbreak (left) while the shrubs planted close to the house deflect the winds and help keep down heat loss due to infiltration (right).

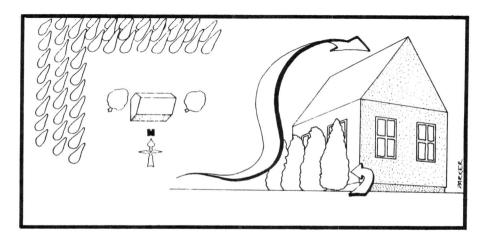

way you did in grade school. If your land is perfectly flat, you can dispense with the model. You don't have to know how high above sea level you are, but a scale model is a great help in showing just how much higher the uppermost part of your property is than the lowest. If there are a lot of contours and sloping grades, make careful note of them. These must be taken into consideration for drainage, many plantings, and any construction that may be affected by seepage, groundwater, or other natural features.

Make your drawings to scale, ¼ inch to a foot for an average plot, but smaller or bigger depending on the size of your property and the drawing. If you don't make a scale drawing, you'll find yourself guessing the area that a deck or garden will occupy in your plot, and that can get you into big trouble. You may find that the deck overwhelms —or underwhelms—the house. What you envision as a spacious tulip bed may hold only a few bulbs if you sketch it in without having made accurate measurements.

It is wise to use any natural formation in a natural way, as opposed to bringing in a bulldozer to create a perfectly level plot. A residual stream bed, a depressed marshy spot, or an outcropping of rock can be changed from a disadvantage into a break in the monotony, and can create a backyard of distinction. Instead of rooting out a clump of rocks, for example, turn them into a rock garden with succulent, alpine, or other compatible plants.

Sloping banks, denuded of topsoil, are common in many housing developments. If the grade is gentle, the soil can be restored to fertility by the use of compost, peat moss, fertilizers, and so on, and turned into a pleasant grassy area. But consider other uses, too, such as a pleasant flower or vegetable garden.

Steep banks can be troublesome. Grass is a poor solution, since the seed will be washed away with the first rain, and even if the grass survives, mowing is difficult and dangerous. Think about covering the steep slope with such evergreen shrubs as low-growing junipers or one of the numerous other groundcovers, or a combination of both. Terraces of railroad ties, stone, or brick will restore the whole area to useful vegetation, but if the bank is in the wrong place or terraces don't fit your own needs and preferences, you may have to consider the bulldozer after all. Sometimes, you can take soil away from one area and fill in another to create a more level plot.

Other structures, on both your property and neighboring plots, should be included in your topographical map. Measure and plot the sizes and locations of garages, tool sheds, play structures, and other manmade obstructions. Since your neighbors' buildings may affect your view, shade, or sun, such structures at least should be noted in your diagram. If they are close to your property line, measure and mark them carefully. Observe and mark the shade patterns of all structures in both summer and winter.

Once again, brainstorm all the possible solutions to the problems on your list of limitations. At this point, write down anything that comes into mind. You can discard the zanier answers quickly, but keep all reasonable solutions on the list for the time being. What seems like a crackpot idea may yet work out to be the best.

SORTING IT ALL OUT

Now you have a sheet of random ideas and wishes and another sheet of problems and limitations with some tentative solutions. You also should have a neatly drawn plan of your property which notes any significant grades and elevations, existing structures, and topographical characteristics.

Preliminary selection now is in order. Using a ledger sheet or similar paper with 3 or 4 columns, winnow out the more outrageous suggestions. Explain to the children that it is impossible to have palm trees in Vermont or a ski run in Florida. Leave in any ideas that are halfway reasonable, grouping them into such categories as "plantings," "structures," "exterior additions" (decks, patios, etc.), "sports areas," or whatever seems to fit.

As you write down an idea, put down any present limitation next to it in the second column, and in the column next to that, put down the ways you think might get around the problem. For example, if your son has his heart set on a basketball court and the next column lists "uneven, rocky terrain," then in the third column put "level off playing area?" Always make it a question, since your son may interpret your answer as a certainty. Leave the fourth column blank for now, or use it for other comments on the situation.

After everything has been noted and put into its proper column, obvious conflicts should be pointed out and discussed. On a tiny plot, for example, it may be possible to have a patio, a tennis court, a garden, an aboveground pool, an outdoor kitchen, *or* a garage—but certainly not all of these things. Choices must be made. Something (in this case, almost everything) must go. Inevitably, there will be some grumbling and bickering, but better now than later.

If you want a pool badly enough you'll find a way to build it. This small plot was handsomely transformed to accommodate a pool, even though most of the backyard is taken up by it.

As more choices are made, however reluctantly, the family members will inevitably focus on what they *really* want. It will also become clearer what is and is not possible under the circumstances. As various items are discussed, however, and prices and space limitations surface, it may become clear that finances and size dictate something a lot less grandiose than first envisioned. This is also the time to get some ballpark estimates and think about whether you'll do the work yourself or hire people. It may turn out that you will do both.

THE FINAL STAGES

When it's finally clear what is and is not feasible, it's time to go back to the map and model and make your final plans. Use the model to gauge the effect of grade and topography, and the map to make sample layouts. Use acetate or tissue overlays on the map to test various layouts and "floor" plans on the map, or pencil in ideas lightly until you are ready for the final version.

Now is the time to test the most favorable alternatives. If, during the selection process, you determined that a rose garden, slate patio, and outdoor kitchen with lighting are what the family most desires, try out various locations. In the beginning, you may have thought that the rose garden should be located next to the patio. After laying it out on your map, however, you may discover that there isn't room —not if you want your outdoor kitchen adjacent to the patio (and you probably do). You may also find that locating the barbecue where you wanted will result in a circuitous route for the outdoor wiring. There is no point in laying down extra wiring around the house if a more direct route is available.

Now browse through the sections of this book that cover the particular projects you have in mind. Read about outdoor wiring, for example. It's foolish to make final plans for a patio before you know where you want the wiring to go. Perhaps you can save a lot of time and money by laying the wires under the patio first, rather than going all around the patio later on. By the same token, if you are planning some new foundation plantings, read the section of Chapter 2 in which mature sizes of shrubs are discussed. Don't jam a bunch of small plants together, only to have them grow up a few years later into a tangled mass. If they look a little puny at first, so be it. Better

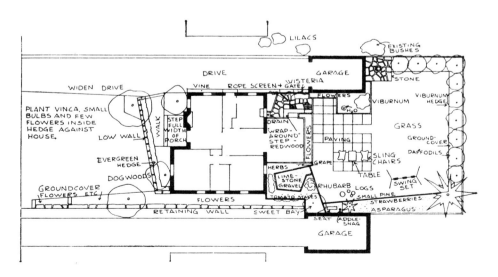

A complete outdoor design, carefully laid out, is the result of intelligent planning.

to live with small plants for awhile than have to cut all the plants down later. If you're impatient for that mature look, spend a little more money and get more mature plants.

If you have a good idea of the sizes of your additions, make cardboard cutouts to scale, and move them around to various locations on your property. Colors will also help you visualize the final result. Paint or crayon your cutouts green for a lawn or tree, for example, red for a rose garden, brown for a deck, white for a patio.

If you are adding a structure or tree—anything that will block the sun—be sure to have at least a rough approximation of the shade pattern. You don't want to erect a tool shed next to a tomato patch.

Your model will make readily apparent such things as drainage and grade. Be especially careful about grade levels when planning anything with a solid surface, like a driveway or patio. Remember that these features, especially when made of concrete, create their own little rivers during heavy rainfall. Poorly conceived patios and driveways that slope the wrong way can result in unwanted man-made lakes, basement seepage, and foundation decay. First read the chapters that discuss installation of concrete, especially the sections on drainage.

Don't expect the first "final" plan to be *really* final. You may be lucky and have everything fall into place initially, but most likely

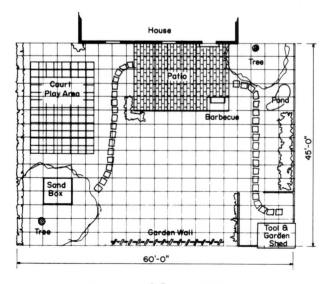

(Each square = 3'-0" on each side)

A scientific plan is based on a grid, with each square representing so many feet (here each square is three feet). Use whatever scale is most convenient for you.

there will be something you forgot to check, some problem which will crop up, or some reasonable objection from someone that calls for alterations. Do the best you can, though, to make everything final on the overlay or penciled drawing. Then go outside and carefully check to make sure there isn't something left out. You may find a boulder you forgot to put on the plan in the very spot where you intended to place a big tree. Or maybe your projected vegetable garden doesn't get as much sun as you thought it did.

Even after checking everything out in the light of day, don't rush out to hire a contractor or buy the materials. Let your final plan simmer for at least a few days, checking everything out one more time. Ask everyone in the family to take a long, last, lingering look.

There is one more task left before you can put the final stamp of approval on your plan. You must get an accurate estimate of costs. Dismaying as it may seem, that longed-for project may be a budget buster, and it's better to know before you begin work.

If the cost of one feature is prohibitive, you don't necessarily have to scrap the plan. Instead of a long line of *Taxus capitata* ("cap" yews), for example, perhaps you can do just as well with some *Juniperus hetzi* (hetzi junipers). They are cheaper and grow faster. Instead of a redwood fence, perhaps you can do with pine or spruce which has been painted or just soaked in preservative and left to weather. Instead of using a contractor, you may well decide to do some jobs yourself. But before you can make any of these decisions, you have to know how to assess the costs of your plan.

ASSESS THE COSTS

You probably have a very rough idea of the cost of any given feature in your plan; now is the time to firm up the estimates. There are two basic approaches to take—hiring a contractor, or doing the job yourself. If you don't have any interest in doing your own work and don't have the time, then you'll probably hire a contractor.

If you are interested in doing the work yourself—or doing some of it yourself—remember this generalization: The more labor-intensive a job is, the more you save by doing it yourself—and this is true all the way down the line. Take decks, for example. If you buy untreated lumber and treat and stain or paint it yourself, the total job will cost a lot less than if you buy prebuilt squares of treated and stained wood or naturally weather- and insect-repellent wood. Building a fence from scratch is a lot cheaper than purchasing 8-foot sections from a fence dealer. The same rule applies to concrete, which by its very nature is labor-intensive. When you buy the cement, stone, and sand and mix them by hand, you save considerably, compared to the cost of premix bags or of trucking concrete to the site. On the other hand, premix is economical for very small jobs, and trucked ready-mix for very large jobs. No matter what the project, you'll save money by avoiding the services of a contractor.

To get accurate up-to-date costs on the materials for a job, prepare detailed lists of everything you'll need and take them to your local building-supply house, nursery, lumberyard, or wherever you'll buy your supplies. The dealer can give you a reasonably close estimate of your costs. Contrast this figure with a contractor's estimate, and you can find out how much you'll save by doing the work yourself. Don't forget to figure in your level of available time, interest, and patience. They count, too.

If you are considering doing some projects yourself and farming some out, you can figure the differences between a contracted job and "D-I-Y" by getting costs for each stage of the work and comparing them with the costs of the materials above. Your savings is the cost of the labor.

One more point about doing the work yourself, if you're so inclined. If you haven't undertaken a great deal of D-I-Y (as seasoned do-it-yourselfers call it), you'll find that outdoor work comes as a pleasant surprise. The backyard is kind to beginners. Gardening, fence building, level concrete work, outdoor carpentry, and similar projects are easy to do by following the simple, step-by-step instructions given in this book. You won't face the complexities of D-I-Y woodworking, furniture building, and other crafts that require fine work and close tolerances. In fact, most of the work in this book requires no more than knowing how to follow instructions and drive a nail, and understanding the differences between up and down on a spirit level. By following the instructions assiduously and working slowly and meticulously, you should be able to do the jobs described here. Some projects will be more difficult, more time-consuming, and more physically arduous than others, but there are very few that cannot be completed successfully with only a rudimentary grasp of the fundamentals of do-it-yourselfing. All it takes is care, planning, and hard work.

Hard work, however, cannot be dismissed lightly. Many of the projects, except gardening, require tough physical labor. More than most D-I-Y work, concrete, brick, and block demand a strong back. Any major task using lumber can involve a great deal of heavy lugging, fastening, and digging. If you have a bad heart or a weak back, you should avoid these heavy major projects.

The list below is necessarily arbitrary because of individual differences and is open to interpretation on the basis of your own experience, but it is a good general guide to the difficulty levels of the various projects described in the following chapters:

EASY FOR EVERYONE

Most gardening
Fences on level terrain
Low walls of stone and ties
Basic outdoor kitchens

MINIMAL SKILLS REQUIRED

Some plantings (large trees, rose gardens, transplanting)
Concrete walks and patios
Brick walks and patios
Blacktop work
Low walls of stone, brick, or block
Low decks
Simple drainage systems

MODERATELY DIFFICULT

Concrete driveways
Simple outdoor wiring
High walls of stone, brick, ties, and block
Simple fireplaces
Low concrete walls
Retaining walls for terracing
Raised or multilevel decks

DIFFICULT

High concrete walls
Complex or extended wiring and water systems
Fancy fireplaces

HIRING A CONTRACTOR

Not everyone, of course, has the interest, time, strength, energy, or skills for every outdoor job. If you don't, you will want to hire an expert to do the work or at least part of the work.

Finding a contractor is easy. Just look in the Yellow Pages or your local newspaper. Insuring that the person you hire is honest, competent, and reasonably priced, however, takes some work. Ask for and check references on any contractor you're considering. Talk to friends, relatives, and neighbors. If contractors are licensed in your area, make sure that yours has a current license. Seek contractors who have been in business for a long time. They have reputations to uphold. Above all, check with local consumer agencies, better business bureaus, and similar organizations for any adverse reports.

Never simply hire the first contractor who appears on the scene. And suspect anyone who calls at your home unasked, especially if he or she promises you commissions for referrals. Suspect any "bargain" price if given for similar reasons.

Always get at least three estimates. If all other things are equal, it makes sense to choose the lowest price, but again, suspect any bid that is unnaturally low. Make sure that each contractor specifies the same quality of materials and guarantees the same amount of work for each job. That way you know you're comparing contractors on the same basis.

When you finally select a contractor, insist on a written agreement specifying the following elements:

- Exactly what work is to be done
- Exactly what materials are to be used, with reasonably accurate amounts
- A method for determining extra charges, if any
- A clause specifying that the contractor will obtain all needed permits and certificates
- A clause requiring the contractor to arrange for any needed inspections
- Insurance to be provided by the contractor as required by law, including workers' compensation and general liability
- Provisions for the contractor to haul away any debris
- Method and/or dates of payment
- Completion dates (optional, depending on size and type of job)

• Performance bond, supplied by contractor (optional, depending on size and type of job)

Method of Payment

It is never a wise idea to pay *anyone* in advance for services to be performed. It is especially unwise to pay contractors or workers in advance. Payment in advance may remove the incentive to complete the job or complete it to your satisfaction.

If the job is a small one, you will usually pay the contractor upon satisfactory completion. Larger jobs, where the contractor must lay out substantial funds for labor and materials, ordinarily require a ⅓–⅓–⅓ payment arrangement. The usual contract specifies that you pay ⅓ of the agreed price when the job is half complete, another ⅓ upon completion, and the balance when all necessary certificates are obtained. It is a good idea, if the contractor will go along with it, to withhold at least a part of the final payment until you have had the chance to live with the job for 2 or 3 months and make sure that everything is up to snuff.

If your contractor is not willing to wait that long for payment— and that's not unreasonable—he or she should instead give you a written warranty.

THE HOMEOWNER AS
CONTRACTOR AND/OR WORKMAN

Many large jobs call for the services of several different contractors. In that event, you the homeowner, or one contractor called the general contractor, will be in charge of the work and will hire other contractors to work as subcontractors.

When a large project calls for the services of masons, carpenters, and electricians, for example, you may feel confident enough to direct the job, perhaps do part of the work yourself, and call in the subcontractors at the appropriate times. Depending on how much is involved, you can save hundreds or thousands of dollars in this way.

Be sure, however, that you know what you are doing before attempting this. A subcontractor—especially one engaged in outdoor work—may do mostly seasonal jobs. He may promise to arrive at your job site on June 1, but if a contractor with whom he does a lot of business tells him he is needed elsewhere on that date, chances are he will put you off to take his business to his regular customer. And you will have to know exactly what tasks each "sub" will perform, what the sequence will be, and what is required of them. Unless you are well versed in this type of scheduling, acting as your own general contractor can be frustrating and risky.

On the other hand, you may be able to work out another arrangement with a contractor that will save as much—if not more—money, yet avoid the risks of dealing with unpredictable subcontractors. You may, for example, be willing and able to spend, a lot of time nailing deckboards to the framing but prefer to leave the planning, sawing, foundation work, and so on to a professional. Ask the contractor if he is willing to "hire" you as a worker and cut his price accordingly, if you do the time-consuming and tedious job of nailing down the deckboards. Many contractors will be skeptical, but if you persist, you may be able to work out a favorable deal. The same applies to other tasks that are less skilled but may require substantial hours of high-priced labor.

GOVERNMENT ASSISTANCE

A note about one possible source of financial assistance is in order here. The projects in this book are not the types that easily lend themselves to government assistance, but don't overlook the possibility. Perhaps a solar collector could be part of your landscape, or a swimming or garden pool could do double duty as a solar device. There are generous federal tax credits for a variety of energy-saving projects. It is also possible that some of your gardening could fall under one of the numerous farm assistance programs. You could be entitled to direct subsidies in certain instances. Fish for your pond or soil-conserving bushes, for example, are available at little or no cost in certain circumstances.

To get the lowdown on various types of assistance, consult your county agricultural agent, local planning board, government publications, or similar sources.

IF YOU ARE STARTING AFRESH

Most people consider their landscaping only after they have bought a home. Although site and location probably play a part in the original selection, the main interest is usually the house itself. Only after they start living with the site do most people begin to consider the shortcomings and difficulties of the grounds.

If you don't already own a home or a building site, though, you have a chance to look for a location that offers the best possibilities for complete indoor and outdoor living. The moment when you first decide to move to a new house is the time to begin the brainstorming and selection process described earlier in this chapter. You will, of course, also be choosing the inside style and shape of the home, but that is not our topic here. Just remember to include the outside activities in your plans.

The factors going into your decision are numerous and beyond the scope of this book, but as far as the outside area of your home is concerned, remember to consider the following:

View. Try to get a house or plot with a pleasant view, at least on one or two sides. The kitchen, where the family spends a great deal of time, should be cheery inside and out. The main gathering area, whether it will be the family or living room, should have at least an inoffensive scene outside the windows. Ideally, the view should be attractive from any room in the house, but this is rarely possible. If you plan a patio or deck, make sure that you have a pleasant site for it to overlook.

Plot Size. As suggested earlier, get a good idea of which and how many outside activities the family would like. If there won't be many, a small plot will do. If you have a large family and all members have different ideas, you should get a plot big enough to handle most of the important activities and projects.

Grade. After you've decided what you want to do with your land, you should have some idea whether you want a level, sloping, or hilly plot, or perhaps some combination. That nice airy spot on top of the hill may be lovely, but how will you get your car up there? The creek at the bottom of the property may be pretty, too, but does it flood in the spring?

Existing Landscape. Although many developers simply ravage the existing landscape, the more thoughtful ones work around trees, rocks, and other impediments to their bulldozers. But how will the landscape fit into your plans? If you are buying an older home, there may be ancient bushes that are overgrown and ugly. Can (and should) you remove them? Can they be cut back? Again, how will the current landscape fit into your future plans? Would it be better to buy a country plot, already cool and luxurious with tall pines? And

how will you get rid of those gorgeous pines if you want to add a driveway or pool? Can you bear it? Ask all of these questions before you buy.

Siting. If the house is already built, where and how will you add the patio? Is there room in the right place? What about the drainage? Does the rain flow into the garage? What about distance from the road? From the neighbors? If you are buying an undeveloped plot, what effect will zoning and building codes have on the home site? What is the grade where the house should be placed? How about locating the driveway? Is there room? Will it be too long or too short? Is the only building area on very low ground, where flooding could be a problem? There are a lot of questions to ask here, and some are tied in with the others. Sure, the plot has a great view, for example, but you may not be able to build to enjoy it if there are too many rocks or setback restrictions.

Soil. This is especially important if the family passion is gardening. Some sites are rocky, some very sandy, some very wet. Grass won't grow well if there are too many trees. You can get a pretty good idea about what will and will not grow if there is already a home with plantings on the property; an empty plot, on the other hand, may be quite a mystery. If you know your botany, you can tell soil conditions from the wild plants that are growing there. But sometimes there is only a thin layer of topsoil. If you dig down and level the land you may find that the backyard is one big sandpit or rockpile. Check with county agricultural agents, or make some test borings yourself.

Type of House. You may have seen those second-story decks that look out on the side of a neighbor's house or worse. They're not only useless, they have a very "tacked-on" look. If a deck is definitely in your future plans, imagine how it would look on an existing home. Most of the projects in this book will blend in with, or can be adapted to, almost any type of house, but before you buy or build, consider the effect of the project. If, for example, you are interested in a passive solar system, the type and location of trees can be vital.

Orientation. This refers to the siting of the home and its components in relation to such elements as the road, sun, breezes, view, and

If the existing landscape poses a problem, there are always ways to work around it. This ingenious redwood deck was built around a lovely old tree overlooking a beautiful view.

surrounding houses. Solar homes should have most or all of the windows facing south, for example. If you will have a spectacular ocean view, the living areas and any deck or patio should face this natural asset. Driveways, especially in snowy areas, should be as short and level as possible. Most gardens should be in full sun. In hot regions, especially, you will want the house to take full advantage of the prevailing winds and not be hidden behind a knoll or other close-in houses. Landscaping should utilize shrubs, trees, and bushes to maximize sunlight and breezes.

NOW TO BEGIN

All the theorizing, brainstorming, winnowing-out, and dreaming should be finished now. You've made your choices, and you know what you want to do. Let's find out how.

Trees, Shrubs, Hedges, and Foundation Plantings

At first, it may seem irrelevant to ask the difference between a tree and a shrub, a hedge and a foundation planting. The answers all seem to be so obvious. Well, maybe yes, maybe no. Arborvitae, for example, is extensively used in foundation plantings. Did you know that arborvitae, if left untrimmed, is a tree, and will overwhelm your house in 10 years or so without annual pruning?

The same applies to certain species of yews and junipers, which are also widely used in foundation plantings. And what exactly is a hedge? According to my dictionary, a hedge is "a row of bushes or small trees planted close together, esp. when forming a fence or boundary." See? I would have thought that a hedge *always* formed a fence or boundary. So it isn't that simple.

And what is a shrub, exactly? Again, according to my dictionary, it is a "woody perennial plant smaller than a tree, usually having permanent stems branching from or near the ground." Now a tree, on the other hand, can be "a perennial plant having a permanent, woody, self-supporting main stem or trunk, ordinarily growing to a considerable height, and usually developing branches at some distance from the ground." But it can also be "any of various shrubs, bushes, and herbaceous plants, as the banana, resembling a tree in form or size." As a matter of fact, there are 13 definitions of a tree.

And how does a "bush" fit into all this? Well, there are 10 definitions of a bush in my dictionary, but a bush, in our sense of the word, is essentially the same as a shrub, although maybe a little closer to the

Intelligently arranged trees and shrubs make this poolside patio a delightful place. (National Landscape Association)

ground, so we're ignoring that term. Then there are "foundation plantings."

Leaving dictionary definitions aside, we'll define the different plantings in our own way, which is according to their use in the landscape. A tree, as used here, is big, a tall "bush" used for shade (usually), in the deciduous, or leaf-shedding, form. Evergreen trees are also big, but they don't shed their needles and are used both for shade and as windbreaks, as well as for year-round beauty.

A shrub, as far as we are concerned, is a bush, deciduous or evergreen. It is any part of the landscape that is smaller than a tree. Used as an accent plant among the trees or in foundation plantings, it comes in many varieties.

Defined by use, a hedge is a simple term. It is a row of bushes or trees, either deciduous or evergreen, used for boundary plantings or to set off one part of the landscape from another. It can also be used as a windbreak. (Evergreens are best for boundaries or windbreaks.)

Foundation plantings are used around the foundation of the home. Intelligent planning requires the use of at least some evergreens, but these can (and often should) be mixed with some deciduous plantings. As mentioned earlier, many of the "shrubs" used in foundation plantings are actually small trees which require pruning to be kept in the desired shape.

ACHIEVING YOUR GOALS THROUGH PLANTINGS

It is assumed that at this point you have established your plan and your goals, at least in general. The purpose of this chapter is to assist you in achieving those goals by the use of trees, shrubs, and other landscaping.

It is time now to think seriously about what your landscape is going to do for you. Is privacy one of your main concerns? If you have a lovely view, how can you alter the landscape to take advantage of it? Is the climate often too hot or too cold? Is your house hidden from view or displayed openly to passers-by? If it is hidden, would you prefer it to be more open? Conversely, would you rather get out of the limelight?

What about the work involved and the expense? Would you like an "instant" landscape, or would you prefer to nurse smaller shrubs and trees for a few years until they grow to more acceptable size? And what about maintenance? Big trees drop a lot of leaves. If you already have, or plan to put in, a nice lawn, remember that leaves must be raked up frequently and discarded each year. To spare you that work, perhaps evergreen trees are preferable for a clean expanse of lawn.

Acquaint yourself with the many types of trees and shrubs and their growing habits. Do they grow quickly or slowly? Are they tall or small at maturity? Are they messy? Are they attractive to birds, and is this good or bad, in your opinion? Most people like birds, but if you have a cat or two, trees that attract birds may not be a good idea. Last, but certainly not least, how will the trees and shrubs react to your environment and one another?

WORKING WITHIN YOUR LIMITS

Closely linked with your goals are your limitations. Geography, climate, grade, plot size, and soil types vary widely. Existing landscaping and structures sometimes can be a hindrance and sometimes an asset.

Although there are trees and shrubs that will grow anywhere—some needle-leaf evergreens such as yews and junipers, for example—there are a great many that will thrive only under specific conditions. Climate is an important limitation. The most obvious examples are such tropical trees as the various palms, the live oak, and fig trees. They won't grow anywhere except the deep south and southwest. Broadleaf evergreens grow very well in warmer climates, in general, while needle-leaf types do not, except for a few pine varieties like the longleaf. On the other hand, there are many trees, mostly deciduous, that do poorly in hot weather. Beech, the birches, aspen, and most maples and oaks are best planted in frost areas. Severe weather is not kind to broadleaf evergreens such as rhododendron and mountain laurel, but frost is a necessity for most fruit-bearing trees and bushes.

Winds can be troublesome if they are too strong. Most evergreen shrubs should be planted away from strong winds. If this is impossible, they should be protected by windbreaks of some sort. To protect their foundation plantings from wind, many people cover them with burlap in the winter. However, you can create a better-looking and more efficient windbreak with screen-type fences or taller evergreens. Burlap pretty much defeats the purpose.

Among large trees, willows and aspens are prone to wind damage, and the English elm may be more resistant to Dutch elm disease than the American variety, but it is much more prone to broken limbs in a windstorm.

Precipitation is another sometimes forgotten weather problem. Cacti and the various succulents are about the only plants that will grow in the desert without costly irrigation. Even palm trees must have sufficient moisture, although they are known as hot-weather trees.

Before investing in trees and shrubs, check out all their characteristics with local experts. Some varieties of a species may have opposite qualities in regard to factors like moisture. Most trees, especially evergreens like pines, require well-drained soil, while the slash pine and Scotch pine may need additional watering.

Soil type is another important limitation. Forget most broadleaf evergreens if the soil is alkaline. Most oaks do well in any type of soil, but the pin oak may turn yellow in soil with a high pH. The golden-rain tree will tolerate mildly acid soil but requires additional lime if the pH is low. Dogwood is another tree that likes the soil somewhat acid. And most trees do best in sandy loam, although some do well in any kind of soil. Soils that are mostly clay will require the addition of peat, compost, or other materials which will break up the soil.

Not only regional differences should be taken into account, though. Analyze any limitations of your own plot. Is it rather small? If so, avoid huge trees which may dwarf the property and impinge on your neighbors. If your lot is on higher ground than the rest of the neighborhood, beware of high winds and the plantings that are injured thereby. If you are lower than the others, don't take chances on plants that don't like wet feet. Again, a soil sample is highly recommended, so that you know what you are dealing with underneath.

A word here for those who are planning a home from scratch, a word of experience. Whatever you do with your existing plot, keep a weather eye on the contractor and especially on the bulldozer operator. Often, the builder brings in his bulldozer and simply tears apart the landscape.

The mature trees in the backyard were left up to provide cooling and energy-conserving shade for the house. The smaller trees were planted to shade the patio. The pool is far enough away so that it has plenty of sun—and no leaves.

Nature has taken decades, even centuries, to grow magnificent tall trees and build up a layer of humus topsoil. Obviously, on a wooded plot, something has to give. You can't build a house in the treetops. The merciless bulldozing of everything in sight, however, is—in my opinion—a crime. As far as I am concerned, the less you disturb a wooded site, the better off you are. If you must take down the trees, site your home so as to leave the bigger ones. They will provide shade in the summer and cool your home, a lovely landscape already in place. You can just sit back and enjoy it, maintenance-free. When the leaves fall, you can leave them there.

Not everyone is blessed (or cursed, if you disagree) with a wooded lot, however. Sometimes new lots are built on old farmland, or the developer has already committed mass mayhem with the landscape. If you want trees and shrubs, in this situation, you have to plant them. And no matter where or when you build, foundation plantings are a must.

SELECTING TREES

Some plans may call for just one tree, others may need several, but it is difficult to imagine any home site, except in arid regions, that would not benefit from at least one large tree. A study reported by the American Museum of Natural History shows that mature trees add as much as $10,000 to the value of a medium-priced home—and that study was made in the mid-1970s. Trees soften the harsh, stark lines of the house, add interest and beauty, attract songbirds, and—most important of all—provide valuable shade when properly sited. When trees protect the house from the hottest rays of the sun, they can lower home temperatures by as much as 20 degrees and can save enormously on the costs of air conditioning.

In view of their potential value, trees should be purchased with great care and foresight. It can be heartbreaking to nurture a lovely tree for many years only to find that it is too small or too big, ill-shaped, messy, or—worst of all—prone to disease and early death.

Many people buy tiny or fast-growing trees in the usually mistaken belief that they are saving money. If the tree is going to mature in a far-off corner of your lot, this may be acceptable, but to buy a tree for shade that will take 20 years to reach 20 feet or to buy a tree that grows fast but dies in 10 years is a waste of most of the tree's value.

Sizes of Mature Trees

Small (up to 40 feet)	Medium (40 to 75 feet)	Large (more than 75 feet)
Arborvitae	American holly	American beech
Brazilian pepper	Blue spruce	Pecan
Cherry laurel	Goldrain tree	Southern magnolia
Desert willow	Hackberry	Sugar maple
Green ash	Honey locust	White oak
Hemlock	Live oak	Willow oak
Jacaranda	Norway maple	
Mimosa	Red maple	
Wax	Scotch pine	
	Valley oak	

Useful Life Expectancies

Short (to 50 years)	Medium (to 75–100 years)	Long (100 or more years)
Arborvitae	American holly	American beech
Brazilian pepper	Blue spruce	Live oak
Desert willow	Goldrain tree	Pecan
Mimosa	Green ash	Southern magnolia
Redbud	Hackberry	White ash
Sydney wattle	Honey locust	White oak
Umbrella tree	Jacaranda	Willow oak
	Norway maple	
	Red maple	
	Scotch pine	
	Valley oak	

The price charged by a nursery to deliver and plant a large tree may seem high, but think about its value to your home for a moment before you rule out this possibility. This is one job, for instance, that you can't possibly do yourself. Nurseries have the equipment to transport a large tree and dig a big enough hole. With a large tree, you begin to reap the benefits of shade and cooling immediately or within a few years, at most. The tree should be guaranteed by the nursery, which is worthwhile insurance.

If you do decide to purchase a large tree, make sure you have chosen a site where it will do the most good. If your object is to cool and frame the house, the tree should probably go on the southwest corner. Trees to shade a patio or deck should be sited where they will provide the most shade at the hottest time of day. The trunk should be centered at a distance of one-half its mature diameter from the house.

Whether you buy a large tree or a small one, there are several factors to be taken into consideration.

Hardiness. Hardiness is a factor which varies with geography, climate, and other aspects of the environment, such as available moisture, contaminants, and competition from human society. In the central city, for example, soils tend to be compacted and poorly drained. The air may be full of soot and other contaminants. Select a tree that is tolerant of such conditions, such as Norway maple, male ginkgo, or London plane tree. Local extension services can be of great help in determining this and other agricultural factors.

Form. The mature shape of a tree should be appropriate for its intended use. A broad-spreading, low-hanging tree such as one of flowering crab apples may be ideal in the front yard but a nuisance next to the driveway. The driveway would look nice bordered by slim, upright trees, such as poplar, which would be unsuitable for shading the house. For specific tree forms consult nursery catalogs or other books that contain illustrations or detailed descriptions of tree forms.

Size. Size is a tricky factor. As discussed above, the more mature the tree, the better use you will get from it. The rate of growth and longevity, however, are also important. How long do you plan to stay in your house? Some trees grow rapidly, yielding shade and screening soon after planting. A silver maple, for example, is a good tree to plant if you don't intend to stay forever in your present house. It grows fast and has a nice form, but it matures quickly and the trunk may split. If you intend to live in a house for a long time or want to plant a nice tree for posterity, select a slower-maturing, hardier tree such as an oak, beech, linden, birch, or red or sugar maple.

By the same token, don't buy a small, slow-growing tree if you need shade rather quickly. Instead choose an ash, birch, aspen, umbrella (chinaberry), or even that silver maple. And for the front of the house, don't buy a tree that will grow into a monster. Ornamental or "understory" trees such as flowering fruit trees, dogwood, or sassafras are better for locations where you don't want the entire area or view obscured. It may seem elementary, but it's been seen all too often—don't plant a real tree such as a pine or fir as a foundation planting.

Personal Preference. This may be the most important factor of all. If you like Norway maples—and they provide nice, dense shade —you may not care that they are only medium in height and live for 75 years or so. You'll surely have plenty of time to enjoy your tree. A tulip tree grows to 100 feet or more, which is too large for the typical suburban plot, but it takes at least 100 years to mature. Its size will do just fine for many decades before that.

Undesirable Characteristics. Watch for low resistance to disease (mimosa) or bugs (birch), shedding nuisance fruits or nuts, and a tendency for roots to clog sewers and uproot sidewalks. It is difficult to find a tree that does not have *some* undesirable characteristic, and the acceptability for residential planting is another personal matter. If planted away from sewer systems, walks, and drives, for example, the shallow-rooted maples are not a problem. And beware the American elm, now almost extinct because of Dutch elm disease.

I once parked my car under a mulberry tree, to my deep regret. I came back to find the car covered with messy, smelly, purple berries. The female ginkgo is also a shedder, although the male ginkgo is a very hardy, unmessy tree, ideal for city streets.

Sweetgum fruits have thorny protuberances that make them a lawn nuisance, but are fine otherwise. Other fruit and nut trees are similar, although not as much of a nuisance as the sweetgum. Beware, however, of an area where there are a lot of children, who use the fruits and nuts as missiles. A horse chestnut through your front window is not a pleasant experience.

Availability. Availability may sound like an unimportant consideration, and it may be if you don't mind a small mail-order tree. But if you are considering buying a larger tree, your choice will be restricted to what's in stock at the local nurseries.

"Local" is a relative term, like "cheap." If the kind of tree you want is many miles away and you are willing to pay the price the nursery wants for transporting and planting it (probably not that much more than a shorter distance), then you may consider the nursery "local." If you can get the type of tree you want only by driving a long distance and bringing it back in your trunk, then this may be "local," too, if you want the tree badly enough.

If you must order your trees by mail, don't worry too much about the somewhat unsavory reputation of the general mail-order business. Most mail-order nurseries have been around a long time and are honest. Some may even provide written guarantees, which apply even if you don't do a good planting job.

Ornamental Trees

We have been talking mainly about shade trees so far. A few words need to be said about ornamentals, which are bought mainly for their beautiful blossoms. In nature's design, of course, there is no such thing as an ornamental tree, but some trees have blossoms, often augmented by hybridization, so lovely that they are planted more for looks than for other purposes.

A prime example of this is the crab apple tree. Like all apple trees —all fruit trees, for that matter—they have such lovely blooms that hardly anyone plants them for the fruit, even though it makes delicious jam. Crab apple trees are most often seen in front of the home or near an entrance, where they won't overwhelm the rest of the scene.

Flowering cherry trees, plum trees, and many other fruit trees are often grown and combined with other species to make lovely blooming trees that grow no fruit. One example is the Kwanzan cherry, which has lovely pink double drooping flowers but bears no cherries.

Another popular flowering tree is the magnolia, which produces huge white flowers during early spring in the northeast. But don't confuse this almost leafless tree with the southern magnolia *(Magnolia grandiflora),* which is a broadleaf evergreen, very tall and long-lived, and which has even larger flowers.

This brings up an important point when dealing with trees, shrubs, and many other plants. It's a good idea to get acquainted with Latin or scientific nomenclature. What is called by one name in one place may be called by another entirely different name in another. What some call a juniper others call a red cedar. (There are at least 5 trees called "cedar.") What is an umbrella tree to some people is a chinaberry to others. Both are actually *Melia azedarach.*

It is especially important to know the proper or scientific name if you are buying by mail. A mail-order nursery may give a common tree a fancy name, so ask for its scientific name. And remember that there are many varieties of the same type of tree. The genus *Pinus* (pine), for example, includes at least 12 varieties. A *Quercus* (oak) can come in at least 24 varieties.

SHRUBS

There are so many kinds of shrubs that it is impossible to describe them all. Like trees, they are deciduous or evergreen. Most evergreens are either needle leaf, such as fir or pine, or scale leaf, such as arborvitae or cedar.

Many shrub evergreens are broadleaf. Notable examples are rhododendron, azalea, holly, and mountain laurel. Most broadleaf evergreens feature lovely spring flowers, but although the leaves do stay on and remain green during cold weather, they're inclined to be "droopy" during severe cold spells, and parts of the shrub may suffer winterkill.

Most evergreens, the broadleaf types in particular, require acid soil (pH less than 6.0). If your soil samples show a sweet pH—that is, neutral to alkaline soil—use fertilizers especially designed to make it more acid.

Deciduous and evergreen shrubs make a lovely contrast to the white brick wall in this appealing entranceway. (AAN)

Evergreen shrubs are used most often in foundation plantings. They are also excellent for holding banks, for use as accent plants, and for creating wind-reducing hedges. Ordinarily, low-growing shrubs such as creeping juniper are used on slopes, where lawns would be difficult to grow. The higher-growing varieties, such as hemlock or upright Japanese yew, are excellent for wind reduction or other hedge use.

There are many varieties of deciduous, or "flowering," shrubs. Some popular varieties are hydrangea, forsythia, weigela, flowering almond or quince, and the fragrant honeysuckle, and mock orange. There are endless newer hybrids and dwarf species, many of which are excellent for low foundations or semi-groundcover. Depending on size, deciduous plants have most of the same applications as do evergreens. They should not be used for windbreaks, however, or as a privacy hedge, since the purpose is defeated during wintertime, when their leaves fall off.

The best place to shop for shrubs is your local nursery. Local nurseries should stock only those species which do well in their area. This is not always done, however. Rarely will you find a shrub that's *impossible* to grow, such as cactus in a northern nursery, but you often may see plants that will give you difficulty, such as acid-loving shrubs in an area with sweet soil. I don't know how many rhododendrons I tried to plant in upstate New York before I realized that the pH was wrong.

Many of the rules for selecting trees apply as well to buying shrubs. Again, think always of mature heights, especially in foundation plantings, and carefully consider climate, form, and pH. Few foundation plantings have undesirable characteristics, and most are widely available, but these attributes still should be kept in mind. In general, all of these considerations become more important as you plant closer to the house. Informal plantings allow a greater degree of freedom than do those around the approaches to your home.

As in planning for trees, weigh the benefits of buying larger, more expensive shrubs. This is a matter of taste and finances, of course, but remember that the more visible the planting, the more a mature plant counts. If you are planting off in the back of the lot, you probably can wait awhile for the shrubs to mature. If you are planting low-growing evergreens to prevent erosion of a slope, perhaps you can plant some annual ryegrass to hold the bank for a time, and intersperse cheap "gallon" junipers until they take over the slope. Indeed, if the bank is a large one, hardly anyone can afford mature plants, so retaining walls and terracing may be the best solution.

If you do buy small plants, be sure to space them to allow for at least several years' growth. You can compensate for the sparse appearance that this creates by using groundcover in between. One popular method of handling small shrubs is to plant thick and thin quick. This is not desirable. The immediate effect may look all right, but inevitably pruning will be neglected, overcrowding will result, and the plants will become misshapen and have to be discarded. If you are fallible, like most of us, you will not "thin quick" when you should, and will wind up with an overgrown mishmash.

FOUNDATION PLANTINGS

For most of your backyard—and front yard, too—informality is generally a good idea. Foundation plantings are quite another matter, however. The purposes of foundation planting are to tie the house into the landscape, avoid harsh edges, and make the home appear to blend naturally into its setting. Poorly designed foundation plantings can make a nice house look out of place in its surroundings.

Here is one aspect of landscape design that must be carefully studied and executed. First, let's discuss some of the fundamental rules.

Don't plant tall trees. Foundation plantings should be shrubs, not trees. The plants should enhance the beauty of the house and not obscure it. Big trees block out light and solar heat. Shrubs can be trimmed to retain their size and shape; in most cases, trees cannot be cut back without ruining their shape. Except for nursery-trained yews and similar evergreens, trees belong away from the house, not in the immediate vicinity.

Don't plant straight rows of one variety. Sameness is boring and monotonous. It may be possible to use just one type of shrub in your foundation, depending on the type and location; never use all the same heights of the same species, however. On the other hand, see the next rule.

Don't plant a botanical collection This is the reverse of the "do not" above. A row of same-size bushes is boring, but a mishmash is bewildering—and also boring. Varied sizes and textures do lend interest. Just don't go overboard, and mix in everything.

Don't plant tall shrubs in front of windows. Tall shrubs do have their place, but they shouldn't be allowed to obscure the windows. What good are windows you can't see out of? Don't let shrubs grow much higher than the bottom sash.

Don't be too bright. The brightness should be in your head, not your foundation plantings. Color is wonderful but should be subdued close to the house. Bright and bizarre colors can be distracting.

General Rules

Since foundation plantings are so important, it is wise to take photographs of the front and other elevations, enlarge them, and cover the pictures with clear acetate or other plastic. For most homes, follow the so-called V principle. Draw two lines, each from the middle of your doorstep to a point about halfway between the ground and a corner eave. (The house need not be symmetrical.) In general, except where windows are located, your foundation plantings should be placed in the two spaces between the ground and these two lines.

If there are already foundation plantings in place and these are above the V-lines, they should be either trimmed or replaced. When the present effect is poor, with badly planned or scraggly plants in place, you may as well pull out the whole batch and start over. This often happens, especially with older homes. There may be nice individual shrubs, but chances are they have grown too big for their location. Salvageable plants may be transplanted to a corner, to a large wall area, or to a border planting.

Evergreen plants that have grown too large will probably have to be discarded. If evergreens are not pruned regularly, not only do they grow too high, but they begin to thin out and resume their original tree shape. Ill-shaped deciduous bushes usually can be saved by cutting them back severely, forcing entirely new shoots from the base. There are some exceptions, however, so consult your local experts or just give it a try. If it doesn't work, *then* throw them out and replace them.

On the positive side, here are some more rules:

• Do plant low-growing shrubs at the entrance and under windows. Also use low-growing shrubs around the porch, unless it is an intensive living area and privacy is required. If the porch is large, use vines or small ornamental trees for shade where desired.

- When an entryway or steps are small, use dwarf plants at the sides, perhaps supplemented by a vine.
- Do plant medium to tall shrubs at house corners, unless the drive, walk, or windows are too close. In that event, substitute vines or a tree-form shrub if you want shade for the windows.
- Do use medium-size shrubs in the foundation where windows are far apart. An occasional vine may add interest.
- Do plant vines such as pyracanthea on a chimney, unless it is narrow. Shrubs also may be planted near a chimney.
- Plants should be mixed, but duplicate and plant some in batches to avoid a disjointed look.
- Use groundcovers or let grass grow to the foundation when planting under windows or waiting for small shrubs to grow to mature size.

Guidelines

The guidelines used here were prepared by Cornell University specifically for New York State but apply to most regions of the northeast, much of the midwest, and the northwest. Check local nurseries and extension services for substitutes where the weather is very hot or very cold. The numbers in the following paragraphs refer to groups in the table.

Entrance Plantings. Entryway plants should give a feeling of easy access, as suggested by low-growing plants. In Illustration A, the windows are fairly close to and equidistant from the door. Use shrubs from Group 3. In B the windows are far from the entrance. Use

(Cornell University)

A   B

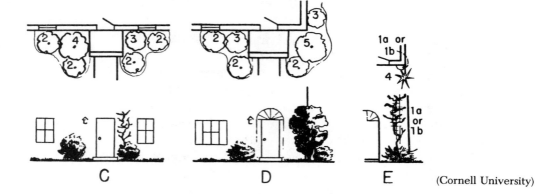

(Cornell University)

groups of shrubs from Groups 2, 3, and 4. In C one window is nearer
the entrance than the other. The plantings on the farther side are a
little larger than the other. Note that a vine on the smaller side offsets
the larger group. If the doorway is near a corner, combine the corner
planting with the entrance planting. In D, a larger shrub is at the
corner. When there is a window, walk, or drive at the corner, use a
vine at the corner (E).

Plantings for Outside Corners. These plantings depend on the
height of the house and closeness of the windows to the corner. The
drawings show shrubs for a two-story home; they should be scaled
down by one or two size groups for a one-story or short side of a
split-level home. Usually, a tree-form shrub or small tree is planted
diagonally from the corner, with smaller plants filling in between.
Illustration A gives suggestions for corners where windows are at
least 4 feet away. In B and B₁ both windows are close to the corner.
Either plant a small tree away from the corner or use low-growing
shrubs close to the house. Some people prefer no shrubbery at all in
this situation.

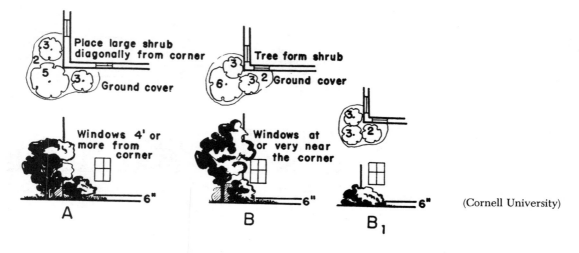

(Cornell University)

Groups and Suggestions for Foundations

This list was adapted from a Cornell University Cooperative Extension bulletin, and lists plants suitable for New York State and areas with similar climates. If you are in a different climate, show the list to your local extension or nursery for adaptation.

Plant	Foliage*	Remarks
GROUP 1A—VINES REQUIRING SUPPORT		
Fiveleaf akebia	SE	Dense, good screener
Jackman clematis	D	Purple showy flowers
Oriental bittersweet	D	Fruit with male and female
Trumpet creeper	D	Orange-scarlet flowers
GROUP 1B—VINES THAT DO NOT REQUIRE SUPPORT		
Bigleaf wintercreeper	E	*Euonymous fortunei* "Vegetus"
Boston ivy	D	Climbs rapidly and tightly
Climbing hydrangea	D	White flowers, best on north side
English ivy	E	Best on north side, protected
GROUP 2—GROUNDCOVERS		
Myrtle (periwinkle)	E	Blue flowers, good in shade
Creeping juniper	E	Dry and sunny locations
English ivy	E	Best on north side, protected
Hardy candytuft	E	Foregrounds, rock gardens
Japanese spurge	E	*Pachysandra,* best in moist shade
GROUP 3—SHRUBS 1½ – 3 FEET HIGH		
Azaleas	D, E	Various colors, acid soil
Drooping leucothoe	E	White flowers, good filler
Flowering quince	D	Dwarf varieties, orange flowers
Flowering almond	D	Pink flowers, watch borers
Japanese yew	E	Dwarf "Nana" *Taxus cuspidata*
Rockspray	D	*Cotoneaster horizontalis,* pink berries
Sargent juniper	E	Full sun, forms dense mound
Slender deutzia	D	White flowers, neat in form
GROUP 4—SHRUBS 4–5 FEET HIGH		
Azalea	D	Various colors, acid soil
Carolina rhododendron	E	Pink flowers, acid soil
Bayberry	D	Gray fruit with male and female
Fragrant viburnum	D	*V. carlesi,* pink flowers, hardy
Japanese barberry	D	Red fruit, very hardy, for hedges
Japanese holly	E	Varied foliage, protected location

Plant	Foliage*	Remarks
Mountain laurel	E	Pink-white flowers, acid soil
Oregon hollygrape	E	*Mahonia aquifolium,* yellow flowers
Spreading cotoneaster	D	*C. divaricata,* red fruit
Weigela	D	Various colors, prune annually
GROUP 5—SHRUBS 6–8 FEET HIGH		
Catawba rhododendron	E	Various colors, acid soil
Doublefile viburnum	D	*V. plicatum,* white double flowers
Japanese yew	E	*Taxus cuspidata,* excellent plant
Regal privet	D	White flowers, good for hedges
Forsythia	D	Yellow flowers, best *Forsythia intermedia*
Hibiscus	D	Althea, *Hibiscus syriacus,* summer flower
Winged euonymus	D	*Euonymus alatus,* very dense, textured
Winterberry	D	Red fruit with male and female
Honeysuckle (winter)	SE	Creamy, fragrant flowers
GROUP 6—SHRUBS 8–15 FEET HIGH		
Beautybush	D	Pink flowers, needs room
Black haw	D	*Viburnum prunifolium,* white flowers
Chinese lilac	D	Rose-purple or white flowers
Star magnolia	D	Showy white flowers before leaves
Mock orange	D	Hardy, fragrant white flowers
Capitata yew	E	Upright with strong center

*D—deciduous E—evergreen SE—semi-evergreen

Illustrations C and D show one window close to the corner and one window several feet away. In these situations, line up the large shrub with the wall having the closer window, bringing it approximately midway between the windows. Use low-growing plants under the windows.

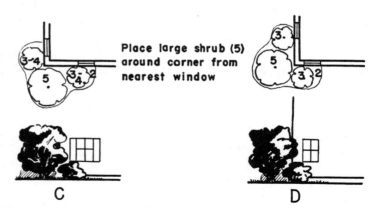

Place large shrub (5) around corner from nearest window

C   D

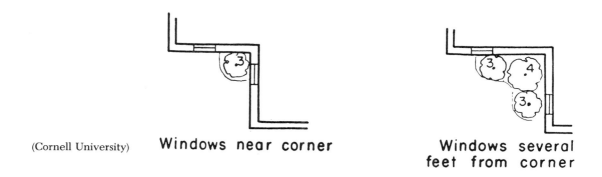

(Cornell University) **Windows near corner**   **Windows several feet from corner**

Plantings for Inside Corners.   Here the plantings are more sub-dued. Use only one low plant where the windows are close (A) or a somewhat larger grouping if the windows are farther away (B). If the inside corner is close to the outside corner, it should be planted in conjunction with the outside corner grouping.

Wall Plantings.   These plantings can vary considerably. Six common situations are shown here; they should be combined and/or altered to meet your specific needs. A typical wall with windows spaced fairly far apart is shown in A. The grouping can be symmetri-cal if desired, but the asymmetrical grouping shown is more interest-ing. Groundcover or flowers can be substituted for the low plants beneath the windows. The same type of wall is shown in B, but with a narrow planting bed bordered by a walkway. A trellised vine pro-vides the needed height without growing onto the walk.

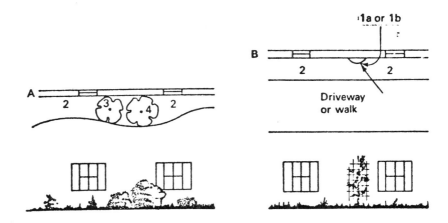

(Cornell University)

In C a large picture is shown. Again, an unbalanced grouping is shown, although the plants can be symmetrical if you prefer it. With a bay window (D), low-growing shrubs not only improve the appearance of the wall but help hide the open area usually left under the bay. If shade is desired, taller plants from Group 6 may be substituted at the sides.

Large chimneys look good with a clinging vine (E) and a low shrub at the corner. Narrow chimneys, however, may be better served with a tall shrub in front. If your house has a high foundation and a basement window with a well (F) and light through the basement window is essential, substitute smaller plants along the sides.

HEDGES

A hedge is a long, usually straight or slightly curved row of shrubs or bushes and occasionally smaller trees. It can be evergreen or deciduous, depending on its purpose. The usual purpose is to establish privacy or a boundary, and this is best achieved with evergreens, certainly if privacy is the main concern.

But hedges can also be used to set off certain areas in the property; they can separate a garden from a play area, for example. In that case, they are usually deciduous, since the hedge has little use anyway in the winter months.

High evergreen hedges are best for privacy. Use arborvitae, Canadian hemlock, or Hick's yew. Privet or hawthorn is most commonly used as deciduous hedges.

There is one type of hedge that has become increasingly popular with the rise in energy costs—the windbreak. This type of hedge is thicker and higher than the typical hedge. It should be made of evergreen trees or very tall shrubs, planted in rows of three or more. Such a hedge, planted on the north and northwest sides (or on whatever side receives the winter winds), is very effective at cutting down heat loss and saving fuel.

A windbreak should be planted at least 50 feet from the house or driveway, if possible, to minimize drifting snow. The shrubs or trees will be effective for a distance of 8 times their height; a row of evergreen plantings 10 feet high, for example, will check the wind for 80 feet on its lee side.

Fir, spruce, or hemlock trees, or tall yews or arborvitae, make the most effective windbreaks. In addition to protecting your home in the winter, a windbreak also directs cooling breezes, which usually come from the south or southwest, to the house in the hot months. For best results, buy trees from 2 to 4 feet tall. They will readily establish themselves and provide early wind protection.

PLANTING TREES AND SHRUBS

Like almost every task in this book, the key to success in planting is doing it right from the beginning. Trees and shrubs are planted the same way, by following the steps carefully and working just a little harder than you think is necessary.

If the soil has poor drainage, dig out more beneath the site than is indicated, and fill with sand and gravel. This will help prevent the plant from getting wet feet. If the soil is poor to begin with, it is wise to dig a bigger hole than needed for good soil, then replace the old soil with new topsoil, or mix peat moss with the old soil in a 1-to-1 ratio. It is always a good idea, in any kind of soil, to dig down deeper than necessary, then pack in good soil under the root ball. This may not be possible, however, for heavy trees with big root balls.

The steps for balled shrubs and trees, assuming fairly decent soil, are as follows:

- Dig a planting hole 2 feet wider than the root ball.
- Dig the hole at least deep enough so that the planting will be set at the same level at which it grew in the nursery.
- Set the planting in the hole. If it sits too high, remove and dig some more. If it is too low, remove and pack in good soil underneath. Heavy root balls should be rocked back and forth while soil is shoved underneath until they are raised to the proper level.
- Untie or cut the strings holding the burlap, and remove the burlap from the top of the root ball. The rest is left on.
- Fill the hole with good topsoil, or mix in peat moss as described above, about halfway to the top. Tamp down soil with your feet, keeping the trunk straight with your hands. Water.
- When the water has seeped through, fill the remainder of the hole with soil and tamp in. Leave a low berm around the edges, and again water.

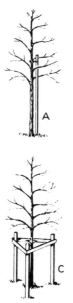

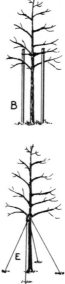

Recommended ways of staking small newly planted trees. (U.S. Department of Agriculture)

- Young trees and tall bushes should be staked.
- For bare-root trees and shrubs, dig the hole wider but shallower. Spread out the roots and dig at least as wide as the roots extend.
- For plantings that come in plastic or metal containers, remove the container by striking the bottom hard with a shovel. If this doesn't work, use metal snips to cut away the container.

CARE

Trees and shrubs fresh from the nursery and properly planted in good soil should not need much attention for the first year. For the first week or two, however, they should be "watered in" with daily soakings. If there are signs of yellowing, apply fertilizer as well as water, as described below. Be careful not to overwater when the soil has poor drainage.

Unlike grass and most flowers and vegetables, trees and shrubs do not need a great deal of fertilizer. One or two applications in spring and/or fall should do for most of these plantings. Most evergreen shrubs benefit from a handful of acid-type fertilizers or from a spraying of a liquid acid-type mix with a special applicator attached to the hose.

Deciduous shrubs need more fertilizer when they are young. Once they are full-grown, an annual application should do nicely. Fertilizers are labeled according to the percentages of nitrogen, phosphoric acid, and potash they contain. Use standard 5-10-5 mix for deciduous shrubs, or spray as above, with (5 percent nitrogen, 10 percent phosphoric, 5 percent potash) liquid fertilizer. Hydrangea, when grown in sweet soil, requires acid-type fertilizer to turn blue or violet; otherwise, the flowers will turn a pale pink or green color.

As always, it is wise to consult local agricultural extension services and to have your soil tested there. Nurseries should be helpful, too.

Reasonably mature trees, again, do not need a great deal of fertilizer. It is good insurance, however, to give them an annual boost of 5-10-5. There are special solid fertilizer plugs available, or you can use a soil auger or crowbar to dig holes 15 to 24 inches deep, beneath the drip-line (outer edge) of the tree about 2 feet apart. Fill the holes with a total of 2 pounds of 5-10-5 for every inch of tree trunk, distributed more or less equally in the holes. Refill the holes with good soil, or mix in sand and peat moss to provide aeration and better watering of the roots.

For established plantings, water when needed, especially during hot, dry periods. The simplest thing is to water the shrubbery at the same time that you water the grass. New shrubs should be watered daily for about 2 weeks, depending on the weather. For new trees, water once a week for the first 2 seasons. Use special plugs or needles for getting both water and water-soluble fertilizer down to the roots, as described above.

PRUNING

While it is possible to become a little lazy about watering and fertilizing and still keep decent trees and shrubs, pruning is one maintenance task that should not be neglected, especially for evergreen shrubs. Japanese yews *(Taxus),* arborvitae, and some forms of juniper will get thin and tall if they are not pruned at least once a year. It is particularly important to keep the desired shape of these evergreen shrubs in foundation plantings. Once they become overgrown, it is impossible to restore their original shape.

Spring is the best time to trim most shrubs. Use a pair of hedge clippers or an electric trimmer to cut off at least half of the new growth on needle-type evergreens. This will keep the bush dense and help retain the original shape, which is the best way to keep these plants (unless you are accomplished at topiary art). Although many people like "square" or "top-heavy" plantings, evergreen shrubs and hedges should be either kept in their original shapes or trimmed with the bottoms wider than the tops for the simple reason that snow collects on wide flat tops and breaks down the branches.

Broadleaf evergreens need little or no pruning. It is a good idea, however, to cut off the flowers after they bloom, to encourage better growth next year. Do not trim or cut off any leaves unless they have turned yellow or brown, in which case the entire branch may have to be removed with a pruning shears.

Pruning deciduous shrubs requires a little more knowledge and skill. Most spring bloomers should be pruned immediately after flowering by removing about a quarter of the new growth evenly from the crown and sides.

Forsythia and hydrangea are exceptions to this rule. They grow their major stems directly out of the soil, and produce blooms on year-old wood. If these bushes are badly overgrown, cut them back to the ground and start over, although you'll have to wait a year for new blooms. If forsythia or hydrangea is in pretty good shape, wait until it blooms, then you can see which parts are dead and cut them out.

Summer-flowering bushes should be pruned well in advance of flowering to encourage profuse blooms. Some examples are Rose of Sharon, honeysuckle, kerria, and spirea. Water and fertilize newly trimmed bushes to help them get over the shock.

Evergreen trees should be trimmed, too, as long as they are small enough so that you can get to the ends of the branches. Cut off half the new growth in spring to help them retain their pyramidal shape. You don't have to seal these cuts, since the natural resin does the job for you.

Shade trees should be kept trimmed and pruned as long as you

For trimming high branches, use a long-handled pruning shears or saw. (Snap-Cut)

are able to reach the branches. To keep the trees healthy, strong, and beautiful, prune often and early. This can be accomplished in the following way:

- Snip off low, undesirable shoots or branches while small.
- Prune away dead, dying, or unsightly areas.
- Remove branches that grow toward the center of the tree.
- Cut off one or both of any branches that cross. When branches rub together, bark is injured, allowing a path for disease.
- If possible, remove V-crotches and multiple leaders. Most trees need one dominant trunk to retain the proper shape.
- Remove any limbs that may interfere with electric or telephone wires, or that block needed sun or breezes.
- When limbs are very large or capable of injury and damage, don't attempt the job yourself. Hire a professional tree surgeon.

The best time to prune trees is late winter, before the sap starts to flow. Small limbs can be trimmed with regular pruning shears, but use a long-handled pruner or saw for cutting above your head.

On large limbs, make one cut about a foot away from the trunk, and about halfway through, working from the bottom with a chain or bow saw. Then make another cut from the top all the way through or until the limb falls of its own weight.

Recent forestry studies have shown that flush-cutting limb stubs may be harmful to the tree. Make your last cut at the "branch bark ridge," a bark-like wrinkle on the trunk of the branch. Start the cut close to that, then saw diagonally—down and slightly outward, to leave a protective "branch collar" on the trunk.

Painting the wound is not recommended either. It is best to leave the cut alone. Tree dressings can be used for cosmetic reasons, but they do no measurable good. House or other paints can actually do harm.

Grass and Groundcovers 3

Although grass and groundcovers are quite different from each other, they are used for the same purpose—to cover up and beautify bare earth. Homeowners have various reasons for choosing one or the other, but when it comes down to it, the bare, brown spots need something to brighten them up. In a newly built or remodeled house, grass or groundcover will repair the damage done by a builder. You can't build a house without disturbing at least part of the landscape, and there will always be some bare earth immediately around the home.

There are other good reasons for growing grass and groundcovers. You may just *like* grass, and neighborhood pressure, in the form of nice green lawns all around, may intimidate you into following suit. If you want to use solar energy, any evergreen trees—and perhaps some deciduous trees, too—that block the sun will have to come down on the south side of the home. Children and animals should have some grassy areas to stretch their legs.

When I was younger, I didn't mind the numerous tasks associated with grass-growing, but there's no question that too much grass is a lot of work. It must be planted or sodded, fertilized several times a year, mowed, watered, weeded, rid of crabgrass, and so on. I now steer away from grass and toward groundcover.

The one nice thing about groundcover is that, once established, it needs little or no care. I am now building another house—a passive solar home—doing most of the work myself, so I can personally supervise the land-clearing and be sure that the beautiful oaks and beeches on my land will be preserved. I want to leave as much of the natural landscape as possible because it is very lovely, and I want to cause as little soil disturbance as possible. I definitely don't want to spend my spare time taking care of a large lawn. Wherever possible, I'll plant groundcover.

Aside from a certain degree of laziness and a desire for a natural look, there are other valid reasons for avoiding grass. Grass doesn't do well under trees. Since the deciduous trees will provide needed shade and coolness in the summer months, I hope to avoid air conditioning for this solar house. With all those trees casting shade and shedding leaves in the fall, grass will be difficult to grow and rake.

But I will need groundcover, around the foundation and in whatever bare spots are left by the bulldozer, and although it pains me, I will have to cut down many of the trees on the south side of the house if we are to take advantage of passive solar heat. So there will be myrtle, ivy, pachysandra, and/or other groundcovers in the area where the trees are felled.

Although I have digressed, the reason for this personal aside is to illustrate how you should be thinking about using grass and groundcovers. Before you plant either, or both, think about it. Think of your overall plan, your wants, and your dislikes before you simply go ahead and put in a big lawn or a mass of groundcover. Don't do anything without a reason.

LAWNS

A well-kept lawn is a thing of beauty. Furthermore grass serves important environmental functions. Grass helps control pollution by absorbing carbon dioxide and other gases and releasing oxygen through plant photosynthesis. A lawn can cool the house by up to 10 degrees on hot days. Grass prevents wind and water erosion and supplies vital organic matter to the soil.

Grass can be walked on, played on, even trampled on, yet it remains in place and springs back up even if neglected. A wide expanse of lawn in front of a home can provide a perfect foreground, delightfully leading the eye to the house itself. On warm days, there is nothing more soothing than stretching out in the shade on a bed of soft grass.

From Bahia to Zoysia

No matter how large your lawn is, it is important to select the type of grass that best fits your climatic conditions. Cool-season grasses grow best in the north, and warm-season grasses are best in the south. Soil pH is also important in choosing grass types or mixtures. Generally, soils below a pH of 6.0 are considered acid. A neutral pH is 7.0. While soil pH does not usually range too far from neutral, some soils have been recorded as being below 4.0, which is very acid. Only Bermuda grass is known to be tolerant of low pH. In very acid soils, the most popular grass—Kentucky bluegrass—will not do well. Kentucky bluegrass also will do poorly in sites that are not well drained. To neutralize acid soil, add 50 to 80 pounds of ground limestone per 1,000 square feet every 5 or 6 years.

Common Types of Grasses and Their Attributes

Grass	Best Planting Time	Seed (lbs. per 1,000 sq. ft.)	Sod (sq. ft.)[1]	Fertilizer (lbs. of Nitrogen per 1,000 sq. ft.)	Height of Mowing (in.)
Bahia	spring	2–3		4	2
Bent grass, Colonial	fall	1–2		4–6	½–1
Bermuda (hulled)	spring	1–1½	5–10	5–10	¾–1
Blue grama	"	1–1½		[2]	1–2
Buffalo (treated)	"	½–1½	25–30	[2]	1–2
Carpet	"	3–4	8–10	2–3	2–2½
Centipede	"	¼–½	8–10	2–3	1–1½
Crested wheat	fall	1–2		0–1	2
Kentucky bluegrass	"	1½–2		3–6	1½–2
Red fescue	"	3–4		2–3	1½–2
Rough bluegrass	"	1½–2		2–4	1½–2
Ryegrass	"	3–4		3–4	1½–2
St. Augustine	spring	None	8–10	4–5	2–2½
Tall fescue	fall	5–6		3–5	2
Zoysia	spring	None	8–10	4–6	¾–1½

[1]Needed to sprig 1,000 sq. ft.
[2]Seldom required on most soils.

Source: United States Department of Agriculture.

Kentucky blue, though, is not the only type of fine grass available. There are many types of acceptable grasses, ranging (alphabetically) from bahia to zoysia. As with other plants, the choice depends primarily upon geography and climate and local pH. The wise lawn grower will take out several soil samples and have them analyzed by the local agricultural extension service. This service is usually free or inexpensive and can provide you with most of the information you need to select the proper type of grass.

Most lawns are planted with grass mixtures. Seed companies have many types of prepared grass mixtures, most of which are quite satisfactory, if you choose the type suited for your lawn. You can, if

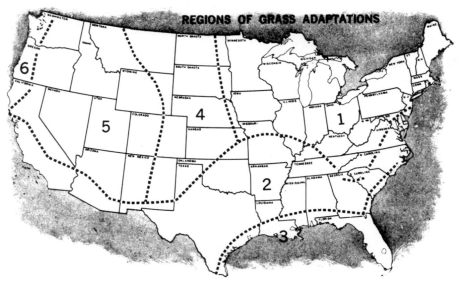

REGIONS OF GRASS ADAPTATIONS

CLIMATIC REGIONS, IN WHICH THE FOLLOWING GRASSES ARE SUITABLE FOR LAWNS:

1. Kentucky bluegrass, red fescue, and Colonial bentgrass. Tall fescue, bermuda, and zoysiagrasses in the southern part.

2. Bermuda and zoysiagrasses. Centipede, carpet, and St. Augustinegrasses in the southern part; tall fescue and Kentucky bluegrass in some northern areas.

3. St. Augustine, bermuda, zoysia, carpet, and bahiagrasses.

4. Nonirrigated areas: Crested wheat, buffalo, and blue gramagrasses. Irrigated areas: Kentucky bluegrass and red fescue.

5. Nonirrigated areas: Crested wheatgrass. Irrigated areas: Kentucky bluegrass and red fescue.

6. Colonial bent, Kentucky bluegrass, and red fescue.

you wish, buy the grasses separately and mix them yourself, but this may be more costly and less effective in the long run, especially if you are not familiar with the grass types.

All mixes are labeled to show the types of grasses and the percentages of each type. See the accompanying figure for the types that do well in your area, and combine this information with the soil type and lawn location (sun, shade, or both).

After Kentucky bluegrass, the most widely used cool-season grasses are red fescue and Chewings fescue. These are especially good where it is humid as well as cool. Colonial bent grass is probably the prettiest grass of all (it is widely used on golf greens), but it is expensive and difficult to maintain. It does very well in New England and the upper West Coast when used alone. When used in a mix, it thrives throughout the northern United States and southern Canada.

In damper regions of the cool-season grass area, choose a mix that has substantial portions of *Poa trivialis* (rough bluegrass). Crested wheat grass is a good selection for the northern Great Plains and intermountain areas or any dry, cool area where irrigation water is not available.

Here is a good, typical seed mix for most cool-season zones where shade is not a problem:

- Colonial bent grass—less than 10 percent.
- Fescues—20–40 percent.
- Kentucky bluegrass—50–70 percent.

Warm-season grasses reach their maximum growth during late spring, summer, and early fall. Frost turns most of them to an unsightly brown, which makes them unsuitable for areas with harsh winters.

Of the warm-season grasses, Bermuda grass is by far the most popular. It is vigorous and withstands heavy traffic, but these same qualities make Bermuda grass an invader of adjacent walks and plantings unless it is periodically trimmed and edged. Some varieties will do all right in the southernmost regions of the northern zones.

In the southernmost warm-season areas, St. Augustine grass is the lawn of choice. Zoysia is used throughout the southern region under limited shade. In the warmer parts of the Great Plains, Buffalo grass is widely used. Most of these are vegetative (started from established plants).

Vegetative grasses do not produce the desired growth when planted from seed. These grasses are planted by such methods as

Colonial bentgrass, the most exquisite of all grass, is widely used on golf greens. Note the closely matted turf.

sodding, plugging, sprigging, or stolonizing. Grasses planted by vegetative methods include St. Augustine grass, centipede grass, creezing bent grass, zoysia, and the improved strains of Bermuda grass.

Wherever the soil is poor, in any region, perennial ryegrass in one of the improved varieties is a good compromise. In general, ryegrass is a poor choice, though, since it grows fast and must be cut often. It also gives grass a coarse, ragged look. Beware of any grass mixtures that contain a lot of ryegrass, and reject any mix that contains orchard grass or timothy.

Starting a New Lawn from Seed

Most cool-season grasses are started from seed. A decent lawn can usually be established by following the directions on the seed package, after selecting the grass type based on proper soil analysis. If you want a really beautiful lawn, you should follow these preliminary steps and precautions.

Preparing the Seedbed. Under ideal conditions, the lawn area should be properly graded to insure adequate drainage. The surface soil should be firm and free of large clods and foreign matter. Into this soil mix well-decomposed organic matter and ample fertilizer.

To soils that have too much sand or gravel, add peat, well-rotted manure, spent mushroom soil, or decomposed sawdust. If the soil is very light, some clay can be broken up and mixed in, too. With a soil that contains a high amount of natural clay, mix in sand, perlite, vermiculite, or peat. Acid soils should receive a liberal dose of lime. When a soil test shows a deficiency of magnesium, add dolomitic ground limestone to provide both lime and magnesium. Be sure to mix in all additives thoroughly, and allow the seedbed to settle for about a week before seeding.

Add "starter" fertilizer to the seedbed to insure an immediate supply of available nutrients. Rake the fertilizer into the seedbed, at the same time giving the topsoil one more mixing and providing a final grading for a smooth, weed-free surface. If you don't have a two-wheel applicator, this is a good time to buy one. It can be used for uniform application of seeds, lawn chemicals, and other materials, as well as fertilizer.

Sowing the Seed. The best way to sow seed is with a mechanical seeder. Small areas can be seeded by hand, but uniform distribution is important, so use hand-seeding carefully if you must seed by hand. It is not a bad idea to mix the seed with equal amounts of sand to achieve better distribution, but adjust the quantities and the mechanical seeder accordingly.

Sow the planting area first in one direction, then at right angles to the original rows to get a complete cover. Carefully hand rake to cover the seed lightly, then firm the seed into the soil by rolling. It is wise to apply a light mulch of weed-free straw or hay over the seedbed. This will help hold moisture and prevent the seed from washing away. The mulch need not be removed; it will gradually deteriorate and provide extra nutrients. Steep slopes are poor candidates for grass, since mowing is difficult and dangerous. If you do plant grass on a slope, use a more sturdy mulch such as cheesecloth, gunny sacks, or commercial mulching cloth. These materials, too, will eventually rot.

Frequent watering is essential in the early stages of lawn development. Once the seedlings begin to sprout, keep them moist but not too wet. Light and frequent waterings are best, although there is little you can do about heavy rainstorms. Keep up the light watering

2 or 3 times a day, until the grass is well established, then water deeply at least once a week, more often during hot, dry periods. The time of day is not as important as the frequency, but mornings are best. This gives the blades time to dry before nightfall, when dampness can cause wilt and mildew.

Planting Vegetative Grasses

Vegetative grasses are planted by several methods, including complete sodding. This expensive method is rarely justified unless your time is very limited or you are planting a steep bank—which is not a good idea anyway.

Spot sodding is the method of choice for some grasses, as outlined in the table on grasses. To spot sod, prepare holes for the small pieces of sod, or plugs, at the recommended intervals, generally 1 foot apart. Set the plugs tightly in the holes and tamp firmly into place.

Strip sodding involves long rows of narrow sod, 2 to 4 inches wide, planted at measured intervals which differ depending on the type of grass. The strips must have firm contact with the surrounding soil.

Sprigging is the planting of individual stolons or runners, spaced at measured intervals. These are made by tearing apart or shredding pieces of established sod. The space intervals are determined by the spread rate of the grass (see the table on grasses).

Large areas of Bermuda grass can be established by shredding stolons at a rate of 90 to 120 bushels per acre. These are then spread over the ground with a manure spreader and disced lightly to firm them into the ground.

All of these methods require that the newly planted grass be kept moist until the lawn is well established. During the first year, light applications of a high-nitrogen fertilizer every 2 to 4 weeks during the growing season will help spread the plants.

CHOOSING GROUNDCOVER

In its generic sense a groundcover is anything that covers the ground, which can include grass, flowers, or vegetables. In the usual sense, a groundcover means a low-growing plant which is used away from normal footpaths because it cannot tolerate too much trampling, but which can withstand many conditions that grass and other plantings cannot.

Groundcovers are used to cover bare spots between shrubs, as in foundation plantings, to cover steep slopes or shady areas and to help prevent erosion. The most popular and useful types of groundcover are myrtle (periwinkle), ivy, and pachysandra (Japanese spurge). These evergreen plants grow rather quickly and multiply in time, covering the entire area with rich, dark shades of green, although they may look droopy and yellow during the winter. They do best in semi-shade but usually can tolerate full shade better than full sun. Myrtle has lovely little blue flowers in spring, and pachysandra sports creamy white blooms.

Don't restrict yourself to these evergreen plantings, however, if you would like a little more color and fragrance in your yard. Many hardy perennials serve very well as groundcovers. I once owned a Victorian house which was surrounded by old lilac and mock orange trees, with lily of the valley in between. In spring I sat on the porch inhaling the scent of all of them and thanking whoever owned the house many years ago and thoughtfully provided the variety of fragrance and color.

Lily of the valley is usually sold in packages of 12 pips at garden centers. If set out early enough, new plants may bloom the first year. Clumps spread quickly and last for years and years, as I can attest from personal experience.

There are dozens of hardy perennial plants that can be planted as groundcover, and I'll mention only a few of them here. For other choices, consult a large nursery or mail-order house. Here are some of the more widely planted varieties:

Barrenwort (Epimedium). A woody herb that tolerates almost any type of soil. It has dense foliage, lasts into winter, and sports white, yellow, and lavender flowers.

Bugle Weed. A perennial herb that can be grown in most soils and becomes very densely packed in a short time, it has blue-purple flowers.

Cotoneaster. A large semi-evergreen which reseeds itself, it does well in most soils but requires full sun and a moderate climate.

Dwarf Geranium. A hardy plant less than 6 inches tall, it blooms profusely with delicate pink flowers in early summer.

Foamflower (Tiarella). Excellent for moist, shady areas and where a woodsy effect is desired, the foamflower blooms with white spikes.

Hosta (Plantain Lily). A tufted plant with broad leaves like the plantain weed, it comes in variegated and other types and is good for shady areas. It needs moist, well-drained soil and frequent division.

Lamium.   Just another weed variety to most people, lamium, like other members of the mint family, grows aggressively and needs cutting back periodically. The deep lavender spikes bloom from May through summer.

Phlox Stonlifera.   One of numerous phlox varieties, this species spreads quickly in light shade. Its soft lavender-blue spikes appear in May and look especially lovely under dogwood and Japanese red maple trees.

Thrift.   A low-growing perennial herb with small pink flowers in spring. Thrift prefers sandy soil and full sun.

Violets.   Another old-time favorite, violets are considered by many to be a pesty weed, but they have handsome foliage beginning very early in the spring and lasting until fall. The blooms are gorgeous.

In addition to the types mentioned, there are some often overlooked evergreen types such as wintercreeper, or *Euonmymus fortunei,* which can be trained to creep up foundations and walls as well as over the ground. Other evergreens which can be bought in low-growing form or be trained as groundcover are Japanese holly, heather, juniper, bearberry, dwarf hollygrape *(Mahonia),* and wintergreen.

Check adaptability of all groundcovers to local climatic conditions.

Planting Groundcovers

Most groundcovers require the same sort of site, soil preparation, planting procedures, watering, and fertilizer. The soil should be dug out to a depth of about six inches, then mixed with ¼ to ⅓ as much organic material such as peat, well-rotted manure, or leaf mold. Spade thoroughly into the soil.

When the planting is on a low to medium slope, no additional preparation is necessary. Retaining walls are needed for plantings on steep slopes, except for junipers and cotoneasters, which can tolerate the dry conditions brought on by water running too quickly down the bank.

Early spring is usually the best time to plant groundcovers. Fertilize the soil according to local conditions, spading it into the soil before planting. Space the plants according to mature size and your budget. Many of the more popular groundcovers, such as myrtle and pachysandra, are slow in their spreading habits, so you may want to plant them close together. This can be prohibitively expensive for large areas. Ordinarily, small plants should be spaced 4 to 6 inches apart.

Most small groundcovers come in flats from the nursery. Use a small garden trowel to separate them, then using the same trowel, dig a hole for each plant as you take it from the flat. If you choose larger plants with root balls, plant them just as you would any other shrub. Use a mulch such as wood bark or chips, bean hulls, peat, or other organic matter to keep the ground free of weeds until the plants begin to multiply. The most efficient way to plant groundcover is by using black plastic mulch. First, lay the plastic over the planting area, staking or weighting down the edges. Next, cut holes in the plastic, and set the plants in place. Make sure that the plants are at the same level as before transplanting, and tamp good soil firmly around the roots. Water each plant thoroughly, then cover the plastic with organic material such as pine bark, wood chips, peat moss, or cocoa hulls.

If weeds do appear, pull them out by hand. Do not dig around these plants; you will break the surface roots and promote weed germination. For the first week or so, water daily, then water on a regular schedule every few days until the plants are firmly established. From then on, 1 inch of water every 10 to 14 days should suffice. During the winter months, when there is no snow cover, plantings in direct sunlight may need occasional watering to prevent thawing out of the plant tissues. Conifer branches or burlap spread over the plants in the winter will also help prevent permanent damage.

Upkeep

Like trees and shrubs groundcovers don't need a lot of care. Grass is another matter. It requires a lot of care.

Grass was made to be cut. You may love it tenderly, but cut it you must. Unlike trees, bushes, and most other plants, grass grows from the lower part of the stem rather than from the tips. Cutting stimulates growth by allowing more sunlight to reach the growing area. It also causes the grass to thicken at the base, thereby helping to crowd out weeds. Regular, frequent mowing, in fact, is the best weed killer there is.

Grass

Each type of grass has its optimum height, as shown in the table on grasses, and it should be cut back to the recommended height before it grows more than 50 percent higher than the optimum. That translates, for example, to about 3 inches for most grasses or less than 1 inch for bent grass. In general, for all grasses except bent grass, it is best to remove only ½ to 1 inch at a time.

One-half inch to an inch at a time can mean frequent mowing during the growing seasons—maybe 2 or 3 times a week. When there is a dry spell, grass may need cutting only once a month. During a drought, in fact, it is wise to allow more growth. In any case, if you want a nice lawn, you really have to check its growth carefully and mow it when it needs it.

In sturdy lawn growth grass blades send out rhizomes through the topsoil, with the roots extending below into the subsoil. (O. M. Scott)

For best results, vary the cutting pattern. Cut in one direction one time, and at right angles the next. If you have to cut twice at one time, go in opposite directions. Once in awhile, try diagonal cutting. If you cut the grass in the same direction all the time, the lawn may develop a slant in that direction.

What about clippings? Even the experts can't agree on whether you should leave them or remove them. Both views are partly right. If you mow often enough, the clippings should be light and act as a mulch. If you let the lawn grow too high, the clippings will choke the grass roots. The lawn does look better with the clippings removed, but they are not that noticeable when they are small. And when clippings decompose, they act as a mulch and add more nutrients to the soil.

My own choice is to buy a mulching mower. This type of mower cuts the clippings up into even smaller units so that they decompose faster. Again, you must keep up a regular mowing schedule when you allow the clippings to remain. A mulching mower may allow you to cheat just a little, but not much. Never leave clippings on if you have allowed the grass to grow above twice its optimum height.

This brings us to mowers. A mulching mower allows you to let the grass grow a little higher before cutting. For those who think they don't have the time or energy to cut their lawns as often as they should, a grass-catching attachment on the mower is a sound investment. Most mowers "throw" the clippings either to the left or right. If you already have a mower of that type and don't want to buy a grass-catcher, try to maneuver the mower so that most of the clippings are thrown to an innocuous area, or back onto the lawn. Avoid, as best you can, throwing the clippings onto walks, driveways, or the swimming pool—and your neighbor's property. If, for example, you have a naturally wooded area next to the lawn, run the mower so that the grass flies into it. Whenever clippings are heavy or unsightly, you will just have to rake them up. Throw them into your compost pile, if you have one.

Just for the record, there is such a thing as a *reel* mower, but you probably haven't seen one except in tandem on a golf course. I had one once, and it did a beautiful job on the grass, cutting it cleanly and gently. In the 1940s and 1950s it was supposed to be the best mower for grass. You had to push it, though, and that was work. Eventually they were manufactured with motors, but this meant the mowers cost more and were expensive to repair. I gave up on mine when the repairs cost more than a new rotary mulching mower. Still, if you have a small lawn and like the exercise, there is nothing like a push-type reel mower for a beautiful lawn. They are still available, but not too easy to find.

For a big lawn a nice riding rotary mower is the most efficient, with a rotary blade, of course.

One more thing—an important thing. The omnipresent rotary mower is a dangerous instrument if not used properly. Be sure to read all the safety instructions that come with a new mower. The newer machines have been designed to eliminate some of the hazards, but always remember at least these points:

- Inspect the lawn for rocks, debris, or other material that could be picked up by the rotor blade and thrown. It could hit you, people near you, or even fly into a window.
- *Never* lift up the machine until the power is off and the rotor blade has stopped spinning. Many fingers and hands have been lost that way.
- Children should not be allowed even *near* a rotary mower. Keep them inside or in another area of the yard while mowing. A thrown stone may hit you in the leg and not injure you too badly. The trajectory of the stone is perfect, however, for the head of a child. It should go without saying that children shouldn't be allowed to operate a power mower until they are old enough to know what they are doing and have been fully instructed.
- Be careful when mowing a slope. The steeper the slope, the more difficult it is to mow. You can cut along a low slope, but steeper slopes may require cutting from the top only, for safety's sake. And, does it need saying? Don't use a rider mower on a steep slope.

In addition to mowing, your lawn needs watering. I've discussed the schedule for new seedlings—watering at least once a day, with two or three times even better. Once the lawn is established, water about twice a week unless there is rain. In the hot summer months during a drought, the lawn should receive a ½ inch of water every 3 days and every 2 days for sandy soils.

To determine how much water you need to supply ½ inch, set out 4 coffee cans or other cans of the same size, scattered around the sprinkling area. Turn on the water for half an hour. Pour the water from all 4 cans into one of them, measure the depth with a ruler, then divide by four to get an average. Adjust your sprinkling time accordingly. For example, if there is 1 inch of water in all 4 cans, the average depth is ¼ inch. You need twice as much water, so double the sprinkling time to an hour.

This example assumes that you have some type of automatic sprinkler, which you should have to do an effective job on your lawn. Hand watering with a hose is not only tedious and hot, it is also unscientific. Best of all, if you can afford it, are underground sprinklers, described in Chapter 5. In any case, when you water, even with a hose, don't just dampen the ground. Soak it to at least a ½ inch. Better to overwater by a ½ inch or so than just to get water to the top inch or two of soil. Underwatering simply encourages weeds and crabgrass. The grass roots extend 5 or 6 inches down. That's where you need the water.

FERTILIZERS AND CHEMICALS

With regard to fertilizers, there's one big "don't." When a lawn begins to turn brown during a hot, dry spell, don't fertilize but *water.* It could also be suffering from a disease such as brownpatch, but that wouldn't be aided by fertilizer either.

The times to fertilize are spring and fall. Ideally, your lawn should receive two doses of fertilizer in the spring. The first should be very early, as soon as the growing season begins, and the second before the really hot months begin. The same applies to autumn. Fertilize once in early fall or very late summer, and again before it starts to freeze. Check the manufacturer's recommendations for amount and rate of fertilizer in your area.

Fertilizers are often combined with other chemicals such as crabgrass preventers or weed killers, which can be applied separately, if you prefer. Indeed, applying these chemicals at all is a matter of need and personal choice. If you plant your lawn carefully and apply water and fertilizer properly, you'll have less need of weed killers than will those who neglect the basics.

If crabgrass is a problem (and it often is), the time to control it is before it appears. First, resolve to take better basic care of the grass, and then apply a pre-emergence chemical early in the game, before the crabgrass appears. A combination fertilizer-preventer such as Turf Builder Plus Halts is the treatment of choice.

Many diseases can affect your lawn, and insects such as grubs and chinch bugs can wreak havoc. Pesticides and sprays for all of these are available, but first you must have a diagnosis. The best bet is to dig up a sample of the sick turf, and take it to your local extension service or qualified nursery.

GROUNDCOVER MAINTENANCE

One of the big advantages of groundcovers is that they need little attention. After initial watering and mulching, watering about every 2 weeks in dry periods should suffice. When the groundcover is near to grass or mixed in with grass, you may as well water the groundcover at the same time. The extra water won't hurt.

Fertilizer should be applied once in spring and once in fall, but some plants can thrive with little or no extra nutrients once they are well established. Fertilizer should be applied by hand to the ground around the plants, and the pellets should not touch the foliage unless it is completely dry.

Weed killers and other chemicals should not be applied to the groundcover bed. Proper mulching until full cover is reached will prevent most weeds. Those that do appear should be pulled out by hand.

Larger groundcover bushes may need pruning, but remove only dead wood, or shear to keep the plants in check. Evergreen plants may suffer winter damage. To prevent this, use an antitranspirant spray in late fall to reduce moisture loss. In direct sunlight, the loss can be more severe. A mulch of leaves, small branches, or other protective material may be necessary during very cold weather.

SOME ALTERNATIVES

If all of this sounds like a lot of trouble, it is. Groundcovers don't take much care but can take a long time to fill in an area. Grass covers fast but demands a great deal of attention afterward.

It is difficult to envision your landscape without any grass or groundcovers at all. Careful planning can keep lawn areas to a minimum, if you prefer to do without much grass. New homes in wooded areas can be built without disturbing the natural landscape more than necessary, drastically reducing the need for new plantings. If lawn areas are too big now or too difficult to keep in good shape, they can be dug up and replanted with shrubs, gardens, groundcover, or whatever suits your fancy.

Difficult spots, such as areas of heavy shade, that are already planted with skimpy grass can be replanted with groundcover or turned into recreational areas. A deck or patio, or perhaps a flower garden, can replace such areas. (If the problem is heavy shade, though, choose flowers with care; the *Impatiens*, for example, flourishes in shade.)

Under trees which inhibit growth of any kind, bare ground can be covered with materials sold at nurseries and garden-supply houses for this purpose. Wood bark, marble chips, or other decorative gravel can be used here or anywhere where the only thing that will grow is a weed.

In analyzing your yard, always remember there is no need to keep a lawn or anything else, if it is too much bother or you just don't want it. Go over your entire plan, decide what you want and don't want, and be willing to start all over again.

4 Gardens

Any veteran gardener knows that there are numerous books, magazines, and other publications devoted to the intricacies of every aspect of gardening. If roses are your special favorite, there are many sources of advice on growing and propagation. For those who fancy tomatoes or zucchini, there are sources much more detailed than this book.

My purpose here, as throughout the book, is to concentrate on overall design and planning. I won't try to tell you how to grow and prepare zucchini, for instance. I will try to help you site your garden or gardens, decide what plants to cultivate, and establish when and where to plant and in general advise on similar subjects of general interest.

Those who want detailed advice should consult the local agricultural society, extension service, and state and federal agricultural departments. The U.S. Department of Agriculture has a great many books and publications available through the Government Printing Office. The GPO operates 25 bookstores in large cities around the country, and publications are available by mail order or phone. For more information and/or a current catalog, write to:

SUPERINTENDENT of DOCUMENTS
U.S. Government Printing Office
Washington, DC 20402

You can also call (202) 275-3050. Publications are available to

Canadians and citizens of other countries for a surcharge of 25 percent.

WORKING WITH YOUR PLAN

Your garden areas, like everything else, should be part of the overall outdoor design. Personal preference, land contour, soil type, climate, geography, and other factors will play a large part in their planning. If you have read Chapters 1 through 3, you should know all these factors by heart.

Some flowers should be part of your landscape, even if they provide only a small splash among the foundation plantings or an edging strip along the sidewalk. Type, color, size, and other considerations are highly personal, so we won't make any specific suggestions.

One important factor in choosing flowers is worth some extended thought. Will the flower bed consist of annuals or perennials or both? Annuals provide a wide choice of brilliant colors, and most of them bloom throughout the growing season. As the name suggests, however, they won't come up next year, and you'll have to start over again. For those who enjoy variety, continual replanting may be good, but annuals consume time and money.

Perennial flowers have the great advantage that their name implies. Plant them once, and you will have blooms every year for a long time (how long depends on what type and on how you care for them). Most perennials are hardy and produce large, beautiful blooms, and some (not too many), like everblooming roses, have flowers all summer. The disadvantages of perennials are that most bloom only once each season, and they have a high initial cost. The variety is much more limited than for annuals, too. Most perennials do not grow true to type from seed and must be taken from cuttings or plant divisions.

There is yet another group that should be discussed when planning your flower garden. These are the biennials—plants that flower the second year after planting. They are grown from seed, and some examples are columbine, foxglove, sweet william, delphinium, and Canterbury bells.

When choosing your garden varieties, don't restrict yourself to just what's available from the nearest nursery. Once again, planning is the key. Examine mail-order and seed catalogs as soon as they are available, usually in early winter. Keep in mind that many shrubs and

Roses make a very special garden. (John Staby/Jackson & Perkins Co.)

ornamental or fruit trees can provide color, too. Spring- and fall-planting bulbs should be remembered when planning a perennial garden. And if it isn't too late, what some gardeners consider weeds can be left where they are or transplanted from the natural environment. Wildflowers, day lilies, ferns, and other native varieties can be transplanted to make lovely accents or can be left in their native habitat. In desert climates, cactus can be used for foundation plantings, and some varieties sport gorgeous flowers. Some vegetables have marvelous blooms and can be mixed right in with the flower bed.

In general, it is wise to provide a mix of annuals and perennials. But choose only a few varieties to avoid the "botanical garden" effect. Pay attention to blooming times, and plan ahead for continuous flowering. Peonies, for example, are a beautiful sight in spring, but not much to look at the rest of the year. If the plants are young and not overcrowded, plant some dahlias, gladiolas, or canna lilies for later color. If the plants are older and closer together, annuals may be better.

Similarly, if you have a bed of crocus, tulips, hyacinth, daffodils, or other spring-flowering bulbs, mix in some annuals or summer-flowering plants for year-round blooms. But remember that spring-flowering bulbs must be planted in fall and that they should be cut down after they have bloomed.

Late-flowering perennials, on the other hand, may be mixed with earlier-flowering annuals or bulbs or spring-flowering perennials. Use windflower *(Anemone japonica)*, New England aster *(Aster noude)*, or sedum with earlier-flowering varieties of your choice.

YOUR GARDEN SITE

The determined gardener can grow flowers almost anywhere, but most flowers and vegetables prefer a sunny location. Some annuals, notably *Impatiens*, do better in the shade and are highly recommended where there is little sun. *Impatiens* are hardy, prolific bloomers and take almost no care whatsoever. They come in a variety of colors and can be grown from seed or nursery seedlings.

Impatiens, here shown in a hybrid dwarf strain, bloom brilliantly in dark, shadowy corners. (Pan-American Seed Co.)

Tuberous begonias also do reasonably well in shade, as do plantain lily, forget-me-not, Jacob's ladder, violets, and lily of the valley. These are all perennials. For other local hardy plants, see your extension agent or visit your nursery.

Except for the areas where shade-tolerant plants will be located, your garden should be planned so that it receives sun for a substantial part of the day. As usual, observe well before you plant. Watch the sun's pattern during the day, and mark the path of the shadows across your plot. If the plant you have in mind requires full sun, don't waste money and energy by setting it in an area that has shade for more than an hour or two a day. "Full sun" means exactly that. The sun should shine on the garden from at least 9:00 A.M. to 3:00 P.M. during the summer months.

The same applies to edible gardens. There are no shade-loving vegetables or fruits. All respond to shade by growing slower and taller and maturing late if at all. The only exception is in extreme desert situations, where afternoon shade can provide a shield from the searing heat and drought.

Remember your overall plan when planting both trees and a garden. Most gardens can tolerate a certain amount of spotty shade from walls, shrubs, or fences. Young, small trees near a garden are generally not a problem, but as they grow bigger, cast bigger shadows, and send out more thirsty roots, they will choke off all growth beneath them.

It's easy to forget that your home itself is a source of considerable shade. Never plant a garden that needs sun within 6 to 8 feet of the north side of a one-story house. Double that distance for a 2-story home. For gardens the south side of the house is best, and west is better than east, because the sun is hotter there. Sun provides not only light for photosynthesis to stimulate plant growth, but it also warms the soil. Since most plants need warmth as well as light, set them close to the house on the east and west, if possible, because they receive reflected heat from the house.

In addition to shade, other natural phenomena to be avoided are high winds, marshy or flood-prone areas, areas of potential erosion, and spots that have unusual fog or frost problems. In urban areas, beware of air pollution, and have the soil checked for possible past contaminants.

Once the sun patterns and climatic and other natural conditions are accounted for, the siting of the garden is a matter of personal choice and common sense. Don't, for example, plant delicate flowers or vegetables next to the basketball or tennis court. And don't plant a rose garden in the path of animals or children. All will be the worse for it.

Good places for flowers are in edgings along walks and driveways and the sunny sides of fences or outbuildings. Rose and other show gardens can be in a sunny area off by themselves, but be sure to allow room for pruning or other maintenance. Paths of brick in sand, gravel, slate, or flagstone will facilitate garden care and make a nice place for walking and admiring.

Vegetable gardens are usually placed in a far-off spot because they are not considered "pretty." There are those who will dispute this view, however. A well-tended vegetable or fruit garden is not an unpleasant sight. If you are proud of your edible garden—and you should be—there is certainly nothing wrong with putting it within easy view, where you can watch the scallions thrive and the beans sprout.

Plantings along a path are attractive and add pleasure to any walk. (National Landscape Association)

GROWING ANNUALS

Annuals are the most versatile of all flowers. Not only do they provide a vast array of colors, but they also come in varying forms, heights, growth patterns, and foliage textures. They bloom from spring or early summer until late fall and are equally at home in formal settings, informal gardens, mass plantings, or small intimate beds.

Use annuals in beds, borders, edgings, among shrubbery, or planted with perennials and biennials. Annuals are ideal for patio tubs, window boxes, hanging baskets, and other planters.

With the huge selection available, there have to be at least a few annuals that will delight every gardener. If you are new to gardening, it is wise to depend on the newer varieties and hybrids, even though they may be a bit more expensive. One good key to quality is the F_1 hybrid designation, which denotes a costly and delicate combination of at least two different true-breeding parental lines, stressing the best characteristics of each.

Hybrids are especially important when planting weaker and disease-prone plants such as ageratums, geraniums, marigolds, pansies, petunias, snapdragons, sultanas, wax begonias, and zinnias. For durability in most of the United States and Canada, some of the hardiest plants are cosmos, four-o'clock, Madagascar periwinkle, marigold, moonflower, spiderflower, and summer cypress.

There are no secrets to growing annuals. Preparation is the common-sense, time-proven procedure. Annuals prefer a loose, porous soil with adequate aeration and moisture-holding capacity. Before each planting, do some deep spading, working in several inches of organic matter such as peat moss, well-rotted manure, or compost.

If the soil is heavy, also add sand or perlite. Shortly before planting time, add enough lime to bring up the pH level to between 6.0 and 6.8. Apply a 5-10-5 fertilizer evenly, and work it shallowly into the topsoil. Rake the bed evenly just before planting.

Large-seeded annuals can germinate reliably when planted directly in the ground. These robust plants, such as balsam, dahlia, marigold, nasturtium, and zinnia, should be sown when the soil is warm and all danger of frost is past. Most annuals, however, particularly those with small seeds, should be started indoors in a hotbed or greenhouse. Unless you are a relatively seasoned gardener with the proper facilities, it is best to buy started plants from a nursery or garden center.

If you plant annuals from seed, be sure to thin them after they sprout. The same applies, but to a lesser degree, for plants bought as seedlings. Water all seedlings lightly and daily until established. An inch of water a week is usually enough for most mature annuals, but more mature plants should be watered to a depth of 7 to 10 inches when the soil is very dry. Light sprinklings, as with grass, only help the weeds. Try to water early enough in the day so that the foliage has a chance to dry off before nightfall.

Almost all annuals become tall and stringy unless the spent blooms are pinched back. Pinching off blooms is especially important for petunias, pansies, ageratums, snapdragons, and zinnias. There are, however, some annuals that should be left alone; among these are poppies, balsam, and cockscomb.

Once annuals are established, mulching helps keep the beds neat, prevents water loss, cuts down on weeds, and adds organic matter. Such organic mulches as peat moss, cocoa shells, and shredded hardwood bark are best for this purpose. In addition to occasional watering and pinching when necessary, this is all the care that annuals need. Once the flowering starts, settle back and enjoy.

PRACTICAL PERENNIALS— PRETTY AND PERMANENT

As you can see, people who praise perennials are prone to poetry. It is true, nonetheless, that the virtue of perennials is that they are not only lovely to look at but ideal for those who want to plan their garden for easy care over a long period of time.

But don't let the word "perennial" fool you. Some plants are more "perennial" than others. Many perennials require some sort of care, and most should be divided and/or replanted every few years. The more "wild" the plant is, the less likely it is to need a lot of work. Plants like day lilies and violets need very little care, but chrysanthemum, fall aster, golden marguerite, lamb's ear, and other members of the artemisia family must be lifted, divided, and replanted every 2 years. Insects and disease may mean short life for such varieties as columbines, delphiniums, and bearded iris. Protect them with appropriate sprays or dusts.

Perennials may be started by several methods, depending on the type and climate. Some can be started from seed, but this is usually tricky and requires indoor starting, as discussed above for some annuals. Others begin life as a bulb, most of which must be planted in the fall, but some in spring or even summer. Others, notably peonies and dahlias, are bought as potato-like tubers. The safest and easiest way to start these and the other types just mentioned is to buy plants already started in containers or pots.

No matter how you start your plants, soil preparation is again the key to successful growth. The ground should be spaded to a depth of 12 to 18 inches, organic matter added, and good drainage provided. Since you want your perennials to last a long time, it is worthwhile to install drain tiles if there may be a problem with wet feet.

New plants should be fertilized in the same way as annuals. After the plants are established, a yearly application of 5-10-5 fertilizer will help them keep their vigor. After an initial soaking, water the plants once a week for a month to make sure that they are well established. After that, water only during dry spells. Always water deep, since light watering only encourages weed growth. Mulching is advisable, too, and insecticides or pesticides may be needed, depending on the susceptibility of the particular plant.

Container plants should be set at the same depth as the pot depth. Bulbs are set at varying depths, as are tuberous plants, which are usually near the surface. Peonies are planted only 2 inches below ground level, 3 inches at most. Form a berm around the crown of new container plants to help catch additional water.

For more information on selecting hardy perennials for your area, consult the sources mentioned previously. In addition to the popular plants already mentioned, other widely available varieties that can be grown in most climates are dianthus (hardy pinks, carnation), bleeding hearts, baby's breath, hibiscus (rose mallow), iris, poppy, hardy phlox, primrose, rudbeckia, autumn stonecrop (a sedum cultivar), yarrow, campanula, and veronica.

It is odd that perhaps the all-time perennial favorite is hardly ever listed as such. Nearly everyone's symbol of beauty (as well as love and romance) is the rose. Since it does grow and flower every year (with care), I, at least, consider it a perennial—and a wonderful one.

Roses take a lot of care in planting, pruning, watering, and other maintenance, but they are worth it. If you want large, long-stemmed roses for cutting, you can plant hybrid tea roses. Most of these require disbudding, which means that you have to pinch off all the buds on each stem except the top one. It can be a tedious job, but the results are spectacular. We highly recommend at least a small rose garden for the serious flower enthusiast.

SPECIALTY GARDENS

Special situations demand special responses. With good planning (and some luck), difficult areas can become showpieces rather than disasters. Steeply sloping banks, for example, can be disastrous if planted with grass. Mowing is both difficult and dangerous. Even worse, however, is to leave a bank stripped of natural vegetation. The first severe rainstorm can cause the bank to come crashing down.

Rock Gardens

One good solution for a bank or any other protruding or high area is a rock garden. If there are natural rocks, all the better, but you can bring them in, if necessary. When selecting rocks for a garden, use at least a few large ones. Some should be at least a foot across, and try for a few two or three feet long. Intersperse the big ones with smaller rocks, but avoid the very small ones.

If you are digging into a slope and setting in the stones, the natural soil should do fine for plantings. Fresh topsoil should be used when you are building up from a more or less level ground.

When the rocks are stratified (occurring in lines, like shale and bluestone) and are moved from their natural location, be sure to set them as they occur naturally, with the grain aligned in the same direction. Boulders and more rounded rocks can be set any way, but if the rocks are glacial in origin, one side will appear more weathered than the others. If so, such rocks will appear more natural with the weathered side exposed. Try to bury all rocks to their approximate natural depth, if they were previously exposed.

No matter what you use for your rock garden, the finished picture should be one of the solidity of the dominant rock mass. This is strengthened by restricting the plantings to low and not-too-luxuriant varieties.

The most pleasing plant arrangements are those which enhance this natural, solid look. If you are a serious gardener, study rock-garden plants in their native habitat, and attempt to duplicate the same look yourself. As usual, assistance from your nursery and others knowledgeable in the field is advised, as well as studying catalog descriptions.

Two types of plantings show to good advantage in a rock garden. The first are those that work best in massed plantings. Some of these are arabis, aubrietia, spreading phlox, low campanulas, sempervivum, *Hypericum repens* (St.-John's-worts), gentians, mossy saxi-frages, and the smaller spreading dianthus. The other type of rock garden planting, and the type that is the delight of enthusiasts, is a plant grown for its intrinsic, but not very showy, beauty. Rarer, more exotic plantings can be used here, such as Lewisias, *Ramonda pyrenaica,* and some of the primulas.

For spring color, low-growing bulbs such as crocus, glory of the snow, scilla (squill), and snowdrop or *Muscari* (grape hyacinth) are often interspersed with perennials. Where the soil is deep, narcissus or tulips can be used, too. Some gardeners like to add annuals, although most prefer rock gardens that require very little planting or maintenance after it is set in.

No rock garden, however small, is complete without at least a few shrubs. Taller shrubs can be used for background, but in the garden itself, very low or dwarf varieties are mandatory. Try to imitate a mountain when choosing shrubs, using conifers where possible. Plant gnarled and spreading forms for the windswept "hilltop," bushy specimens for the lower slopes, and tiny, spiky trees for the sheltered bottom of the valley.

Herb Gardens

Herbs have long been a favorite of serious gardeners, especially those who favor organic gardening. Many are beautiful to look at, as well as wonderful cooking aids.

Herbs will grow well in any garden where vegetables thrive and can be grown among shrubs or in flower beds, borders, and boxes. All they need is good drainage and at least six hours of sun a day. Most herbs require an alkaline soil, so add lime if soil tests show a pH much below 7.0.

The soil is prepared as it is for vegetables, using similar fertilizers and mulches. Although herbs can be propagated in many ways, you'll get the best results by sowing annuals directly into the beds and by buying perennials as plants or taking cuttings from friends or neighbors. Herbs are especially resistant to disease, but inspect all new plants for evidence of disease before purchasing. Insects are not usually a problem for established plants, since bees, ladybugs, and praying mantises protect as well as pollinate these plants.

Herb gardening is a specialty unto itself, with many varieties available, and their selection depends as much on your palate as it does on their horticultural virtues. Listed here are a few favorites, though, with some of their characteristics.

Basil. A tender annual, so plant seeds when all danger of frost is gone. Harvest when flower heads appear, pinching back the flower heads for further growth. Basil has a clovelike flavor with a special affinity for egg dishes, tomatoes, and salads.

Chives. The most delicate-tasting member of the onion family. A very pretty perennial, with lavender flower heads that can be dried for winter arrangements. Chopped fresh finely, it can be used in salads or to garnish numerous dishes.

Dill. A hardy annual that is planted as seed in early spring or in autumn for an early start. It easily reseeds itself if allowed to mature. Green flower pedicles are distinctive in arrangements.

Sweet Marjoram. A tender perennial planted as an annual, it can be bought as small plants from nurseries. Two harvests are possible by cutting back stems to an inch above the ground after first bloom. A delicious, spicy, aromatic herb, sweet marjoram is used to flavor poultry, lamb, and herbal teas.

Rosemary. An evergreen perennial, but a very tender one that needs winter protection until well established. Great as a greenhouse plant. Buy young plants, and take cuttings in late summer. Use as you would sweet marjoram.

Sage. Another evergreen perennial, but very hardy. Needs lots of sun and good drainage. The strong woodsy flavor enhances cheeses, poultry, dressings, sausages, and pork.

Sorrel (French). A hardy perennial, used fresh to add a nice sharp taste to greens, spinach, and soups. It can be grown from seed or root divisions. Broad leaves are cut and used throughout season.

Tarragon. A tender perennial requiring root protection during severe winters. Buy young plants from a reputable source, or propagate from cuttings or root divisions. The robust flavor is derived by drying leaves in the oven. Used extensively in vinegars, sauces, and salad dressings and on fish, turkey, and vegetables; it gives the distinctive taste to sauce Bernaise.

Thyme. A hardy perennial best grown from divisions bought at a nursery. Needs sun and good drainage. A low, bushy plant with lovely blooms. Its stimulating flavor is used with almost any food.

Other popular and delicious herbs are garlic, Egyptian onion, lovage, various mints, oregano, salad burnet, the savories, and, of course, parsley.

Cactus Gardens

Cactus is a succulent, meaning that its leaves are fleshy and absorbent, allowing them to survive many days of drought without water. Cactus is the best-known of the succulents, but other varieties are crassula, a family of hardy succulents which includes jade, sedum, sempervivum (house leeks), and kalanchoes.

Succulents can be grown as house plants in colder climates and are excellent for sunny areas such as solariums or solar greenhouses. They thrive on neglect, needing only some, but not too much direct, sunlight to survive and very little water. Overwatering, in fact, is the one thing that will ruin them. Unlike most other house plants, they actually love overcrowded roots, so they rarely need repotting.

For outdoor gardening, there are only a few places where cactus gardens are possible. The rule of thumb is: if cacti grow naturally where you are, they will grow in your garden. With few exceptions, cold winters will kill them.

Unfortunately, the king of the cactus, the saguaro, is an endangered species, and you can't buy them. Some preferred varieties are *Gateria, Caphalocereus* (old man cactus), and a strange prickle-less breed, *Rhipsalis,* which grows in trees and comes from deep in the tropical jungle. This *does* need watering.

VEGETABLES FOR VICTORY

During the scarcities of World War II, the home vegetable garden was known as a victory garden. There was a huge upsurge in home-grown foods, which opened many people's eyes to the advantages of fresh fruits and vegetables. Though we are not at war, these advantages have not changed. Supermarket produce is all right, but pales by comparison to right-off-the-vine tomatoes, beans, peas, or cucumbers.

In addition to the pleasure of fresh produce, you'll also save money. Studies have shown that for every quarter invested in a vegetable garden, you get a dollar's worth of groceries in return.

Planning Your Edible Garden

When you plan a vegetable garden, hard-nosed practicality, rather than form and beauty, is called for. The first thing is not to overdo it. Most people make their garden too big, and wind up with a weed patch by late summer. It's fun to set the plants and contemplate beautiful, tasty results, but meanwhile there is a lot of work to be done. Most of us just aren't up to it.

If you have a lot of space and a garden tractor, you can feed a family of 4 very amply with a 50 × 50-foot plot and have food left over for freezing and canning. The vast majority of us, though, have only our spade, our hoe, and a few other hand tools. When you have to use muscle power, limit your vegetable garden to 20 × 25 feet at most, and avoid such space-takers as squash, pumpkins, and corn. Unfortunately for us corn-lovers, kernels must be planted in at least 2 rows, side by side, for cross-pollination. That takes quite a bit of space which is better served by smaller plants.

But use your imagination. It isn't necessary to have a big vegetable garden. A small plot can yield plenty of juicy tomatoes, snappy green beans, and pungent radishes. And why not use window boxes or planters for carrots, onions, lettuce, or whatever? If you want to pretty them up, plant some annuals in front. In foundation plantings, try some tomatoes, eggplants, or vine crops for added color as well as good eating. Try training cucumbers or melons up railings, trellises, or fences. A cucumber vine will do very well in only a cubic foot of soil if you use liquid plant food every two weeks.

Luscious beefsteak tomatoes are a beautiful sight for the gardener. (Geo. J. Ball Inc)

A Selection of Vegetables and Their Climate Requirements

Cold-hardy Plants for Early Spring Planting		Cold-tender or Heat-hardy Plants for Late Spring or Early Summer Planting		
Very Hardy (Plant 4–6 Weeks before Frost-free Date)	*Hardy (Plant 2–4 Weeks before Frost-free Date)*	*Not Cold-hardy (Plant on Frost-free Date)*	*Requiring Hot Weather (Plant 1 Week or More after Frost-free Date)*	*Medium Heat-tolerant (Good for Summer Planting)*
Broccoli	Beets	Beans, snap	Beans, lima	Beans, all
Cabbage	Carrots	Corn, sweet	Cucumber	Chard
Lettuce	Chard	Okra	Eggplant	Corn, sweet
Onions	Mustard	Squash	Melons	Soybeans
Peas	Parsnips	Tomato	Peppers	Squash
Potato	Radish		Sweet potato	
Spinach				
Turnips				

Hardy Plants for Late Summer or Fall Planting Except in the North	
(Plant 6–8 Weeks before First Fall Freeze)	
Beets	Collards
Kale	Lettuce
Mustard	Spinach
Turnips	

Farmers plant successive crops each year, and so can you. Try an early-yielding vegetable in the spring, and plant a late-blooming one for a later harvest. Check your extension office for suggested varieties. The chart shown here is available free to all residents of Suffolk County (New York) from the Extension Association. It applies to all states in the Northeast. Similar information should be available for your area.

Your vegetable garden must be planted where it soaks up as much sun as possible. It is especially important to steer clear of black walnut trees. I personally love black walnut trees, for their wood if

Home Garden Vegetable Selections and Characteristics
(northeast United States and lower Canada)

Vegetable	Quan-tity	Will Plant	Plant- or Hill-spacing in Row	Distance between Rows—Hand Cultivation	Planting Time		Plants Outdoors
					Seeds Indoors	Seeds Outdoors	
Asparagus	Pkt.	75 ft.	1–2 in.	20 in.		April-early May	April
Beans, Bush	½ lb.	75 ft.	2 in.	2–3 ft.		Late May-mid-July	
Beans, Lima	½ lb.	75 ft.	8–10 in.	2½–3 ft.		May 20–25 or after June 10	
Beans, Pole	½ lb.	50 "hills"	3 ft.	3½–4 ft.		Late May	
Beets	1 oz.	80 ft.	2 in.	14–18 in.		Late April-mid-July	
Broccoli	Pkt.	200 plants	1½ ft.	2½–3 ft.	Late March-April	May-June	Early July
Brussels Sprouts	Pkt.	150 plants	2 ft.	3 ft.		Mid-May-June	Early July
Cabbage, Early	Pkt.	250 plants	1 ft.	2½ ft.	February-March		Late April-May
Cabbage, Late	Pkt.	250 plants	1–1½ ft.	3 ft.		Mid-May-June	Early July
Cabbage, Chinese	Pkt.	40 ft.	1½ ft.	2 ft.		July	
Carrots	½ oz.	150 ft.	1½–2 in.	1½ ft.		Late April-mid-July	
Cauliflower	Pkt.	160 plants	2 ft.	3 ft.		Mid-May	Early July
Celery, Early	Pkt.	400 plants	6 in.	3 ft.	Late February		May-early June
Celery, Late	Pkt.	400 plants	6 in.	3 ft.	Mid-April	Early May	June-early July
Corn, Sweet Early	½ lb.	500 ft.	1 ft.	3 ft.		Late April-early May	
Corn, Sweet Late	½ lb.	600 ft.	1–1½ ft.	3 ft.		Mid-May-late June	
Cucumbers	Pkt.	20 "hills"	1–2 ft.	5–6 ft.		Late May-late June	
Egg Plant	Pkt.	100 plants	2 ft.	3 ft.	Late March		Late May or early June
Endive	Pkt.	30 ft.	8–12 in.	1½ ft.		Mid-July	

Home Garden Vegetable Selections and Characteristics (northeast United States and lower Canada) *(Continued)*

Vegetable	Quan-tity	Will Plant	Plant- or Hill-spacing in Row	Distance between Rows—Hand Cultivation	Planting Time		Plants Outdoors
					Seeds Indoors	Seeds Outdoors	
Kale	Pkt.	25 ft.	10–12 in.	2 ft.		Late April-mid-July	
Kohlrabi	Pkt.	40 ft.	6 in.	1½ ft.		April-July	
Lettuce, Head	Pkt.	100 plants	12–15 in.	1½ ft.	March-April	April-July	Late April-early May
Lettuce, Leaf	Pkt.	30 ft.	6 in.	1½ ft.		Late April-August	
Muskmelon	Pkt.	20 "hills"	2–3 ft.	6 ft.	Late April early May	Late May	Early June
Water-melon	Pkt.	8 "hills"	4 ft.	8 ft.	Late April early May	Late May	Early June
Onion Seed	½ oz.	100 ft.	1–3 in.	1–1½ ft.		Late April-mid-May	
Onion sets	1 lb.	50–75 ft.	2–3 in.	1–1½ ft.			April-mid-May
Onion plants	100	35 ft.	4–5 in.	1–1½ ft.			April-mid-May
Parsley	Pkt.	30 ft.	4–6 in.	1½ ft.		April-May	
Parsnips	½ oz.	75 ft.	2 in.	2–2½ ft.		April-May	
Peas	½ lb.	50 ft.	½–1 in.	2½–3 ft.		April-early May	
Peppers	Pkt.	75 plants	1½ ft.	2½ ft.	Late February or March		Late May-early June
Radishes	Pkt.	25–30 ft.	1 in.	1 ft.		April-May-August	
Rutabaga	Pkt.	50 ft.	6–8 in.	2 ft.		Early July	
Spinach	1 oz.	80 ft.	3–6 in.	1–1½ ft.		April-August	
Squash, Summer	Pkt.	6–8 "hills"	3–4 ft.	3–4 ft.		Late May-late June	
Squash, Winter	Pkt.	3–4 "hills"	6–8 ft.	6–8 ft.		Late May-mid-June	
Swiss Chard	Pkt.	15 ft.	8 in.	1½ ft.		April-July	
Tomatoes	Pkt.	150 plants	2–3 ft.	4–5 ft.	Late March-early April		Late May-mid-June
Turnips	Pkt.	50 ft.	2–3 in.	1½ ft.		Mid-July-August	

Courtesy Joseph Harris Co.

nothing else, and they are a great investment if you have a lot of low-lying acreage. But black walnuts give off a toxic substance through their roots called juglone. Don't plant a vegetable garden within 30 feet of a black walnut tree.

Before planting, prepare the soil as you would for any garden. The soil should contain plenty of organic matter. Compost is excellent for both soil-conditioning and providing nutrients. Your vegetables should have additional fertilizer, too. Any balanced fertilizer containing nitrogen, phosphorus, and potash will do. Add some before you plow. Liquid fertilizer is a good alternative, applied at planting time and 2 or 3 times more during the growing season. Slow-release fertilizers are also available. Use them only once before planting.

Timing is all-important in planting vegetables. Find out the best planting times from local sources, or use the information on the seed package. And buy only treated or certified seed. Cheap seeds only create problems and cost more in the long run. If you buy started plants, ask the nursery about the best time to plant.

Mulching can prevent a lot of cultivating and weeding. Black plastic mulch is excellent for vegetables. Place the sheets flat on the ground and weight the edges with stones. You can sow seeds through the plastic by slashing long slits in it or cutting holes for individual seedlings. The plastic will hold water that seeps through the holes, and it hastens ripening by increasing the soil temperature.

FRUITS AND NUTS

Not many of us think of fruits and nuts when planning our gardens, and for good reason. Most grow on trees, and we think of trees only for shade and ornamentation, even though many of the ornamental trees are really fruit trees or hybrids thereof. But even nut trees can be a good investment for shade as well as the nuts. Many of them, such as walnut or pecan, yield beautiful and expensive woods if you ever cut them down.

Some fruits can be grown on a smaller plot. Excellent apples, peaches, pears, or cherries can be grown in just 3 or 4 years from dwarf trees. These trees grow to only to 8 or 10 feet, but they are cultivated to maximize fruit production on every limb. These are sold mostly through mail-order nurseries and generally cost less than $10 each.

Berries of all sorts are another excellent investment. Newer ever-bearing strawberry hybrids are very hardy and produce berries over a long period of time. It is almost impossible to find blackberries, gooseberries, currants, boysenberries, and other old-fashioned berries in the market. If you can buy raspberries—to many the tastiest of them all—the prices are mind-boggling at the market. There may be difficulties in growing some of these (except for blackberries, which grow wild in many places), but they are well worth the extra time and effort. And they don't take up much space.

Space, too, prevents our going into the intricacies of selecting and growing fruits and nuts, but plenty of information is available on the subject from the sources previously mentioned.

PESTS AND WEEDS
AND HOW TO KILL THEM

By far, the best way to handle pests and weeds is to prevent them from appearing in the first place. Do this by buying clean, sturdy plants, plant them in good, well-prepared soil, and keep them healthy by regular watering, feeding, pruning, cutting, and whatever else the plant needs to stay robust.

But nobody's perfect. Weeds and bugs will appear even in healthy plantings. No one has found a way to prevent Dutch elm disease or ward off gypsy moths, chemically or otherwise. So, no matter how careful you are, there will be crabgrass, dandelions, leaf spot, mildew, aphids, borers, beetles, and slugs.

Everyone today is afraid of chemicals. Hardly a day goes by without news of some ecological disaster. But what do we do when our plants are dying and our fruits are being consumed by insects?

There *are* ways of controlling many of these problems without using chemicals. Bugs can and should be picked off by hand. If you incorporate bird-attracting plants into your garden, the birds will gladly lend you a helping hand. Worms, too, are helpful little rascals in the soil, keeping it loose and aerated. Many bugs are positively beneficial and should be encouraged in the garden. Ladybugs love aphids and other smaller insects. The praying mantis, lacewing, spiders, ground beetles, and some types of wasps and mites will eagerly rid you of harmful pests.

But, assuming that you have done all you could to keep your plantings healthy, and you have utilized all the biological controls available, scabs may still attack your apple blossoms. The leafhopper may still devour your lettuce. Reluctant as we may be to use chemicals, even the most fervent environmentalist or organic gardener may be forced to use them to save his plants.

Proper timing is important in the application of some pesticides and herbicides. If you don't dust your roses regularly, they will almost certainly develop black spot and be crawling with aphids. Weeds and bugs will take over if you don't apply the proper chemicals at the proper time.

If timing sounds like our old byword "planning," that's exactly what it is. Protection of your plantings is first and foremost a matter of intelligent design. These are the basic steps:

- Buy only quality stock.
- Keep your plantings healthy by proper watering, mulching, and the like.
- Determine what natural biological controls will prevent problems.
- Know what pests are likely to attack each type of planting.
- Use preventive measures such as pesticides and herbicides and apply them promptly and religiously.
- If and when disease strikes, remove all diseased plantings and burn them.
- Save the remaining plants by discovering promptly what the problem is and applying the proper chemicals or other controls. If you have researched and planned properly, you should be able to recognize the problem and take the necessary steps. If not, take the diseased plant to your local extension agent or nursery.

Most of the above suggestions have the approval of organic as well as "inorganic" gardening experts. The use of chemicals is generally disapproved by true organic gardeners. There is one microbial pest- and disease-control agent which is recommended by organic gardeners because it has no known deleterious effect upon any aspect of the environment. That is *Bacillus thuringiensis,* which is extremely effective against the grub stages of many harmful insects such as the cucumber or Japanese beetle. For other aspects of organic pest and disease control, consult any publication devoted to this subject. Rodale Press of Emmaus, Pennsylvania, has many helpful publications on this subject.

COMPOST

The compost pile or heap has been referred to several times already. But what is it exactly, and how do you create one?

A compost pile consists of relatively fine, homogeneous organic material produced from the decomposition of such plant refuse as lawn clippings, old plants, weeds, and kitchen garbage. The resultant humus material, created by the disintegration caused by bacteria and fungus organisms, is usually about ⅓ of the original volume.

Now what about that garbage? Who wants garbage and weeds in the garden? First, the garbage is organic refuse only—coffee grounds, egg shells, corn cobs and husks—things that naturally decay. Second, if you alternate the organic matter with layers of soil, which you should, there is ordinarily no offensive odor. Last, by the time the whole heap has disintegrated, any weed seeds that have been included are no longer viable.

To make a compost pile, construct an open container out of slats and/or open wire or wood fencing. Start the pile with a 6-inch layer of plant material. Any coarse plants or long stalks should be cut into pieces no longer than 8 inches. Sprinkle in a pint of fertilizer for each square yard of the pile. (Organic gardeners prefer 5 pounds of dried manure.) Top that with a layer of soil about an inch thick.

Repeat this process with as many layers as you can make with available refuse, and add kitchen garbage. Grade the layers so that the center is lower than the outside, to catch as much rainfall as possible. When rainfall is lacking, water the pile to help promote decomposition.

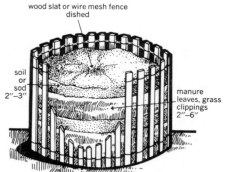

wood slat or wire mesh fence
dished

soil
or
sod
2"–3"

manure
leaves, grass
clippings
2"–6"

The model for a compost pile.

About every 3 months, turn the material over with a pitchfork or garden fork. In warm weather, the compost will be thoroughly decomposed after 4 to 5 months. It will take another month or 2 where it is cool or dry.

That's about all there is to it. Because of the possibility of odors or unsympathetic neighbors, the compost heap should be located in a far, sheltered part of the lot. Although a compost pile is a great help in soil conditioning, mulching, and keeping the plumbing free of coffee grounds, it isn't exactly a pretty sight. In fact, it looks a lot worse than it smells.

MAIL-ORDER NURSERIES

Most mail-order nurseries and seed companies are honest and reputable. Below is a list of some of the best-known, reliable companies. Some specialize in seeds and others in live plants; many have both. Send for catalogs to find out more. (Omission of a company from this list doesn't mean that it is not reliable. These are just the better-known companies.)

W. ATLEE BURPEE CO.
Warminister, PA 18974

GURNEY'S SEED &
NURSERY CO.
Yankton, SD 57079

JOSEPH HARRIS CO., INC.
Moreton Farm   Rochester,
NY 14624

HERBST SEEDSMEN, INC.
1000 North Main Street
Brewster, NY 10509

KELLY BROTHERS
Dansville, NY 14424

MILLER NURSERIES, INC.
Canandaigua, NY 14424

MELLINGER'S
2310 West South Range
North Lima, OH 44452

GEORGE W. PARK SEED
CO., INC.
P.O. Box 31
Greenwood, SC 29646

STARK BROTHERS
Louisiana, MO 63353

STOKES SEEDS, INC.
737 Main Street
Buffalo, NY 14240

HENRY FIELD SEED &
NURSERY CO.
Shenandoah, OH 51602

5 Water Management

With the landscaping in place, for many homeowners the most important concern about water usually is keeping their grounds easily and well watered. Most people take water for granted. However, water, or the lack of it, plays a vital part in every home, no matter where the home is located. In the western United States, fierce battles for water rights have raged from the time of the first settlers, and even today are bitterly fought in court cases and referendums.

Conversely, other areas suffer, if not exactly from a surplus of water, then from water which doesn't go where the homeowner would like it to. According to the U.S. Department of Agriculture, drainage problems occur in about 20 percent of the land in the United States, the result in most cases of excessive rainfall. Drainage problems can also be caused by flooding, springs, seeps, ponding of surface water, and low soil permeability. Given the range of water-related problems a homeowner may face, this chapter will begin with the question of how to keep your grounds easily and adequately watered and then turn to how to deal with excess water.

SPRINKLER SYSTEMS

It is a rare homeowner who doesn't have at least a small patch of lawn on the property. And as everyone knows, keeping that patch of lawn —be it large or small—in good condition is no easy task. That expanse of green requires a great deal of care in the form of fertilizing, mowing, and proper watering. Statistics show that only 4 percent of the lawns in the U.S. do not need supplemental watering. Watering can be a chore, especially if the weather is dry and the lawn is vast.

Precise lawn watering is quite a scientific matter. Underwatering can leave your lawn brown and weed-ridden, while overwatering can ruin a lawn by keeping the roots too soggy. If you must do one or the other, overwatering is preferred, but that can be expensive and time-consuming.

If you'd like an easy way to avoid either dehydrating or drowning your lawn, consider an automatic sprinkler system. These systems aren't cheap, but you can save quite a bit of money by installing yours yourself. With the new types of plastic tubing available, it's a lot easier than it used to be. And because the automatic system delivers just the amount of water needed at just the right time, you may be surprised to discover that you are actually saving money on your water bill. There is no wasteful, expensive, and possibly erosive runoff, and you don't have to worry about having the lawn brown out when you go away. The system is usually programmed to go on late at night, when you aren't doing other things in the yard, water pressure is best, and wind evaporation is least.

A Typical System

The typical automatic sprinkler system consists of underground plastic pipe controlled by a solid-state computer-like gadget that is programmed like a clock radio to turn various sprinkler heads on and off at various times. (Sensors, which measure the groundwater content, tell the controller to stop if there's been a recent rain, and other advanced technology is also available.)

At the other end of the plastic pipe are the sprinkler heads, which are installed flush with the ground but pop up when the controller tells them to. There are a number of types of sprinkler heads available, in heavy-duty plastic or brass, and all are designed for lifetime use. There are sprinklers that distribute water over squares, rectangles, circles, and partial circles. They are permanently installed in strategic locations to provide complete lawn coverage, and all are recessed out of the way of toes, mowers and lawn games.

Sprinkler heads can pop up and spray water all around or in a specific direction, or can merely give off a gentle mist (mostly for delicate shrubbery). Some heads are gear driven; others are water

Well-placed automatic sprinklers eliminate time and work and cut down greatly on wasted water. (Rainjet)

driven and whirl around. With a little effort you can find a sprinkler head for almost every type of use and location.

Two types of pipe are in general use for lawn installations. In the sunbelt, semi-rigid plastic tubing is usually recommended. In colder climates, where freezing is common, a high quality polyethylene tubing is recommended; it should bear the stamp of approval of the National Sanitation Foundation (NSF). If in doubt about which type to use, ask your dealer for a recommendation. The polyethylene is usually a safer bet, because all tubing is installed only 6 to 8 inches below ground level, and polyethylene will expand and remain leak-proof even if some water inside freezes. PVC must have all water removed by blowing compressed air through the system, if there is any chance of freezing. Galvanized or copper pipe has been used in older systems, but plastic has largely replaced metal pipe for this type of installation.

Controllers are being improved almost as fast as you can write about them, so check with your dealer to see what new features have been recently made. As stated, in general they work like a timer or clock, telling the sprinklers when to go on and when to shut off. You can program the controller to do almost anything you want it to do. If there is a prolonged period of rain, you can turn the system to "off," so that it won't work at all until you want to reactivate it.

Most systems have various zones, so that some sprinklers will operate at one time, others at another. During a dry spell, for example, one zone may be turned on 3 times a week and work for 45 to 60 minutes. Another zone that needs less water can be turned on once or twice a week for a half hour. You can do anything you want to with each zone, even turn it to manual if you just want to leave the sprinkler going on a hot day to give the kids something cool and wet to run through.

Depending on the water pressure, which should be about 60 psi (pounds per square inch), you may be able to operate only 1 or 2 zones at a time, but you can operate the zones in sequence, so that numerous zones can be watered in a single night. A half-acre property is typically divided into 8 zones.

Can You Do It Yourself?

If you have the right equipment, which can be rented or—if you are lucky—borrowed from the dealer, it is not all that difficult to install an underground sprinkler system. You should not try to plan the type, size, number of sprinklers, or their placement by yourself, however. Get on-site inspections from 3 or 4 dealers, and pay close attention to their recommendations. Ask each for a written estimate for both dealer-installed and do-it-yourself systems.

A dealer can install the average system in about a day. It may take you several days, mainly because of inexperience, but the savings will be about ⅓ of the dealer's price. Time and prices will run higher if there are lots of obstacles to work around, complicated topography, and so on. Have a good diagram and plan available.

Your plan should show the spray patterns for each sprinkler head and the location of the piping. Make sure that you study the type of heads available and that any obstacles (and how to get around them) are shown before you begin.

The key to laying the pipe is the special machine which you will get from the dealer. It is a tractor-like wonder which saws a vertical slice in your lawn and puts in the plastic pipe at a rate of about 50 feet a minute. Follow your plan and dig and lay the pipe at the same time.

In most systems, T-joints are fitted onto the pipe below the spot where a sprinkler head will be located. The fitting is easily attached with slip nuts, O-rings, and expanders. The riser is then connected to the T-joint in the same way, and the sprinkler head is attached to the end of the riser in much the same manner. Specific instructions will be included with each system and may vary according to brand and model.

All of the tubing, of course, eventually runs back to the house, where each zone is connected to a solenoid-activated valve. The valves are then attached to the controller. Most of the piping in this part of the system is copper or galvanized and is located inside the house to prevent freezing. Obviously, your dealer will provide more specific information about installing the controller, valves, and other programming aspects of the system.

The pipe-laying machine, incidentally, leaves only a thin cut in the turf, which is readily covered over by new grass in a short time. No backfilling is necessary, and the slit becomes invisible very quickly.

Although it is a rather difficult job, sprinkler heads can be moved to new locations if necessary. It is also possible to start with a smaller system, then make additions later. This raises the overall expense considerably, however. If you do choose this method, make sure that the controller will be able to handle the entire job when it is completed. Making additions to the lines is easy, but changing the controller is difficult, costly, and wasteful. As always, plan thoroughly in advance.

OTHER METHODS

If you have only a small space to water or can't afford an automatic sprinkling system, don't despair. While there is no denying the ease and luxury of the automatic systems, without them you don't have to resort to standing with the hose for hours each day.

Lawns can watered quite efficiently by the proper use of portable sprinklers. The common circular two-arm sprinkler is the simplest and cheapest type. The better ones are adjustable at each end, so that one end can throw a finer spray for close use and the other a longer, coarser spray. These are usually quite adequate for smaller lawns and gardens.

Since most lawns are square or rectangular, the oscillating sprinkler is favored by many homeowners. Settings on the dial enable you to spray different-sized areas, such as full or partial, as the long, curved head swings back and forth in an arc. Most can also spray just to one side, which is helpful near a public sidewalk. You can water your lawn without dousing the passers-by.

Modern impulse sprinklers, which spray, more or less, in "spurts," have many adjustments, which allow them to spray from a 20- to 40-foot radius or in partial circles. Many sprinklers are available with spikes so that they can be set for the season into the ground where you want them. Others can travel along the garden hose to spray the entire lawn without moving the set-up.

If worse comes to worst, you can always use the old hose by hand. Adjustable hose nozzles can vary the spray pattern. And, for the long, narrow lawn or garden, soaker hoses do an excellent job.

If grounds maintenance is your major concern as far as water goes, the rest of this chapter may not be of immediate interest to you. However, for homeowners with water problems or for those planning new or second homes, here is a brief survey of other water-related questions.

A SURVEY OF DRAINAGE PROBLEMS

If you live in a home that has been standing for some time and has never had a drainage problem, chances are that you won't be bothered in the future. If, however, you make any significant changes in the landscaping, you should be aware of what can happen. Even more caution should be exercised if you're buying a new home, especially if the home is located in a new development where unavoidably there will be disturbances to the natural vegetation and topography.

Ideally, a home should be built on a well-drained knoll where a minimum amount of grading and subsurface drainage will be required. In urban areas, sewer systems have eased drainage problems on poorer sites, but as housing moves further away from cities with sewers and elaborate drainage systems and the pressure increases for more development, topography is being reshaped to squeeze homes into areas where natural water movement is disrupted. Homes are built on plots that are less desirable in terms of drainage, and natural water patterns are changed.

All of the problems discussed below are difficult to deal with in the best of circumstances. It is strongly recommended that local agricultural experts, landscape architects, reliable contractors, and other specialists be sought out for help and advice.

Testing for Drainage Problems

Most drainage problems are subject to seasonal variations, in some cases very wide ones. Although local conditions may vary, the best time to evaluate difficulties is November through April, when evaporation and transpiration are very low. If you are building a new home, try to make these observations before you start so that you will not only be able to design your water-control systems more accurately, but you will also choose the optimum site for building your home.

If you are planning a new home or making any significant changes in your current landscaping, you should begin with a soil evaluation. Detailed information on the soil conditions can—and should—be gathered from test borings. These should be made at the highest and lowest elevations of the plot, during the wet season, and in depressions and at the bottoms of abrupt slope changes. Obvious spongy or ponded areas which may affect existing turf or shrubbery should also be explored by test bores. Each bore should be 3 to 5 feet deep to determine the presence or absence of low-permeability soil layers or a high water table.

Profiles of well-drained soil will show a high proportion of sand or gravel. Color will gradually change from a dark topsoil to a light brown at about 3 feet, with no "free" water. Vegetation at the site will have deep, uniformly distributed roots. Soil profiles that show abrupt color changes and small blotches within 3 feet of the surface indicate restricted internal drainage. The soil will be composed of sand, silt, and clay in a wide range of proportions and will appear cemented or densely packed. Poorly drained soil will exhibit a dark, highly organic surface layer with an abrupt change to a light gray or

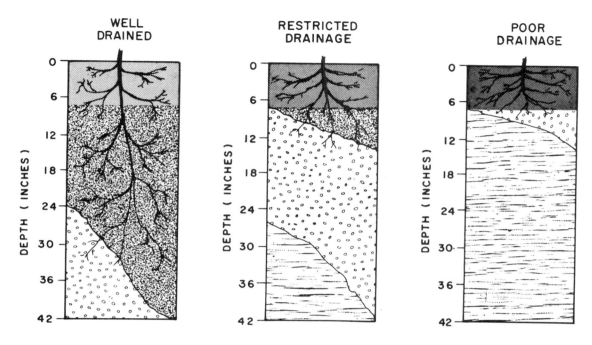

Soil profiles show the type of drainage present on your property.
(Cornell University)

brown mottled zone 6 to 8 inches down. Natural vegetation will consist of shallow-rooted plants such as willow, alder, sedge, or red maple.

Proper Foundations

If soil samples show well-drained soil, this does not mean that drainage precautions should not be taken. Even the driest climates occasionally have a heavy rainstorm which can devastate poorly drained homes. So despite the fact that soil shows good drainage, lay perforated pipe or field tile around the foundation at the outside of the footings. The drain tile should be backfilled with at least a foot of clean gravel and laid with a grade of 1 inch per 10 feet leading down to a storm sewer or suitable dry well.

When the soil permeability is restricted or poor, good foundation drainage is even more important. It is wise, especially with poor drainage and hydrostatic pressure from underground streams or a high water table, to install drain tiles *inside* the footings or somewhere underneath the basement floor. A granular fill also should be

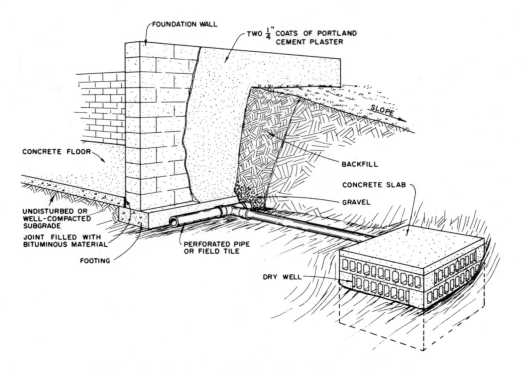

FOUNDATION WALL

TWO $\frac{1}{4}$" COATS OF PORTLAND CEMENT PLASTER

SLOPE

CONCRETE FLOOR

BACKFILL

CONCRETE SLAB

GRAVEL

UNDISTURBED OR WELL-COMPACTED SUBGRADE

JOINT FILLED WITH BITUMINOUS MATERIAL

PERFORATED PIPE OR FIELD TILE

FOOTING

DRY WELL

Even on well-drained soils, construction should include provisions for removing excess water. Here, drain tiles carry water to a dry well or storm sewer, if available. (Cornell University)

added under the basement floor before pouring it. Bituminous coatings should be added to the foundation walls up to grade level, and gravel fill installed to within 1 foot of finished grade on top of the drain tile outside the foundation.

Over time, erosion of fill material from the foundation wall may occur and lead to wet basements. Backfill will often settle in, creating a natural ditch around the foundation where water collects. Foundation walls should be checked periodically, especially if the home was recently built, and new topsoil added, to form a gradual slope away from the foundation. Again, especially with newer homes, this may also mean that existing foundation plantings should be dug up and replanted to make them level with the new grade.

Sloping Banks

Sloping banks, particularly those created by contractors to make homesites level, can be a huge and expensive headache for any

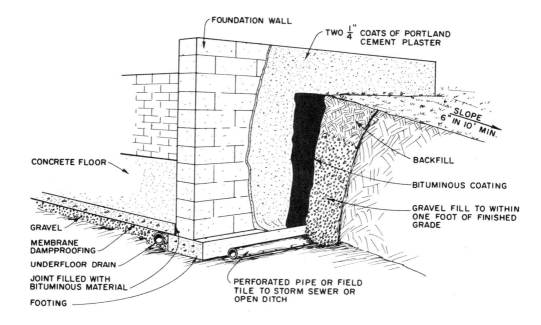

FOUNDATION WALL

TWO ¼" COATS OF PORTLAND CEMENT PLASTER

SLOPE 6" IN 10' MIN.

CONCRETE FLOOR

BACKFILL

BITUMINOUS COATING

GRAVEL FILL TO WITHIN ONE FOOT OF FINISHED GRADE

GRAVEL

MEMBRANE DAMPPROOFING

UNDERFLOOR DRAIN

JOINT FILLED WITH BITUMINOUS MATERIAL

FOOTING

PERFORATED PIPE OR FIELD TILE TO STORM SEWER OR OPEN DITCH

When soil drainage is poor or restricted, extra steps must be taken to insure proper drainage. Note the additional drain inside the footings, bituminous coatings around the foundation, and gravel backfill, as well as gravel under the basement floor covered by a dampproofing membrane. (Cornell University)

homeowner. Quick-growing grass is often the developer's answer, and does provide temporary relief, but such grass is often impossible to safely mow and may die out after the first year. The best permanent solution is extensive use of terracing with retaining walls, but this can be very costly and time-consuming.

Once an erosion pattern becomes evident (and it will soon enough), drain tile can be laid along the natural waterway and covered with gravel and earth, and some sort of groundcover or permanent plantings can be started. Unfortunately, these often wash away in heavy rains. Sometimes the only method is the use of interceptor drains, which divert and carry off the water to a storm sewer located away from the house and the natural water path.

Sometimes poor planning results in *un*natural water paths. If you follow the instructions in this book for building walks, driveways, and patios, this should not happen. If poor drainage already exists, however, you may have to install drain tile and/or a dry well to divert water accumulation.

PERFORATED PIPE
IN GRAVEL BED

SOLID PIPE TO
DISPOSAL AREA

Sometimes the only way to deal with a steep slope is to install interceptor drains along it to divert the water away from the house to a safe disposal area. (Cornell University)

As you may have noticed in highway building and other construction where steep banks are common, it is possible to establish a fairly steep bank with the proper groundcovers. The types of vegetation that will survive and develop a dense, protective cover are limited, however. Consult Chapters 2 to 4 for some suggestions, and seek professional advice about seeding mixtures, fertilization rates, seedbed preparation, mulch, and similar questions.

Exposed Tree Roots

Where trees have been retained on a new building site, roots may have been exposed, or, at the opposite extreme, smothered by several feet of raw fill. Such trees will look healthy for a time but will eventually die.

When a tree has had its roots exposed or soil dug out from around it, you may be able to save it by erecting retaining walls on one or more sides. Chances of saving the tree are much greater if it is on a slope and only one side of the tree is affected. If the entire root system has been damaged, it may be possible to keep the tree alive by erecting a large, well-drained, soil-filled wall all around the tree. This is more likely with trees with deep taproots than with shallow-rooted varieties.

General Maintenance

Gutters and downspouts should be inspected and cleaned yearly. Any leaves, toys, baseballs, or other debris should be removed. Bent, broken, or rusted sections should be fixed or replaced. Shallow spots in the lawn should be filled in and resodded. In areas that are prone to ponding, especially near the foundation, elevated beds should be constructed for flowers, shrubs, or ornamentals. Use "mini" retaining walls of brick, stone, or ties, and slope drain tile away from the foundation, if that's where the problem is.

If soil permeability is poor, roof runoff should be deflected across a wide lawn area by careful placement of gutters and downspouts. Splash blocks may also be necessary. If ponding results from these solutions, the runoff should be connected to a storm sewer or drainage ditch. Dry wells are a poor but sometimes necessary choice.

CONSTRUCTING A DRY WELL

Dry wells may be indicated in a variety of circumstances. For example, as discussed, a dry well may be adequate to capture runoff where the soil is very well drained. This type of dry well is similar to a septic tank and, when it is the only method of flood protection, it should be built by professionals.

Sometimes, however, there are certain low areas that can be cured of ponding by the use of a homemade dry well. In sandy, well-drained areas where there are no storm or sewer drains and septic tanks are the norm, a dry well can often relieve some of the load caused by an inadequate septic system.

When the problem is minor, an adequate dry well can be built by digging a 6-foot-deep hole and placing a 55-gallon drum in the ground, either at the center of a low spot or connected to it by a drain. Drill holes in the bottom and sides of the drum so that the collected water will eventually percolate into the soil, which must be well drained to begin with.

Commonly, a dry well is put in for a specific purpose such as draining a clothes washer in an area where septic tanks are used for primary drainage. Many people do not realize the enormous amount of water that is discharged by a typical washing machine. Large-capacity washers can use well over 100 gallons of water for each load. If you multiply that amount by the number in your family, you can see that the washing machine adds an enormous burden to your existing system. The dry well would be filled to overflowing with just half a load.

A dry well designed to drain a washing machine or other large load should be built of concrete block. A sandy, well-drained soil is essential. Construction is not an especially complex job, but is not easy on the back. There is a lot of digging to be done.

Proper size is difficult to determine. An undersized dry well will bubble up at the top and be as much of a problem as a filled septic tank. But if you build too big a well, you've wasted a lot of time, work, and money. An engineer or other expert in this type of work should be consulted.

Sometimes an intelligent estimate will have to suffice if you can't afford professional advice. Dig a test hole, then measure the rate at which the water level drops. Your local board of health or extension agent should have percolation tables for your area, and you should be able to figure out from these the approximate size of your intended dry well.

When the size has been determined, dig an appropriate-sized hole by hand or machine. Line the bottom of the hole with concrete block, with the cores facing down, then build up the sides with standard 2- or 3-core block or special block made for this purpose. When you get to within about 2 feet of ground level, have your masonry dealer deliver a concrete cover and place it on top. Connect the drain to your washer (or whatever) and cover the dry well with dirt.

Planning a Patio or Deck 6

Of all the improvements and projects in this book, a deck or patio is probably one of the most pleasant to think about. These outdoor living rooms have taken the place of the porches where our parents or grandparents used to relax on warm evenings, sitting, enjoying the breeze, and watching the world go by.

Both decks and patios are similar in purpose, serving as nice-weather living rooms. The basic difference is that a deck is above the ground, while a patio is at ground level. Decks are almost always made of wood, while a patio can be constructed of almost anything —including wood. But the question is which—deck or patio or both? Sometimes the answer is very easy. If you live in a seaside area, perhaps California, where many homes are built on the side of a cliff, you'd better put in a deck, because there isn't any place to put a patio. On the other hand, if you live in a low house on level ground, there really isn't anywhere to put a deck, a ground-level deck being, for all practical purposes, a patio. In making your choice, there are several factors that should be taken into account.

FACTORS TO CONSIDER

Grade. Take a look at the grade of your property. In general, the steeper the grade, the more likely it is that a deck is the better choice. A patio, whether concrete, brick, or stone, should be nearly level. In some cases, that may mean extensively digging into the landscape,

This imaginative California multilevel deck makes the most of irregular terrain, starting from the second story of the home and descending.
(California Redwood Association/Ernest Braun, photographer)

building up some parts of the land or leveling other parts. Sometimes you can do both at the same time, removing earth from one area and filling it in at another, but the more land you have to disturb, the more difficult and expensive it becomes to install a patio. When regrading gets to the point at which retaining walls are necessary, you also must consider esthetics. Retaining walls are not necessarily ugly, but the higher they get, the more of an eyesore they become. Decks, on the other hand, fit more easily on sloping property.

View and Site. No matter what type of outdoor living area you want, it is important that the surroundings be pleasant and easy on the eye. The site of the house and the view beyond are critical factors in your choice of deck or patio. If the view beyond the home is not much to look at, it is usually best to keep the outdoor area as low as possible, so a patio is usually better. Put up a fence for privacy, landscape the area, add some flowers, and you've essentially created your own view. A low deck may be all right, but if it gets too high, you will inevitably see the unpleasant view beyond.

This charming, irregular patio of stone in concrete is enhanced by a brick privacy wall. A clump of birch has been left in the center. This design won a Certificate of Merit for Puddephatt Landscaping, Little Rock, Arkansas.

This inviting deck saves existing trees and looks harmonious on the modern-style home.

Where the long-range view is good, a deck almost always should be chosen to take advantage of it.

Type of House. Most contemporary-style homes adapt well to either a deck or patio. It is difficult to build a deck to blend in with older styles of architecture, however, unless it's added out of sight in the back. If you're thinking about a patio for an older home, note that concrete areas don't add much to older homes. A better choice for paving is brick or flagstone, which would blend better, especially at the front of the house.

Also consider the lines of the home. Squarish houses can be stretched out by the addition of a deck. The deck takes away the boxy look and may help the house fit in better with the landscape. Place the deck where it doesn't make the house look awkward. Try to envision the house with the deck attached. How will it look? Better yet, take several pictures of the house and draw in the deck at various sites. If you can't get a deck to look right on any site, consider a patio.

Present Landscape. When choosing a site for a patio, you must consider the landscaping you already have in place, for it will have to be removed to make room for the patio. Will your patio site mean the loss of a favorite rose garden? You can build a patio around a single tree, but not around several of them. In selecting the site for a patio, make sure you aren't taking away something you can't bear to lose. A high deck will leave the existing landscape in place, but remember that you will lose sunlight below the deck.

What about the type of soil? If you have to dig down or regrade the area, be sure to test-bore in a few places. You may find that there is nothing but rock underneath. At the opposite extreme, you won't want to put a patio over boggy or marshy soil. It'll soon sink into the swamp.

Price. Talking about actual prices is always risky, but we can make comparisons.

Generally speaking, patios are cheaper to build than decks. Concrete patios are the cheapest, although prices can rise quickly for elaborate contractor-installed concrete such as exposed aggregate or mixed-in color. Going up the ladder in cost are brick in sand, patio block, brick on concrete, and flagstone.

Decks are more expensive generally, but you can save more money by building your own deck than you can by installing your own patio, since more labor is involved in deck construction. Although I don't recommend it, using some of the less expensive woods

This traditional home, with its paneled windows, is enchanced by a patio made of brick and wood.

can considerably lower the cost of a deck. If you do use the cheaper woods, each piece should be individually dipped in a wood preservative, which is very time-consuming and does bring up the cost somewhat. Pressure-treated wood decks are less expensive than red cedar or redwood, although they are not as attractive and are more likely to split.

Can You Do It Yourself?   If price is a factor in your decision, you might consider building a deck or patio yourself. These are not projects that call for great skill, and building them yourself can cut the cost by ⅓ to ⅔, depending on the design. Again, the more labor-intensive a project, the more it will cost to hire someone to build it.

In general, though, decks are a little more difficult to build, mainly because safety is a prime factor. Building a deck demands close attention to instructions, and proper construction techniques, but care and attention should enable you to build a safe, sturdy deck. If you intend to do the work on a deck or patio yourself, however, and you don't feel confident that you can do it right, it may be better for you to build a patio or ground-level deck.

Family Considerations. Ordinarily, the sizes and ages of family members don't affect the choice of patio or deck. But if you have young children or a family member confined to a wheelchair, a deck does present some problems. The deck can be made safe and comfortable with such alterations as guardrails designed to prevent children from slipping through and a smooth surface for wheelchairs. A brick or flagstone patio also may present problems to someone who has difficulty walking or uses a wheelchair; smooth concrete in these cases may be preferable.

In the last analysis, personal preference is the most important factor. If you *must* have a concrete patio installed over a boggy area, then you'll figure out a way to have it. If it has always been your dream to have a deck outside your bedroom, then you will undoubtedly build one, even if the view is not perfect.

But do try to use your head. Consider the other factors before insisting upon your favorite choice. And search around for alternatives. Read the next section on the various types of decks and patios before you make a final decision. For example, if every other factor dictates a ground-level patio, but you love the look and feel of wood, remember that you can have your deck—just try that ground-level deck we talked about.

PATIO AND DECK MATERIALS

The word "patio" almost automatically connotes "concrete." And concrete *is* the most popular material for patios. Before you routinely select concrete, however, at least consider other material. Brick and flagstone, though more expensive, have a more elegant look. Maybe that's why they're often called terraces, while a concrete terrace is a patio. And if you have decided on concrete, remember that there are several variations of concrete (discussed below). Sometimes a little creative brooming or a few well-placed divider boards

An example of exposed aggregate concrete.

can mean the difference between a dull-looking and a pleasant surface.

Remember, too, that a deck doesn't necessarily have to be a plain rectangular row of boards. It can be two-level, multilevel, low, high, round, hexagonal, diagonal, parquet, or almost any shape or pattern you can imagine. Some of the variations are shown on these pages and discussed at length in the following chapter.

Concrete. Poured concrete is a long-lasting and care-free material. I think that plain, unadorned concrete makes a patio look too much like a driveway, but the popularity of this type of patio attests to its comparatively low price and durability. A few simple measures can eliminate the driveway look. You can construct a grid of redwood or other weather-resistant lumber to frame the concrete. Scribing a pattern in the concrete in the final finishing is another good touch. The best-looking concrete patios are made using the exposed aggregate technique. Then, too, there is no need to stick with rectangles. Concrete can take any form you wish, including curves. Plantings, whether in pots or built in, also provide interest and break up the monotony.

Brick. There are two basic types of brick patios. The simpler and less expensive type is brick in sand. This is an ideal project for the do-it-yourselfer. You simply lay down a bed of sand and put the bricks into it one by one. It is a little tedious and time-consuming, but the result is well worth the effort.

Although brick in sand is simple and good-looking, the bricks may be disturbed by heaving due to frost or dislodged by an errant table leg. Resetting is simple enough, but the problem can be avoided altogether if you lay the brick onto a concrete slab, with mortar between the bricks. This is more work and, of course, more money, but the brick is better anchored.

Patio Block. This type of cinder or concrete block is intended for level installation. It comes in different sizes, one of which looks very much like brick. Brick "pavers," in fact, can also be used in the same way. Many people prefer these materials for fancy patterns because the construction is modular. It is difficult, for example, to construct a herringbone pattern with standard brick in sand. Common brick comes in odd sizes to allow for mortar, and will cause gaps in herringbone and most other patterns. Patio block is generally laid down without mortar.

Flagstone. Flagstone is handsome, but quite expensive. Dressed flagstone, cut into uniform sizes, is even more costly. "As-is" irregular stone has a rustic, natural look, but is more difficult to lay out without gaps. Both kinds can be laid in a sand bed, but undressed stone is quite difficult to work with because of variations in thickness. It is best to put down a concrete slab first, then lay the stones section by section in a thick bed of wet mortar. Dressed stone is also laid on a slab with a thinner mortar layer, and uniform mortar joints.

Wood. Decks are almost always made of wood, although I have

This eye-catching design is made of patio block. The wall and fountain pool are made of concrete masonry.

seen decks made of perforated steel and a few other exotic materials. Decks vary mainly in the type of wood used, the various levels, and the location.

Other Materials.   Almost any weather-resistant material can be used for a patio. Among these are tile, wood blocks, and outdoor carpeting.

LOCATION

Patios

The best location for a patio is directly off that part of the house that you use the most. This may be the family room, kitchen, living room, or wherever you do most of your relaxing and entertaining. In other words, the patio is usually placed where it is most convenient. The fewer the steps, the better the hot dogs taste and the more cooling the drinks are. It's also a good idea to have a patio located where you can keep an eye on the children and the barbecue and take advantage of any cooling breezes. Usually, sliding glass doors with screens connect the patio to the living area.

Easy access is not the only factor to consider when deciding the location of your patio. The design of your home may not invite an

A patio should be situated where it will get the most use. Usually, the most convenient spot is next to the house, near the kitchen or family room. The patio usually is entered by means of sliding glass and/or screened doors.

Sometimes an attractive spot in a well landscaped garden is the most inviting place for a patio. This attractive brick in mortar sunken terrace, covered by a wood pergola and backed by a brick screen wall, is an outdoor conversation pit. This patio won a Residential Design Award for the Atlantic Nursery of Freeport, New York. (National Landscape Association)

attached outdoor living area. You may want to place a patio in a far corner of your lot, for privacy or to gain a better view.

One of the most important considerations in locating a deck or patio is the relationship to the sun. Depending on geography, you will want to locate your deck or patio to take advantage of, or possibly block, the sun. A patio that faces south will almost certainly need a roof or some other sun screen. For those who enjoy outdoor breakfasts in the pleasant morning sun, an attachment that faces east may be best. A westward-facing deck or patio will get the hotter midday sun, which may be fine in cool regions but uncomfortable in warm climates. In climates where it is very hot most of the year, consider a north-facing patio, so the house will provide shade most of the day.

Prevailing breezes are another important consideration, and it's a good idea to consult local weather authorities for wind patterns. A west-facing location is usually best for cool breezes. If this is not practical, southern or northern sites are second best. East-facing sites usually get the fewest breezes. Mountains or other natural barriers may alter this, of course. And if you are in a chilly area, where you wish to avoid cool breezes, reverse these directions. To change the flow of breezes toward—or away from—your outdoor living site, plan your landscaping carefully.

Decks

Deck location should be based on the same considerations as patio location, except that a deck can be built above ground level and thus can serve rooms other than the primary living areas. In fact, decks can be built off any room or *every* room, as they sometimes are in vacation homes, where one large wrap-around deck or several small decks encompass the entire house. With this built-in flexibility in deck choices, think about a deck off the dining room, bedroom, or bath. For private sunbathing a bedroom or bathroom deck is a good choice. A small screened-in deck off a child's room gives extra space for "outdoor" sleeping in warm weather. In vacation homes where several generations or several guests gather, bedroom decks can provide a little privacy and luxury.

In addition, a deck can be built on one or several levels, adding architectural interest to the house. An upper-level deck can create downstairs storage space or a play area. A deck also can be built where a patio is impossible, such as over a sloping or rough area.

Before you make your final choice, remember to at least give a passing thought to less conventional deck and patio sites. A brick patio can be built in *front* of the house, which is not the usual place; it may just happen to be a pretty, private area with trees overhead and a commanding view. And consider a detached deck. Again, this is not typical but is a nice design that could lend itself well to a secluded spot in the corner of a large plot.

7 Building a Patio

If you decide to build a patio, you are among the vast majority of homeowners who long for a pleasant, private place to enjoy the great outdoors. But there are still choices to come. Unlike decks, patios can be built of a wide variety of materials and can come in many forms.

CONCRETE PATIOS

A concrete patio is basically a slab, and directions for building one are given in detail in Chapter 11. The various types of finishes also are described there and should be decided on before you draw up your final plans for a patio.

A major problem in planning a concrete patio is drainage. A concrete slab is flat and impermeable. Drainage may be only a minor problem if your patio is small, but be aware that large, uninterrupted concrete surfaces often cause rather severe runoff. Rain will collect on the slab and rush off to a lower level in big rivulets unless you build the patio in a hollow, which is certainly not a good idea.

A patio must be pitched at a slope of ¼ inch per foot, toward a neutral area such as a field or well settled lawn, where accumulated rainwater will do more good than harm. Avoid sloping toward your garage, your house, your garden, or your neighbor's yard. If there is no area adjacent to the patio where runoff will not be a problem, you may have to create a drainage system. Another alternative is to intersperse the concrete areas with planted areas. This not only helps with drainage but also makes for a very handsome patio.

The methods for ground preparation, forming, pouring, and other concrete-laying chores employ the techniques discussed in Chapter 11. If the patio is connected to the house, an isolation joint (pages 159–60) should be used. Planting areas, built-in sandboxes, or other interruptions should be located on joints or where the joints intersect. Forming of these areas is the same as for exterior forming.

Since a patio often incorporates a network of wood grids, we shall describe here in detail the technique of laying them. After the subgrade is prepared, the gridwork is constructed of 2 × 4 redwood or red cedar, using all-heart grades of lumber. Pressure-treated lumber (grade 0.60) or cypress can also be used. Face nail the 2 × 4s together using 16d hot-dipped galvanized nails, and toenail where necessary with 8d nails. Also add 16d galvanized nails on 16-inch centers to help "tie" the wood to the concrete. The grid should be in dimensions that look best for your patio and its surroundings. Two-foot squares may be all right for a small patio but wouldn't be big enough for a large one. Four-foot squares are most common, but rectangles, larger or smaller squares, or a random pattern—whatever provides the best accent and design to the area—can also be used.

When forming the interior sections of the grid, drive the stakes down below the top of the wood at least 1 inch so they will be invisible after the concrete is poured. This type of patio may be worked in easy stages. Each section can be poured individually or a few sections can be poured at a time. The wood grid makes striking off, or leveling, easy. Just use a board long enough that it can be pulled along the top edges of the gridwork. Before pouring the concrete, run masking tape along the tops of the boards. Remove it after

This detail of wood gridwork shows how nails should be driven in to help tie in the wood to the concrete. (Portland Cement Association)

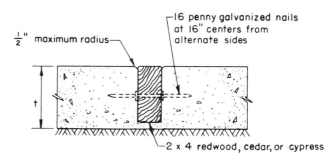

When using wood gridwork, run masking tape over the tops of the wood to prevent staining. (Portland Cement Association)

the concrete starts to set. Then run a damp cloth along the tops of the wood to remove spilled cement and prevent staining.

There is one other note to be made, about concrete patios that are adjacent to a pool. Make sure that the final finish is of a non-skid type. Either use exposed aggregate, or broom the surface well, to prevent accidents caused by wet, careless feet.

BRICK PATIOS

The two main types of brick patios are brick set in sand and brick set on a concrete slab. There is, however, an intermediate type which combines some of the best features of both. For this type, mix equal

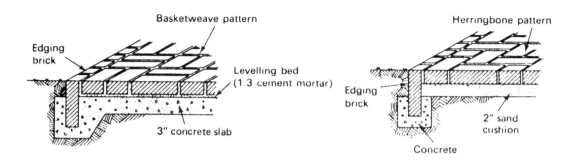

Construction details for brick in mortar (left) and brick in sand (right).

amounts of Portland cement and sand for your base. When this mixture is hosed down after spreading, it hardens into a mortar—not as strong as regular mortar, but a more stable base than pure sand. The method of laying bricks on this mix is the same as for sand alone, so I will make no further mention of sand-cement mixes in the directions.

Brick in Sand Patios

Brick in sand patios are easy but time-consuming to construct and are very handsome and relatively inexpensive. The technique is often used for walkways, too. Sand is used both as a base for the bricks and for filling in the cracks. It does a surprisingly effective job of holding the individual bricks in place, and if some of them do work loose, it is a simple matter to pull them out, relevel the sand, and put the bricks back in place.

When selecting brick, you will find mostly "common" or "standard" brick, which generally measures 2¼ × 3¾ × 8 inches. This size is perfect for building walls and for other standard uses but will cause you trouble if you try to use it for elaborate patterns in your patio. If you plan a design other than the running bond shown in the photographs, look for patio block, or paving brick, which is exactly twice as long as it is wide. The popular, good-looking parquet or herringbone pattern is much easier to lay with paving brick or patio block. There are lots of other types of brick, but stay away from them for projects like this.

Used brick looks nice, but in many areas it is almost as expensive

This handsome poolside patio is made of brick and sand. The design was by Ireland's Landscaping in East Norwich, New York. (National Landscape Association)

as new brick and the pieces of mortar that often cling to the old brick make it difficult to work with. If you use old brick, knock or scrape off the mortar with a brick hammer or chisel.

The best source for brick is a masonry or building-supply dealer, who can give you good advice and arm you with the proper tools. With your layout in hand, the dealer should be able to determine the proper number of bricks. For common brick, 5 per square foot is about right, since there will be some waste from cutting. Curved or herringbone patterns result in up to 10 percent more waste than other patterns. If you're using brick for edging, figure on 3 bricks per linear foot.

You will need some special tools for cutting brick. A "bolster," or wide brick chisel, is the best tool for this work. Hit the chisel with a mash (hand-drilling) or ball-peen hammer. Do not use a bricklaying hammer or a regular carpenter's claw hammer to hit the chisel.

You will also need some line, a line level, a mason's or carpenter's level, a folding or metal rule, a garden rake, a garage broom, and a square-ended garden spade for digging. You can buy stakes or improvise by cutting up scrap wood and chopping the pieces so they're pointed. Safety goggles are recommended for cutting brick, and galvanized nails, 20d or larger, are needed if you will be nailing ties together. Use a mash hammer or sledgehammer for the ties, too. Sand needn't be the fine type used for mortar. Coarse or "bank-run" sand is good enough. When ordering sand, figure on 25 cubic feet of sand for every 100 square feet of area.

Determine the layout of your patio. A brick in sand patio can be level or almost so, because rainwater seeps down through the sand, thereby eliminating any drainage problems. To begin, set stakes to the same height at all corners or at short intervals for curves. Since ground is seldom truly level, choose a starting spot along the perimeter somewhere near the median, then drive the first stakes there. Use the line level to ensure that all heights are the same. The line can be set any height you want, but about 10 inches above the final surface works pretty well. Run the line very taut between each of the stakes, using the line level in the approximate center.

No matter what height the line represents, add 2 inches for the sand and then add the height of the brick (probably 2¼ inches) to that to determine the excavation. If, for example, your line is set 10 inches above the top of the finished patio and you are using standard brick, add 2¼ inches for the brick and 2 inches for sand (4¼ inches total), and dig down 14¼ inches below the line throughout. Exact dimensions are not really critical in this construction, and you can always make up for any errors by adding or subtracting sand.

Some form of edging for the patio is desirable. Good choices for materials are creosoted railroad ties, pressure-treated lumber, redwood, red cedar, or bricks set in mortar sailor-fashion, on their ends. For the edging, dig down a little more. A 6 × 8-inch trench is usual for railroad ties, but measure the depth of the material you have, and add 2 inches more for a sand bed. Brick edging should be in the soldier position, with the long side vertical. These should also be laid in a 2-inch bed of sand, so dig a trench 10 inches deep and about 4 inches wide for common brick. (If you prefer the sailor position, it is best to embed the edging in concrete.)

Whatever you use for edging, set the material carefully in the trench, paying close attention to the depth as measured from the line. If the edging is level or at whatever pitch you have determined, the field brick will be easier to lay. For either ties or brick, pack sand between the joints and under any low spots to set them as firmly as possible.

When the edging is finished, lay down a heavy plastic liner over the level area. This will help a great deal in holding down the growth of weeds that can poke up in the sandy cracks between the bricks. (If your grade is perfectly level, poke some holes in the plastic to facilitate drainage.) Now shovel in your sand bed to make a 2-inch layer. Rough-grade it with the spade as you go along, then use the back of a rake to get the bed as smooth as you can. Minor imperfections can be corrected later.

If you have planned carefully, you should be able to start working from a corner of the patio. Otherwise, begin in the center and work out toward the edges. The former method is preferable for this type of work, since you can use the edging as a leveling tool. When you must start at the center, run more line between the corners, on the diagonal, to insure a level starting spot.

No matter how well you've planned or what bond you use, some cutting of the brick will be necessary at the edges. With the "running bond" pattern shown in the photographs, half bricks must be cut for every other row. To cut a brick, place it in the sand, hold the bolster in the center, then give it a solid, quick rap with the hammer. The brick should break into two almost even sections, although your line

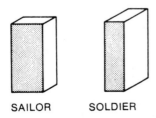

SAILOR   SOLDIER

Brick used as edging can be set either soldier- or sailor-fashion. Soldiers, with the narrowest side facing the patio, do not usually need any type of footing except the sand. If you prefer sailors, it is best to embed them in concrete.

won't necessarily be neat and straight. This type of patio is rustic by definition, so a little jaggedness can be tolerated. If that's not your style, the brick can be cut more precisely by scoring all around before breaking.

Set one brick at a time (I warned you that it was time-consuming), leveling each one by either scraping away excess sand underneath or adding more if it's too low. "Eyeballing" will work up to a certain point for leveling the brick, but check progress every so often with a carpenter's or mason's level. Don't get too concerned if there are a few slight hollows or high sections. As mentioned, drainage should not be a problem, and a little bit of waviness can even have a certain charm.

Lay each brick as close as possible to its neighbor. Each brick is not a perfect rectangle, though, and you may not be the perfect bricklayer, so there will be gaps between bricks, some fairly large, most quite small. To make sure that all the bricks are locked tightly together, spread sand over the whole surface and work the grains down between the bricks with a wide broom.

You may wonder where the sand goes as you work it down and watch it disappear. A lot will filter under as well as between the bricks. But if you think the sand did a disappearing act this way, wait until you start watering; the last step in the "locking" process. Use the fine spray on the garden hose and water the whole area. Much of the sand will wither away under even the most gentle watering. Spread more sand around, broom it down again, and rewater. In most cases, this process must be repeated three or more times before the sand finally stops disappearing.

Brick in Mortar Patios

For this type of patio, use the techniques discussed below for flagstone. Also see pages 177–81 for the bricklaying procedures.

FLAGSTONE PATIOS

Stone is our most ancient building material. The pyramids, Mayan temples, and other ancient buildings are testimony to the durability and workability of stone.

For a patio we're less concerned with the durability of stone than with its beauty and ease of construction. It's nice to know that the patio will last a lot longer than the house itself, but it's even nicer to know that once the patio is complete, it will be an attractive outdoor living area.

Despite its advantages, however, there are several negative aspects to stone. One is price. For your patio, you will need ashlar stone at the least, and most people prefer dressed stone, which is the most expensive of all.

Precut, or dressed stone is ordinarily sold in nominal sizes from 12 × 12 to 24 × 36 inches, with 6-inch increments in between. Sometimes smaller sizes, cut from scrap, are also available. The actual size of the stone is usually ½ inch less than the stated size in each dimension to allow for mortar, which should be used with this type of stone. Order flagstone in square feet, multiplying length by width. But you can't put mortared stone on bare ground. You must pour a concrete slab beneath (see Chapter 11 for details of slab construction). However, the slab can be as thin as 2 inches (3 is preferred), and there is no need to be fussy about the finish, since you will be covering it.

Dressed stone is elegant and formal. Uncut or irregular stone is rustic, and for some tastes more comfortable. Irregular stone also lends itself more readily to laying in a sand bed, like brick. Flagstone

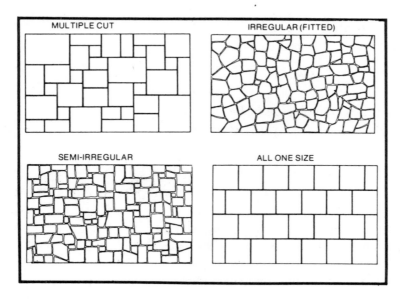

Many patterns can be used for level stonework. (BSI)

Dressed, or precut flagstones come in various-sized squares and rectangles, making a good-looking, easy-to-lay patio.

is much more difficult to level than brick, however, and heaving is a bigger problem because it is more difficult to correct. Stone dust, which usually can be bought where you buy stone, is a good material for "dry" (without mortar) patio construction. It is about 25 percent higher in price than coarse sand. It is very fine and is used in the same way as sand.

In dry construction, follow the instructions given for the brick in sand patio. When using irregular stone, plan your layout carefully, selecting the individual pieces beforehand and establishing the pattern before you actually begin construction. You can use other materials, such as ties or redwood, for edging, but you can also use the stone itself. For this purpose, choose pieces with straight edges —there should be some—and try to choose the thicker pieces for stability. This type of stone usually comes in varying thicknesses; thicker is better for laying in sand. If you can't find enough straight-edge pieces, you can cut them as described in Chapter 10, under "Working With Stone."

Leveling the stones can be very frustrating. One side of each stone should be reasonably level, and this one will go on top. The bottom can be quite bumpy, so you will have to adjust the sand or stone dust bed to fit the contour as best you can. Trial and error is really the only method, and once you have the stone reasonably stable, go on to the next stone. Watering will help fill in the spaces that you may have left.

Work on one section at a time, checking with your level as you go along. Don't worry if one stone is a little high or low or even a little tipped. The overall effect will be level as long as you take care to check it as you proceed.

After all the stones are laid, spread a heavy layer of sand or stone dust over all the cracks and water it in. Do this at least 2 more times, until all the stones are set solidly. If any of the stones still rock or seem unsteady, lift them up and relevel them. Then water in several times as before.

Wet flagstone patios are laid in a bed of mortar consisting of 1 part Portland cement to 3 parts fine sand, mixed to the consistency of mud. Thin stone (½ to 1 inch thick) works best here. Again, make sure that the pattern is carefully laid out in a "dry run," because it will be next to impossible to remove any stone once it has set in the mortar.

The concrete slab must dry for at least 24 hours before setting the stone. (Complete curing is not necessary.) Lay a bed of mortar about 1 inch thick over an area of not more than 2 or 3 flagstones. Place the stones carefully into the mortar and tap them on top with the handle of a trowel or with a rubber mallet. Push down on one side or the other to level, if necessary. Check level, make any adjustments as necessary, and proceed to the next stone.

Keep laying the stones, 2 or 3 at a time as described above, until the patio is complete. You can use the same mortar mix, adding a bit of fireclay, or mix up another batch with 1 part fireclay to 2 parts mortar mix, to fill between the joints. Use a small pointing trowel to

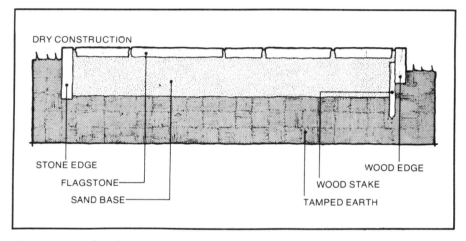

Construction details for stone in sand patio, which is dry. (BSI)

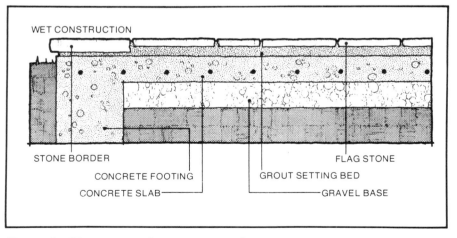

How to build a stone patio, wet construction. (BSI)

*This unusual poolside patio is made from cut-off pieces of redwood
4 × 4s. The poolhouse also is made of redwood, which is nicely set off
by the irregular stone in the wall and chimney.* (California Redwood
Association / Joseph W. Molitov)

force the mortar well into the joints, then level off or otherwise
"point," as described in Chapter 10. The mortar can be flush with or
slightly below the stone, but should not extend above it. If you are
using precut stone with regular joints, concave pointing produces a
nice neat joint. Be sure to wipe off excess mortar with a damp rag
before it dries and stains the flagstone. If the cleaning doesn't remove
all the mortar, a muriatic acid bath should remove the stains later on.

OTHER TYPES OF PATIOS

Although most patios are built of the materials above, you can fashion a patio out of almost any material that will withstand the elements. Once again, a ground-level deck is really a patio, and directions for building one are given in the next chapter. You can even make a patio out of blacktop, although it doesn't generally make a very appealing surface.

Paving brick and patio blocks can be laid in much the same way as regular brick or stone. Other good patio materials are quarry or patio tile, also laid in a similar fashion. When the patio is directly linked to a room, such as a kitchen, where tile is already used, both rooms can be paved with the same tiles for a connected indoor-outdoor look. Ask your dealer for any variations in technique when using any of these materials.

Precast concrete blocks or rounds also can be used in patios, although they are more often used for walkways. Another possibility is a wood-block patio, which is made from either tree rounds, cut crosswise across the trunk, or from end-grain wood cut from ties or other squared, weather-resistant lumber. These can be laid in sand using the same methods discussed above.

PLANTINGS

In making your overall plan, you should already have determined how many plantings you will want around your patio, if any. This, in turn, will depend on whether you want to shut off or enhance the view, keep out or retain the sun, and so on. If your patio is large, it is usually a good idea to have the best of both worlds. Keep one part of it sunny and provide shade for the rest.

Large evergreen shrubs will protect against wind and sun. Ornamental trees usually are medium size and provide shade as well as color. Large deciduous trees near a patio allow sun during winter months and give shade in the summer. They may, however, provide more shade than is desirable unless the patio is quite extensive, or the trees are strategically located.

Sometimes, especially if you use concrete, it is a good idea to blur the edges of the patio with low evergreen shrubs, such as ground-hugging yews or junipers. These shrubs are also ideal for small plantings within the patio itself, where unpaved spots may be provided. Mix in some annuals for summer color, and put in some bulbs for springtime freshness. In southern climates, cacti make good in-between plantings. (Northerners can use potted cactus plants, if they like the look.) All such plantings should be low-growing, so that they don't break up the patio into separate enclaves.

Generally, high shrubs and trees should be used only for screening out unpleasant sights or for privacy. When the edge of a patio is right next to a neighbor's house or patio, choose a fast-growing hedge such as privet. If you prefer evergreens, buy reasonably mature hemlock, black pine, hetzi juniper or Hick's yew, and plant them quite close together. Otherwise, it will be a long time before these plants grow enough to give you the desired feeling of isolation.

In warm weather, delicate plants such as cactus or house plants can be taken outdoors in redwood or ceramic pots to enhance a snowbelt patio. Since they will have to be shifted back inside when winter comes, make sure that the pots are not too big. When filled with dirt, even medium-size pots are heavy.

When space is at a premium, flower boxes hung on the wall of the house next to the patio can provide needed color. You can also install a flower bed along the edges of the patio.

I cannot emphasize too strongly the importance of planning. If you consider the plantings in the beginning, when you first plan the patio, everything will fall into place. After you build the patio, it may be too late to make up for a lack of color and greenery.

PATIO COVERS

Covering a patio may seem like wearing a raincoat in your bathroom shower, but patio covers do serve a useful purpose. It all depends on what you want from the patio. If your main purpose is to soak up some sun, obviously a patio cover will not be wanted. On the other hand, if you live in the Southwest or similar area, where the sun beats down mercilessly most of the time, you may very well welcome a little respite from the rays that northerners so avidly seek.

Potted plants add color and texture to this ground-level deck and can be taken inside, if necessary, during cold weather. (California Redwood Association / Ernest Braun)

Remember last year's barbecue disaster, when the rainstorm washed out both the steaks and the good times? If you had a patio cover, you could have fired up the coals and forgotten the elements. So if your patio is large enough, cover the cooking and dining area.

Where the sun is a problem and you would like to keep it out altogether, a standard shed roof, attached to the house and supported by sturdy posts, is the treatment of choice. If you combine this with a screened-in enclosure you will have a great spot for sleeping on warm nights.

If you want protection from rain and the worst of the sun, but you want light and an open feeling, consider tinted fiber glass panels. Construction is relatively simple.

Screen-type or louvered roofs are an effective compromise. They deflect some of the sun's hottest rays but allow more light and breeze than the solid types.

Building a Deck 8

If your idea of a wood deck is an ungainly tacked-on structure that makes a house look lopsided, take a look at the photographs in this chapter and elsewhere in this book. A deck can be a very sophisticated addition that enhances both the beauty and livability of a home.

At one time, a deck was seen as simply an area for outdoor recreation or a way to overcome the deficiencies of a sloping lot. Now, decks are used to give an exterior accent to the contemporary look of a multilevel house and come complete with hot tubs, conversation or barbecue pits, planters, outdoor furniture, and built-in landscaping. Railings have been modernized and harmonized with the settings, and on low decks they have been replaced by perimeter benches or planters. Instead of straight wood decking you can use eye-pleasing designs such as diagonal lines, parquet designs, and varying patterns, and you can use a variety of materials where possible.

The best improvement of all is that decks now are designed to blend in with, rather than obscure, the natural landscape. Wood patterns are pointed toward a pleasing nearby feature, and multiple levels make a more gradual union with the surroundings.

The ideal way to plan a deck is to hire a landscape architect. An experienced landscape contractor who has designed good-looking decks would be a good second choice. It's certainly possible to plan your own, perhaps with the help of a contractor or building-supply dealer. Discuss with your designer the purpose, size, location, and type of deck you want to be sure he or she knows what you have in

A complex deck with many levels, plus benches, a hot tub, and a quarry-tile patio at the bottom level. Design by landscape architect James Babcock (California Redwood Association / Ernest Braun)

mind. If you don't want to hire an architect or contractor to design your deck, your lumber dealer will be happy to help you select the materials and figure out quantities. But keep modern design principles in mind. The deck should enhance your landscape, not detract from it. Study the photographs and designs on these pages and adapt them to your own uses. You may be able to use some of these plans as is, but always remember that anything can be enlarged or changed to fit your individual preferences. What's right for one home is not necessarily suited to another.

PLANNING PRINCIPLES

Foremost in your mind as you're planning your deck should be its purpose. Why are you building it? How do you expect to use it? These questions are vital in assessing location, size, and type. If, for example, you are a sun-worshipper and your main reason for a deck is to have a private place to sunbathe, take a good look at where your house gets the most sunshine. Although it may seem heretical to place the deck in front of the house, that may be the best location, provided you can achieve some privacy. Or maybe it's better away from the house, all by itself, where trees, fences, and shrubs won't block the sun.

If summer entertaining is the main reason you want a deck, you'll need room for tables, benches, or other seating, a service area, and perhaps a bar, lighting, and some sort of cover to protect against a sudden rainstorm. You've got to plan big. The deck should be a minimum of 300 square feet; 400 or more is even better. When a deck gets that large, it may resemble a large platform, which could be unattractive if not planned right. Consider 2 or more levels, or try a rectangular rather than square shape, or add some other variations to break up the monotony. And place it where you get the most breeze.

On the other hand, don't clutter up small decks with these accessories. Keep small decks simple, and try to use long pieces of wood, to avoid breaking up the lines of the deck by butting smaller pieces together. One trick is to run the deckboards diagonally, using longer pieces in the center and progressively shorter pieces as you go toward the edges, saving the cut-off pieces for last. This is an eye-pleasing design. Generally, a small deck—less than 150 square feet —attached to the house should be rectangular.

A small, easy-to-build ground-level deck in the back of this lot takes advantage of the sun. (National Landscape Association)

If the land slopes down away from your house, you don't necessarily have to build a large platform with long steps to the ground and sturdy railings. Depending on the grade, it may be more pleasant, and safer, to follow the grade with several different levels all the way to the ground. That way you provide broad steps which can be used as seating or extra living space.

When do you need railings? You need them whenever there's a chance of injury from falling off the edge. The level of risk may vary considerably with each family. Children should be protected at all times. A fall of even 1 foot onto rocks or concrete can be dangerous but is probably harmless if onto grass or into soft bushes. Where the edge is 1 or 2 feet off the ground, perimeter benches or planters are visually more appealing than railings. Whenever you get more than 2 feet—3 at most—off the ground, railings are a must. As always,

This deck, located on a sloping grade, follows the natural contours of the land. (California Redwood Association)

check building codes. They may define a safe height as being a lot lower than you would expect.

You don't necessarily have to build the entire deck at one time. The deck should be *planned* as an entirety in the beginning, but if you can't afford to do it all at once, do it in stages. This is much easier to do if you are using more than one level or material. Attaching a section to another on the same level with the same materials can lead to a tacked-on look, so plan on building only as many levels as you can complete. Or change to a different material for new sections of the same level if you are building pretty much on level ground. In that case, consult Chapter 7 and make the other section of the deck some version of a patio.

Decks, or parts of them, can be covered. Any covering should be done only over a portion of a large deck, to provide shelter in case of rain. The covering should be of wood, preferably of the same type used on the deck. Trellises or open wood screening may enhance a deck, and they are good for hanging plants or lights.

TYPES OF WOOD

Theoretically, you can build a deck out of any type of wood. As a practical matter, however, it is wise to build your deck using a wood that is as weather-resistant as possible. Redwood is the best and most expensive wood for deck-building. It is virtually impervious to the elements, insects, decay, and splintering. You even can embed the heartwood of certain redwood grades in the ground, and the wood won't be affected. Heartwood comes from the center of the tree.

Nearly as high in durability is red cedar. It is less expensive, but not as widely available. Red cedar's qualities are the same as redwood's, except it may be somewhat less durable. These 2 woods are the only ones that can be used untreated. (An exception is cypress, which is generally sold only for posts.) Although both have a reddish cast when new, they tend to fade to silver-gray if left to the elements. This color is not unpleasing, and many people prefer it. Preservatives or stains will preserve the reddish-brown color.

The only other recommended wood for "naked" outdoor use is pressurized, or pressure-treated, lumber, which is injected with chemicals to make it durable. This is that greenish wood you see in lumber yards. It is often referred to as Wolmanized lumber, after a trademark of its principal manufacturer, the Koppers Company.

This deck is built of Wolmanized pressure-treated lumber, which is rapidly gaining acceptance for decks and other outdoor uses. (Koppers)

Pressurized lumber has the same applications as redwood and red cedar, but it is considerably less expensive—about 30 to 40 percent cheaper than redwood. It is more prone to splintering, however, than either redwood or red cedar, being made of southern pine. You may like the greenish tone, but if not, pressurized wood can be stained or painted like any other wood.

You can, if you wish, use other woods, but unless you want to see the deck disintegrate in a few years, the wood must be treated with preservatives. This is definitely the least expensive way to go but the most time-consuming. And no matter what preservative you use, and how you apply it, the longevity will be considerably shorter than for the long-lasting woods. At most, preserving adds only 5 to 10 years to the life of the wood. A typical preservative is "penta" (pentachlorophenol), which was formerly available under various brand names. New environmental regulations now forbid homeowners from applying penta or creosote directly. Woodlife I, for example, should now be off the market. Woodlife II, however, is still available, since it does not contain penta. Always apply preservative before the wood is nailed and after the piece has been cut to size to ensure that all surfaces are fully covered. If you wait to apply preservative until after the wood has been fastened, you may leave many parts untouched by the chemical.

The best way to apply preservative is to dip the wood into the chemical, allowing it to soak in overnight. You can use a large barrel for this, turning the pieces over the following day if they are too long for the barrel, or you can pour the preservative into a long trough. A piece of gutter with the ends closed can be used for this. The best method of dipping lumber, however, is to dig a trench in the ground long enough for the longest pieces (after cutting) and wide enough to accommodate several pieces at once. Find an out-of-the-way spot which needs new grass or is otherwise not in good shape, and dig your trench about 2 inches deeper than the thickest piece of lumber. (If 4 × 4s are the biggest lumber you're using, for example, dig the trench 6 inches deep.)

Lay some thick sheets of polyethylene in the trench extending about a foot beyond all sides, and use double layers over any seams. Fill the trench with the preservative, lay some of the boards inside, and place bricks or stones over the edges of the plastic and on top of the wood so that it won't float to the top. Leave the cut pieces of wood in the preservative overnight, remove, and add more pieces. Add more preservative as it soaks into the wood, and save any liquid that is left over. It can be reused indefinitely. To retrieve the liquid, either scoop it out, or dig a hole nearby beneath the level of the trough, insert a bucket or other container, and dig a trench to the bucket so that the preservative will flow into it.

Suiting Lumber Grade to Purpose

For most deck-building purposes, # 2 grade (common) lumber is acceptable, but any wood that will be in contact with the ground must be a better grade than normal. Posts, unless they are set on aboveground concrete piers, should be heartwood or, if pressurized lumber, should be grade 0.60, which has the highest concentration of preservative. Other pressure-treated wood, if it has any contact at all with the ground, should be grade 0.40. Grade 0.25 is acceptable for wood if it will be aboveground.

Remember that the higher your deck is above the ground, the more important it is that you follow sound construction practices and use good quality materials. Be sure to study the allowable spans and sizes given in the tables, particularly if your deck will be over 3 feet high. Follow the attachment directions explicitly, and don't try to skimp on time or materials. If you build it right, your deck will not only be safer, but will last a lot longer.

ATTACHMENTS

The diagram on the following page illustrates the attaching devices that you will be encountering in the deck construction techniques described in these pages. If you have never worked with lumber outside, you should now familiarize yourself with the non-corroding nails and other rustproof attachments that are available.

Simple decks, particularly those that are built close to the ground without too much superstructure, are built mainly with nails. For exterior use, hot-dipped galvanized nails are best, although aluminum, stainless steel, or other non-corroding nails also will suffice. "Common" (straight shank) nails are used most often, but a better choice, if available for exterior use, is a deformed shank nail such as annular grooved (ring shank) or spirally grooved. These nails retain their withdrawal resistance even after repeated wetting and drying cycles.

Wood screws made of brass or other non-corroding materials can almost always be substituted for nails, although the cost may be prohibitive. No nail holds quite as well as a wood screw, and if the deck is relatively small, the investment may be worthwhile. The usual approach is to attach deckboards to joists or beams with flat-head screws, which insure a tight, long-lasting platform. Variable-speed drills with a screwdriver bit, or an automatic screwdriver, will drive the screws in quickly and securely.

Use 8d (8-penny) nails or 1½-inch screws for attaching nominal 1-inch lumber to other lumber. For attaching nominal 2-inch boards, use 16d nails or 3-inch screws. Larger-size wood requires other con-

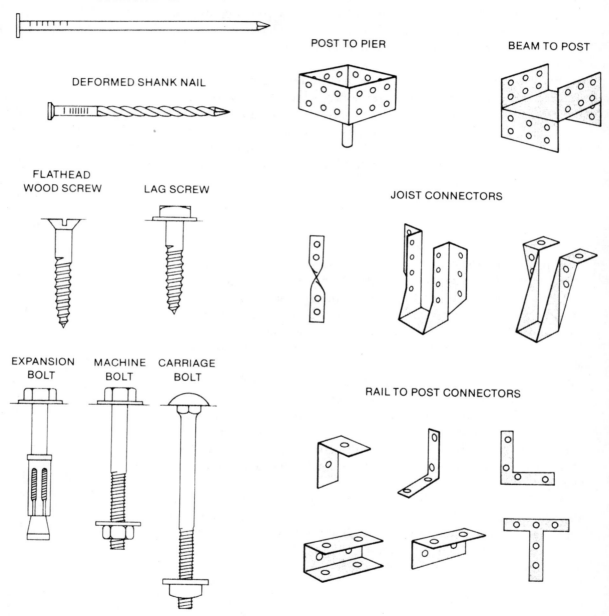

COMMON NAIL

DEFORMED SHANK NAIL

POST TO PIER

BEAM TO POST

FLATHEAD
WOOD SCREW

LAG SCREW

JOIST CONNECTORS

EXPANSION
BOLT

MACHINE
BOLT

CARRIAGE
BOLT

RAIL TO POST CONNECTORS

The main types of deck-building connectors. (Koppers)

nectors, depending on size and on what is being connected to what. The illustrations and instructions will suggest the proper attaching device, but following are some general rules about the various connectors and how to use them.

Lag Screws. Lag screws are large screws which look like, and are turned like, a bolt. They have a bolt head which is used to turn the screw into the wood using an appropriate wrench. These are used primarily for heavy joints, such as in attaching a 2 × 6 to a 4 × 4, where a through bolt cannot be used. A lead hole is drilled first, and the lag screw is turned into the hole. Use a large washer under the head so that the head doesn't penetrate the wood. Holes should be drilled to almost the full length of the screw. The diameter should be ⅔ of the screw diameter for soft woods such as redwood and cedar, and ¾ of the screw diameter for hardwoods and for denser softwood species such as Douglas fir.

Bolts. There are two types of bolts, machine bolts and carriage bolts. Machine bolts are used with washers under the head. Carriage bolts are used without washers under the head. A squared section at the bolt head resists turning as it is tightened. Both types are used to clasp two framing members together by extending completely through the wood and attaching with a nut and washer on the other end. Bolt holes should be drilled the same diameter as the bolt.

Bolts are used in many combinations, but mainly when making connections of two relatively thin pieces of wood, such as railings to posts. They are sometimes used with metal connectors to fasten larger pieces of timber.

Metal Connectors. Metal connectors come in various forms and are used for a number of purposes. Some of these devices come with the recommended attaching devices, such as nails or screws; some do not. The recommended fastenings are detailed in the instructions that follow. In general, 6d common galvanized nails or 1-inch roofing nails are used where the stress is not great and there are many holes in the connector. Where the stress is higher and the holes fewer, larger nails or even lag screws or machine bolts may be required. Check with your dealer if you have any questions.

SITE PREPARATION

Depending on the height of the deck, most or all of the ground beneath it will be deprived of any useful sunlight. Weeds are undoubtedly the only vegetation that will grow in this hostile environment, and can create not only an unsightly mess, but a rise in the moisture content of the wood, leading to possibly hazardous decay where decks are close to the grade.

Where this is going to be a problem, either remove the soil in the immediate area and transplant sod and plantings, or use a weed killer and cover the area with heavy polyethylene sheets. If the soil is removed, replace it with sand or gravel on top of similar plastic sheeting which is laid down after removing the soil. In either case, punch some holes in the sheeting to allow for drainage.

Drainage is, in fact, the only thing you have to worry about in preparing the site for your deck. Make sure that no water will be allowed to collect in damp pools underneath; regrade if necessary. Try to avoid disturbing the natural terrain as much as possible, and grade just enough to insure that water runoff will run in the right direction.

If you are digging out the soil, you may as well dig any needed postholes at the same time. Use an appropriate posthole digger, depending on the type of soil (see Chapter 10, under "Setting Fence Posts"). Either the clam-digger type or auger type can be rented. Some dealers will give you a "loaner" if you buy your lumber there. Holes should extend at least 2 feet into the ground, with the actual depth depending on the height of the post and on the frost line. Consult local building or planning boards for frost-line requirements. A rule of thumb is that about one third of the post should be in the ground.

When you build a ground-level deck or wood patio, it is essential to thoroughly prepare the site as discussed above. Weeds and other vegetation will surely cause problems with a deck at or near ground level.

GROUND-LEVEL DECKS

Simple Low Decks

Several sample plans for low decks which can suggest designs for your own deck are given here. Note how the simple deck transforms the drab back of the house, shown on the next page, into a lovely area. This is a very easy deck to build.

The deck is 10 × 12, with 4 × 4 posts either sunk in the ground or resting on precast concrete piers at each outside corner and in the

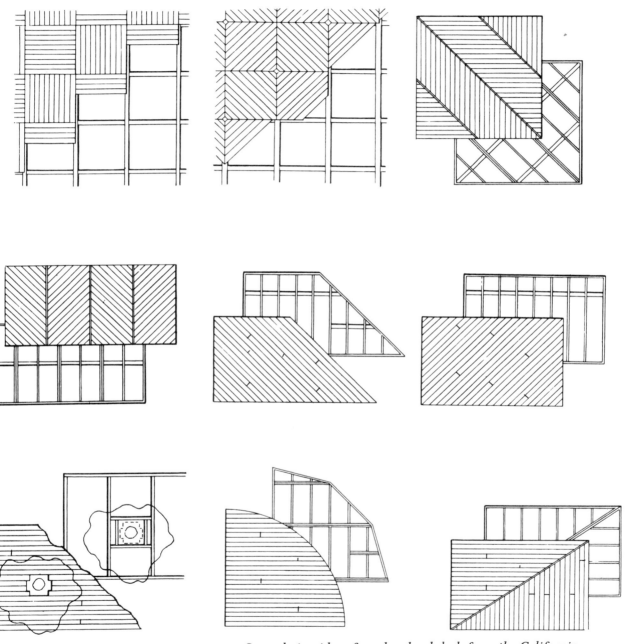

Some design ideas for a low-level deck from the California Redwood Association.

A redwood deck transforms a rather drab backyard into a pleasant spot. (California Redwood Association).

middle—five in all. The inside end of the deck is attached to and supported by the house. A piece of 2×12 is nailed to the house, with 2×6 joists hung to that by means of metal joist hangers.

At the outside edge of the deck, joists are attached with nails driven through a 2×12 which has been attached to the posts with lag screws. On both sides, 2×12s are first attached to the posts with lag screws, and then 2×4s are attached to the 2×12s with carriage bolts and are toenailed to the posts using 10d nails. The 2×4 decking is nailed into the joists and into the 2×4 ledgers on both sides.

As noted in the illustration, joists are spaced 2 feet o.c. (on center, or 2 feet measured from the middle of one joist to the middle of the next). The spacing of the deckboards is an individual matter, with

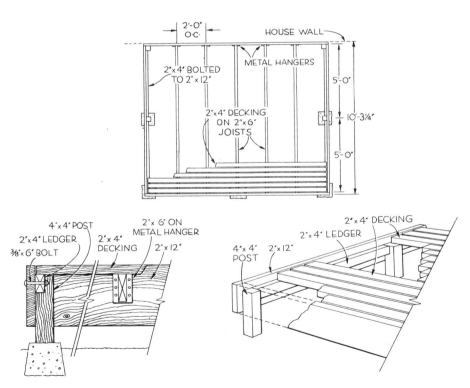

A deck of parquets built on a redwood frame.
(California Redwood Association)

some people preferring ¼ inch or more between boards and others butting the boards closely together. One good way of achieving good even spacing is to use a 12d galvanized nail between decking as you nail it. This provides an almost perfect ³⁄₁₆-inch space between boards, which is just about right for most people.

If you prefer a deck with no space between the boards—and if it's high up, this might be a good idea because the space makes people nervous—be sure to plan your deck so that there is a gradual slope toward the most innocuous side. About ¼ inch per foot is a good grade to allow for ample runoff.

Parquet Decks

One of the nice things about parquet decks is that you can build the components during the cold months or on rainy days. Once you start to lay the parquets, they go up fast, and you have a nice deck in no time.

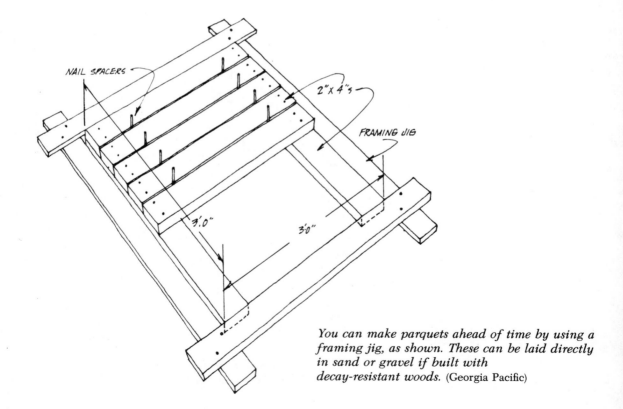

You can make parquets ahead of time by using a framing jig, as shown. These can be laid directly in sand or gravel if built with decay-resistant woods. (Georgia Pacific)

There are many ways of laying a parquet deck, and here I'll briefly describe just two of them. The parquets shown here can be built as independent units, to be laid directly in a bed of sand for a ground-level deck. You can more or less free-lance your way, adding a unit here and there, going up or down a level or two, skipping some shrubbery in between, and so on. This type of deck must be built of completely weather-resistant materials because much of it will be right on the ground.

Making uniform parquet units can be a little tricky. I am using 36-inch parquet squares here, but the same principle I am about to explain applies to any size you choose. The "beams" here rest directly on the ground, preferably sand or gravel, and consist of two 2×4s exactly 36 inches long. Since a 2×4 is only 3½ inches across the top, nine 2×4s laid side-by-side measure only 31½ inches (9 times 3½). That leaves 4½ inches for spacing, or ½ inch between each deckboard.

If you want uniform spaces between boards, the end boards are placed at only half the desired spacing, or ¼ inch, from the outside edges of the section, which achieves the desired ½-inch space when the 2 end boards are butted together (¼ inch at each edge equals ½ inch). It sounds complicated, although it really isn't. All you have to do is study the illustration and follow instructions, and it will become clear. The only reason I'm explaining it here is that it sounds peculiar, and I wouldn't want you to construct a garage full of wrongly cut parquets before the snow melts. As soon as you abut one square against another, you will see the logic of it all.

Anyway, to make a perfectly square parquet unit, cut each of the deckboards per unit to a length of 35½ inches. Lay the nine 2×4s out so that the boards are ¼ inch from the ends of the boards on all sides. In other words, start the first board ¼ inch in on both ends, and ¼ inch in from the ends of the 3-foot "beams." When you began to lay the square, you will see that this results in a ½-inch space all around, so that all deckboards are uniformly spaced. After you make the first parquet, lay some scrap wood on all 4 sides and make a framing jig for the rest of the squares.

The deck shown next is also a parquet deck, but instead of assembling the modular units on the ground, you build a frame to hold the parquets. Here again, you get involved in framing peculiarities, but of a different sort.

If you have ever built a wall, you know that studs are to be placed on 16-inch (or 24-inch) centers. You may have been surprised to find that the end pieces of paneling or gypsum drywall (or Sheetrock, a trade name) were a little short on the ends. That's because "centers" apply only when the framing member is actually in the center—away from the end. It is correct to build your wall so that the center of each stud is 16 inches away from the center of the next one—except when you get to the end stud. If the center of the end stud is also 16 inches away from the next one, the end of the paneling or drywall will fall where you measured it—in the center of the end stud. When it comes to the end, you want your wall covering to *reach* the end, not fall in the middle of the stud.

All of which is meant to explain why the edge members of all deck frames must be brought in half the width of the joists, beams, or whatever, as opposed to the centers used in the middle or field beams. This is a difficult concept for the beginning woodframer to understand. I hope the explanation helps, but if it doesn't, don't despair. Just trust the instructions, and everything will work out fine.

The diagram shows a square deck made up of flat 2 × 4s laid out in squares of 30 inches each. Since the actual dimension of the flat

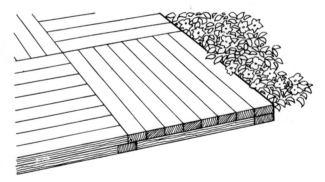

A parquet deck made of flat 2 × 4s laid out in a separately constructed framework of 30-inch squares.

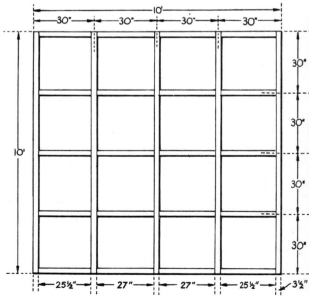

side of the 2 × 4 is 3½ inches, the edge framing members must be brought in 1¾ inches (half the width) so that the end of the edge decking will be flush with the edge of the frame.

To put it another way, as shown in the diagram, the spaces between the field frames will be 27 inches, while the spaces between the perimeter frames and the adjacent "beams" will be 25½ inches.

To make a 10-foot-square deck, cut five 10-foot framing members out of 2 × 4 stock and lay them parallel on the ground. Cut 10 pieces 27 inches long and toenail them between the 3 center rails. Cut 10 more pieces 25½ inches long and use them for the shorter end rails, as shown. Drive 16d nails into end grain where possible, and use 8d nails for toenailing. Check for level and square as you proceed.

Decking consists of 128 2 × 4s, each 30 inches long. Each of the 16 squares of the grid should be covered by eight parallel 2 × 4s spaced ¼ inch apart. Form the parquet pattern by laying each square in the direction opposite to the last one. Use two 12d nails at each end to nail the decking to the frame. To avoid cracking or splitting, predrill nail holes at the ends of each piece.

ABOVEGROUND AND MULTILEVEL DECKS

The higher a deck, the more potential there is for trouble or injury. If you follow the recommendations given here, your deck should work out fine, but it may be wise to check out your plan with an experienced contractor or architect. And be sure that all connections are tight and solid.

The primary safeguards in planning and building an aboveground deck are trying not to span too great a distance, resting it on sturdy footings and posts, and attaching it securely to the house. A thorough study of construction principles should enable you to adapt any type of plan or design your own deck from scratch.

Framing Spans and Sizes

The allowable spans for decking, joists, beams, and the sizes of the posts depend not only on the size, grade, and spacing of the members, but also on the type of wood. Woods such as Douglas fir, southern pine, and western larch allow greater spans than do cedar, redwood, and some of the less dense pines. Normally, deck members are designed for about the same load as are floors in a dwelling.

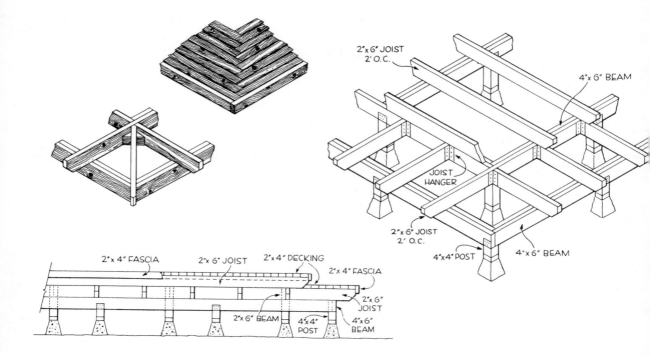

The low, multilevel deck shown here can be adapted to any terrain with a mild grade. The drawing shows basic construction details, with 4 × 4 posts set on concrete piers, facenailed double 2 × 6s forming 4 × 6 beams, 2 × 6 joists, and 2 × 4 decking and fascia. Beams are 5 feet on center, with joists 2 feet apart. Garden-grade redwood is used throughout.

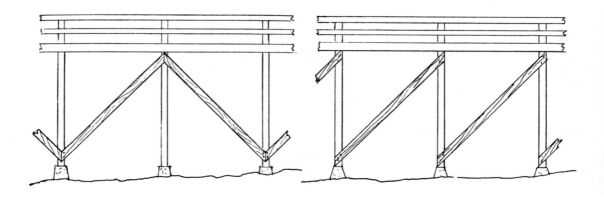

High free-standing decks should have some form of additional bracing.
(U.S. Department of Agriculture)

The arrangement of the structural members can vary somewhat because of orientation of the deck, position of the house, slope of the lot, and so on. Basically, however, the posts, anchored to footings, support the beams, which in turn support the floor joists. The deckboards are then fastened to the joists. When beams are spaced more closely together, the joists can be eliminated if the deckboards are thick enough to span the beams. When the deck is fastened to the house in some manner, the deck is normally rigid enough without bracing between posts. In high free-standing decks, it is best to use some form of bracing.

Minimum Post Sizes

Species Group	Post Sizes	Load Area Based on Beam Spacing × Post Spacing									
		36	48	60	72	84	96	108	120	132	144
1	4×4	up to 12-ft. heights_____up to 10-ft. heights____up to 8-ft. heights_____									
	4×6					up to 12-ft. heights_____up to 10-ft. heights					
	6×6								up to 12-ft. heights		
2	4×4	up to 12-ft._____up to 10-ft. heights_____ up to 8-ft. heights_____									
	4×6			up to 12-ft. heights_____ up to 10-ft. heights_____							
	6×6						up to 12-ft. heights_____				
3	4×4	up to 12-ft. up to 10-ft._____up to 8-ft. heights._____ up to 6-ft. heights_____									
	4×6		up to 12-ft. _____up to 10-ft. heights_____ up to 8-ft. heights_____								
	6×6			up to 12-ft. heights_____							

Example: If the beam supports are spaced 8'6" o.c. and the posts are 11'6" o.c., then the load area is 98; use next larger area 108.

Maximum Allowable Spans for Spaced Deckboards

Species Group	Maximum Allowable Span					
	Boards Laid Flat				Boards Laid on Edge	
	1 × 4	2 × 2	2 × 3	2 × 4	2 × 3	2 × 4
1	16	60	60	60	90	144
2	14	48	48	48	78	120
3	12	42	42	42	66	108

Maximum Allowable Spans for Deck Joists

Species Group	Joist Sizes	Joist Spacing		
		16" o.c.	24" o.c.	32" o.c.
1	2 × 6	9'-9"	7'-11"	6'-2"
	2 × 8	12'-10"	10'-6"	8'-1"
	2 × 10	16'-5"	13'-4"	10'-4"
2	2 × 6	8'-7"	7'-0"	5'-8"
	2 × 8	11'-4"	9'-3"	7'-6"
	2 × 10	14'-6"	11'-10"	9'-6"
3	2 ×6	7'-9"	6'-2"	5'-0"
	2 × 8	10'-2"	8'-1"	6'-8"
	2 × 10	13'-0"	10'-4"	8'-6"

Key to species groups—1: Douglas fir, western larch, and southern pine. 2: western hemlock and white fir. 3: western pines, cedar, redwood, and spruces.

Post Sizes. The common sizes for wood posts used as supporting beams and floor framing are 4 × 4, 4 × 6, and 6 × 6. The size of the post is based on the load, the height of the post, and the span and spacing of beams. Most decks are designed for a live load of 40 pounds per square foot, with an additional allowance of 10 pounds per square foot for the weight of the material, or 50 pounds per square foot altogether. The suggested sizes of posts required for various heights using several beam spans and spacings are listed in the tables. Normally, the minimum dimension of the post should be the same as the beam width to simplify the method of fastening the two together. A 4 × 4 beam, for example, might use a 4 × 4 or a 4 × 6 post depending on the height and the other factors shown.

Beam Spans. The nominal sizes of beams for various spacings and spans are shown in the tables. These sizes are based on such species as Douglas fir, western larch, and southern pine, for Group 1; western hemlock and white fir for Group 2; and the western pines, cedars, redwood, and spruces for Group 3. Recommended lumber grade is # 2 or better.

Joist Spans. The approximate allowable spans for joists used in outdoor decks are listed in the tables for both the denser species of

MINIMUM SIZE TABLES—UNTREATED LUMBER

The tables on this list are for non-pressure-treated lumber, and it is recommended that all species except redwood and red cedar be soaked in preservative as described on page 138. Tables all assume a live load of 40 psf (pounds per square foot) and a dead load for the wood itself of 10 psf.

Minimum Beam Sizes and Spans

Species Group	Beam Sizes	Spacing between Beams									
		4	5	6	7	8	9	10	11	12
1	4×6	up to 6-ft. spans _____								
	3×8	up to 8-ft. _____		up to 7'	up to 6-ft. spans _____					
	4×8	up to 10	up to 9'	up to 8'	up to 7-ft. _____		up to 6-ft. spans			
	3×10	up to 11'	up to 10'	up to 9'	up to 8-ft. _____		up to 7-ft. _____		up to 6-ft. _____	
	4×10	up to 12'	up to 11'	up to 10'	up to 9-ft. _____		up to 8-ft. _____		up to 7-ft. _____	
	3×12		up to 12'	up to 11'	up to 10'	up to 9-ft. _____		up to 8-ft. spans _____		
	4×12			up to 12-ft. _____		up to 11'	up to 10-ft. _____		up to 9-ft. _____	
	6×10					up to 12'	up to 11'	up to 10-ft. spans _____		
	6×12						up to 12-ft. spans _____			
2	4×6	up to 6-ft. _____								
	3×8	up to 7-ft. _____		up to 6-ft. _____						
	4×8	up to 9'	up to 8'	up to 7-ft. _____		up to 6-ft. _____				
	3×10	up to 10'	up to 9'	up to 8'	up to 7-ft. _____		up to 6-ft. spans _____			
	4×10	up to 11'	up to 10'	up to 9'	up to 8-ft. _____		up to 7-ft. spans _____		up to 6-ft.	
	3×12	up to 12'	up to 11'	up to 10'	up to 9'	up to 8-ft. _____		up to 7-ft. spans _____		
	4×12		up to 12'	up to 11'	up to 10-ft. _____		up to 9-ft. _____		up to 8-ft. _____	
	6×10			up to 12'	up to 11'	up to 10-ft. _____		up to 9-ft. spans _____		
	6×12				up to 12-ft. spans _____			up to 11' ___		up to 6-ft.
3	4×6	up to 6'								
	3×8	up to 7'	up to 6'							
	4×8	up to 8'	up to 7'	up to 6-ft. _____						
	3×10	up to 9'	up to 8'	up to 7'	up to 6-ft. spans _____					
	4×10	up to 10'	up to 9'	up to 8-ft. _____		up to 7-ft. _____		up to 6-ft. spans _____		
	3×12	up to 11'	up to 10'	up to 9'	up to 8'	up to 7-ft. spans _____		up to 6-ft. _____		
	4×12	up to 12'	up to 11'	up to 10'	up to 9-ft. _____		up to 8-ft. _____		up to 7-ft. _____	
	6×10		up to 12	up to 11'	up to 10'	up to 9-ft. _____		up to 8-ft. spans _____		
	6×12			up to 12-ft. _____		up to 11-ft. _____		up to 10' ___		up to 8'

Example: If the beams are 9'8" apart and the species in Group 2, read the 10-ft. column—3×10 up to 6-ft. spans, 4×10 or 3×12 up to 7-ft. spans, 4×12 or 6×10 up to 9-ft. spans, 6×12 up to 11-ft. spans

Sizes and Spans—Pressure-Treated Lumber

The sizes below apply to pressure-treated (Wolmanized) lumber.
The load assumptions for the previous table apply here.

Minimum Beam Sizes

Length of Span (ft.)	Spacing between Beams (ft.)						
	4	5	6	7	8	9	10
6	4 × 6	4 × 6	4 × 6	4 × 8	4 × 8	4 × 8	4 × 10
7 .	4 × 8	4 × 8	4 × 8	4 × 8	4 × 8	4 × 10	4 × 10
8	4 × 8	4 × 8	4 × 8	4 × 10	4 × 10	4 × 10	4 × 12
9	4 × 8	4 × 8	4 × 10	4 × 10	4 × 10	4 × 12	*
10	4 × 8	4 × 10	4 × 10	4 × 12	4 × 12	*	*
11	4 × 10	4 × 10	4 × 12	4 × 12	*	*	*
12	4 × 10	4 × 12	4 × 12	4 × 12	*	*	*

*Beams larger than 4 × 12 recommended. Consult a designer for appropriate sizes.

Minimum Post Sizes

Height (ft.)	Load Area (sq. ft.) = Beam Spacing × Post Spacing				
	48	72	96	120	144
Up to 6	4 × 4	4 × 4	6 × 6	6 × 6	6 × 6
Up to 9	6 × 6	6 × 6	6 × 6	6 × 6	6 × 6

Vertical loads figured as concentric along post axis. No lateral loads considered.

Maximum Allowable Spans for Deck Joists

Joist Size (in.)	Joist Spacing (in.)		
	16	24	32
2 × 6	9'-9"	7'-11"	6'-2"
2 × 8	12'-10"	10'-6"	8'-1"
2 × 10	16'-5"	13'-4"	10'-4"

Maximum Allowable Spans for Spaced Deckboards

Maximum Allowable Span (in.)		
Laid Flat		Laid on Edge
2 × 4	2 × 6	2 × 4
32	48	96

Though able to support greater spans, the maximum spans will result in undesirable deflection or springiness in a deck.

Group 1 and the less dense species of Groups 2 and 3. These spans are based on the same loads as those for posts.

Deckboard Spans. Deckboards are usually laid flat using boards of nominal 2-inch thickness in widths of 3 and 4 inches. Decking also can be made of 2 × 3s or 2 × 4s placed on edge over longer spans, or of 1 × 4 boards in shorter spans. Deck spans are listed in the tables.

Footings and Posts

Concrete footings below the surface are normally used for weather-resistant or treated posts. Use either a prepoured footing upon which the wood members rest or a poured-in-place type. The minimum size for preformed concrete footings in normal soils is 12 × 12 × 8 inches. Where spacing of the poles is over 6 feet, 20 × 20 × 10 inches or larger sizes are preferred.

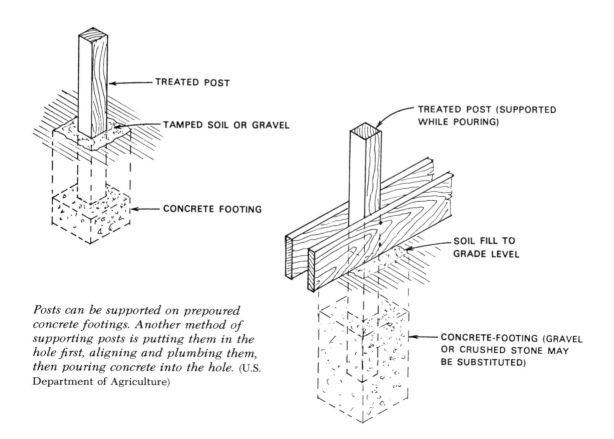

TREATED POST

TAMPED SOIL OR GRAVEL

CONCRETE FOOTING

TREATED POST (SUPPORTED WHILE POURING)

SOIL FILL TO GRADE LEVEL

CONCRETE-FOOTING (GRAVEL OR CRUSHED STONE MAY BE SUBSTITUTED)

Posts can be supported on prepoured concrete footings. Another method of supporting posts is putting them in the hole first, aligning and plumbing them, then pouring concrete into the hole. (U.S. Department of Agriculture)

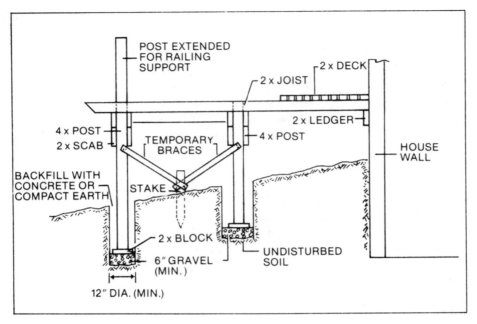

This diagram shows the initial stages of deck-building. (Koppers)

With poured-in-place footings, the poles are prealigned, plumbed, and supported above the bottoms of the excavated holes by one of the methods shown here. Concrete is then poured below and around the bottom of the pole. There should be a minimum depth of 8 inches of concrete below the butt-end of the pole. Soil may be added above the concrete when necessary for protection in cold weather and for cosmetic purposes.

To avoid excavation and concrete-pouring problems and contact of the end-grain of the wood with wet concrete, you can use precast footings with built-in hardware for attaching the posts. These exposed footings should extend at least 6 inches above grade.

The proper fastening of supporting posts to footings with top surfaces above grade is important, as the posts should not only resist lateral movement but also uplift stresses which can occur during periods of high winds. These anchorages should be designed for good drainage.

Beam-to-Post Connections

Beams are framing members which are attached to the posts. Depending on design, the floorboards may be directly attached, or

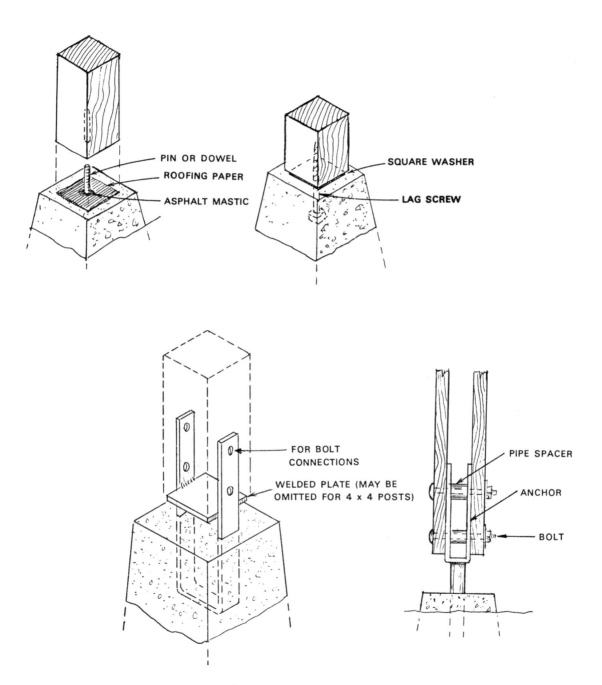

PIN OR DOWEL
ROOFING PAPER
ASPHALT MASTIC

SQUARE WASHER
LAG SCREW

FOR BOLT
CONNECTIONS

WELDED PLATE (MAY BE
OMITTED FOR 4 x 4 POSTS)

PIPE SPACER
ANCHOR
BOLT

How to attach posts to precast concrete piers. (U.S. Department of Agriculture)

there may be an intermediate network of joists. Beams may be single, large or small, framing members, or may consist of 2 smaller lumber units (usually 2-inch lumber) fastened to each side of the post.

Single beams of nominal 4-inch lumber usually bear on top of a post. When this system is used, the posts must be trimmed level so that the beams bear evenly on all posts. Use a line level or spirit level attached to a long, straight board to establish this alignment.

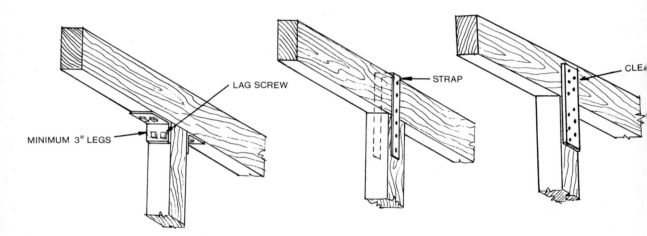

Various ways of attaching beams to the tops of posts.
(U.S. Department of Agriculture)

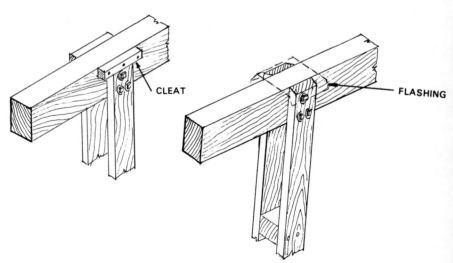

Attaching a beam between double posts of 2-inch lumber.

To attach wide single beams, use two angle irons with 3×3-inch or larger legs, fastened by lag screws. You can also use a 3-inch strap, ⅛-inch thick, preformed to insure a good fit. For smaller lumber sizes, use 10d ring-groove nails to attach the strap, or ¼-inch lag screws for larger lumber. Still another method is to cut long cleats out of 1×4 lumber or ¾-inch plywood (exterior grades) and nail them to each side of the post with 8d annular nails.

When double posts are used, such as two 2×6s, a single beam is usually placed between them. Double or split beams are normally bolted to the tops of the posts, one on each side. Notching the top of the beam provides greater load capacity. A piece of asphalt felt or a metal flashing over the joint will provide some weather protection for the post end.

It is sometimes advantageous to use the post that supports the beam as a railing post. In such a design, the beam is bolted to the post, which extends above the deck to support the railing members.

Beam- and Joist-to-House Connections

When the deck adjoins the house, a sturdy means of connecting beams or joists to the house is required. Recommended connections are metal hangers, wood ledgers, or angle irons, or use of the top of the masonry foundation or basement wall. The deck should be designed so that the tops of the boards are just under the sill of the door leading to the deck. This will provide easy access to the deck as well as protection from rain.

Beams.   Metal beam hangers can be used to connect the beam to the house. These may be fastened directly to a floor framing member, such as a joist header, or to a 2×8 or 2×10 which has been bolted or lag-screwed to the house framing. Use 6d or longer nails or the short, large-diameter nails often furnished with commercial hangers for fastening. Hangers are available for all beams up to 6×14.

Beams also can be secured to the house by bearing on ledgers which have been anchored to the floor framing or to the masonry wall with expansion shields and lag screws. The beam should be fastened to the ledger or to the house with a framing anchor or a small metal angle.

Joists.   When joists of the deck are perpendicular to the side or end of the house, they are connected in much the same manner as

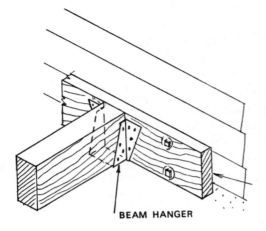

The beam hanger is bolted or lagged directly to the house frame. (U.S. Department of Agriculture)

BEAM HANGER

Attaching joists which bear directly on the beam (left). If a header is used at the end of the joist, attach as shown at right. Header should overhang the beam by ½ its width. (U.S. Department of Agriculture)

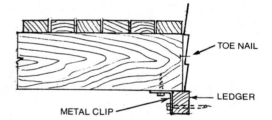

TOE NAIL

LEDGER

METAL CLIP

beams, except that the fasteners are smaller. Joists are toenailed to the ledger and the house or fastened with small metal clips.

Joists also can be fastened to a 2 × 8 or 2 × 10, lag-screwed to the house, by means of joist hangers. Six-penny nails or 1¼-inch galvanized roofing nails are used to fasten the hangers to the joist and to the header. When joists are parallel to the house, usually no ledger or other fastening member is required. If the joists are supported by beams, then the beams, of course, are connected to the house, as previously discussed.

Bracing

On uneven sites or sloping lots, posts up to 5 feet in height do not ordinarily require bracing. When the deck is not attached to the house, it is good practice to use bracing between higher posts to provide lateral resistance. Treated poles or posts embedded in the soil or in concrete footings usually have sufficient resistance to lateral forces, and such construction normally requires no additional bracing. However, when posts rest directly on concrete footings or pedestals and unsupported heights are more than 5 feet, some system of bracing should be used. Braces between adjacent posts serve the same purpose as bracing in the walls of a house.

Joist-to-Beam Connections

When beams are spaced 2 to 5 feet apart and 2 × 4 Douglas fir or similar deckboards are used, there is no need to use joists to support the decking. The beams thus serve as both fastening and support members for the 2-inch deckboards. However, if the spans between beams are more than the recommended spans in the tables, it is necessary to use joists between the beams or to set the 2 × 4s on edge for decking. To provide rigidity to the structure, the joists must be fastened to the beams in one of several ways.

Joists bearing directly on the beams may be toenailed to the beams with 1 or 2 nails on each side. Use 10d nails to avoid splitting. When there are uplift stresses in high wind areas, supplementary

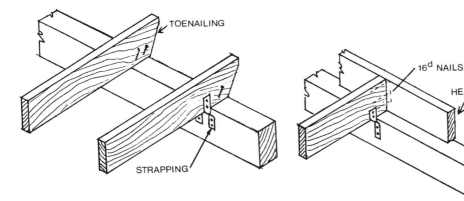

A perpendicular joist fastened to the house.
(U.S. Department of Agriculture)

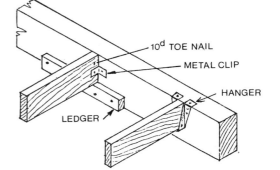

*Attaching joists between
and flush with beams.*

metal strapping might be used in addition to the toenailing. Use 24- to 26-gauge galvanized strapping and nail with 1-inch galvanized roofing nails. When a header is used at the joist ends, nail the header into the end of each joist. Have the header overhang the beam by ½ inch to provide a good drip edge.

Joists located between beams and flush with their tops may be connected in either of two ways. A 2 × 3 or 2 × 4 ledger can be spiked to the beam. Then joists are cut between beams and toenailed to the beams at each end. This joint can be improved by the use of small metal clips.

Or, a metal joist hanger can be used. The hanger is first nailed to the end of the joist with 1-inch to 1¼-inch galvanized roofing nails and then is nailed to the beam.

DECKBOARDS

Use two 8d nails at each framing member to fasten 2 × 3 and 2 × 4 decking laid flat. For 2 × 3s or 2 × 4s on edge, use one fastener per joist. Use two 12d nails for 2 × 3s on edge, and 5-inch flathead screws for 2 × 4s set on edge.

Ordinarily, you should space all deckboards, flat or vertical, ⅛ to ¼ inch apart; use 8d nails for ⅛-inch, 12d for ³⁄₁₆-inch, and 16d for ¼-inch. End joists of flat deckboards should be made over the center of the joist or beam. Always place flat-grain boards with the "bark" side up. When the upper face gets wet, it crowns slightly, and water drains off more easily. End joints of any deckboards on edge should be made over a 4-inch or wider single beam or a nominal 2-inch joist with nailing cleats on each side. Leave ¼ inch between the ends of butted deckboards.

When screws are used for fastening, and when all fastening points

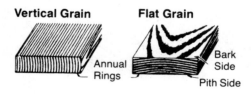

If boards are vertically cut (left), either side can be laid up. When the grain is flat, the bark side goes up (right).

of the deckboards are placed on edge, it is a good idea to predrill ends of 2 × 3 or 2 × 4 flat deckboards when building with the denser species or whenever there is a tendency for the wood to split, as may be the case with very dry wood or such species as spruce when nailed near the end.

RAILING POSTS

Usually low-level decks located just above the grade require no railing. However, if the site slopes, adding to the height of the deck, some type of protective railing or system of balusters might be needed at the high end(s).

The key members of a railing are the posts. Posts must be large enough and well enough fastened to provide strength to the railing. Railings should be designed for a lateral load of at least 20 pounds per linear foot. Posts must be rigid and spaced properly to resist such loads.

One easy method of providing posts for the deck railing is extending the posts which support the beams. When single or double beams are fastened in this manner, the posts can be built above the deck floor, and serve to fasten the railing as well as other horizontal members. Railing heights may vary from 30 to 40 inches or higher when a bench or wind screen is involved. Posts should be spaced no more than 6 feet apart for a 2 × 4 horizontal top rail and 8 feet apart when a 2 × 6 or larger rail is used.

When supporting posts cannot be extended above the deck, a joist or beam may be available to which double posts can be secured. Posts can then be arranged as shown here. Such posts can be made from 2 × 6s for spans less than 4 feet, from 4 × 4s or 2 × 8s for 4- to 6-foot spans, and from 4 × 6s or 3 × 8s for 6- to 8-foot spans. Each post should be bolted to the edge beam with two ⅜-inch or larger bolts, depending on the size of the post.

This system also can be used when the railing consists of a number of small baluster-type posts. When such posts are made of 2 × 2s or 2 × 3s and spaced 12 to 16 inches apart, the top fastener into the beam should be a ¼- or ⅜-inch bolt or lag screw. The bottom fastener can then be a 12d or larger nail. Predrill when necessary to prevent splitting. Wider spacings or larger-size posts require 2 bolts. A ⅛-inch to ¼-inch space should be allowed between the ends of floorboards and posts.

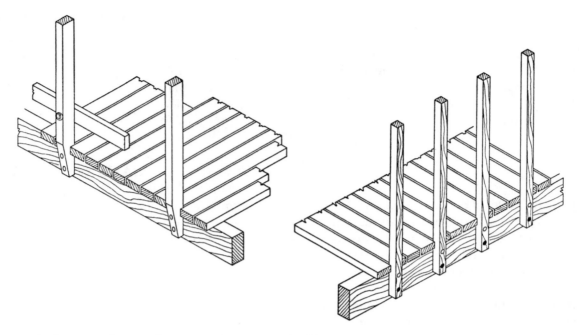

Methods of attaching railing posts, by use of a double post attached to beam ends (above), or by standard balusters securely fastened to outside beams (below). (U.S. Department of Agriculture)

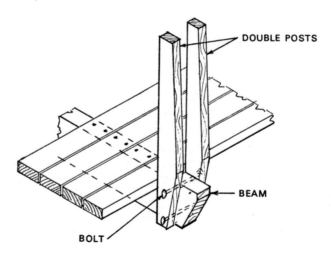

DOUBLE POSTS

BEAM

BOLT

DECK BENCHES

High-deck Benches. At times, it is possible to combine utility and protection. by using a bench along the edge of a high deck. The vertical back supporting members (bench posts), spaced no more than 6 feet apart, are bolted to the beams or can be fastened to extensions of the floor joists. When beams are more than 6 feet apart, the bench posts can be fastened to an edge joist in much the same manner as for fastening railing posts. The backs and seat supports should be spaced no more than 6 feet apart when nominal 2-inch plank seats are used.

Low-deck Benches. Benches also can be used along the edges of low decks. These can be simple plank seats which serve as a backdrop for the deck. Such bench seats require vertical members fastened to the joists or beams with cross cleats. For 2 x 4 seats, vertical supports should be bolted to a joist or beam and be spaced no more than 6 feet apart. A single wide support (2 x 10) or double supports (two 2 x 4s) can be used.

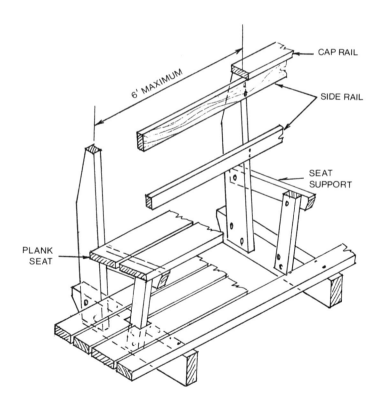

Construction details for building high-deck benches. (U.S. Department of Agriculture)

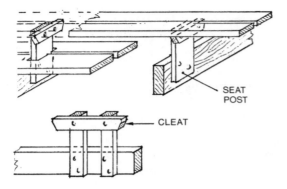

SEAT POST

CLEAT

One way of building low-deck benches. More freedom of design is allowed here because secure attachment to the deck is of little or no importance. (U.S. Department of Agriculture)

RAILINGS

Horizontal Railings. The top horizontal members of a railing should be positioned to protect the end grain of such vertical members as posts and balusters.

The upper side rail, which is usually a 2 × 4 or wider, should be fastened to the posts with a lag screw or bolt at each crossing. The cap rail then can be nailed to the edge of the top rail with 12d nails spaced 12 to 16 inches apart.

When railing posts are spaced more than about 2 feet apart, additional horizontal members may be required as a protective barrier. These side rails should be 2 × 4s when posts are spaced no more than 4 feet apart. Use 2 × 6s when posts are spaced over 4 feet apart.

Rail Fastenings. When the upper side rail is bolted to the post, the remaining rails can be nailed to the posts. Use two 12d nails at each post and splice side rails and all horizontal members at the center line of a post. Posts must be more than 2 inches thick to provide an adequate fastening area at each side of the center splice.

STAIRWAYS

Stairways are often needed for access to a deck or between sections of multilevel decks. Exterior stairs are much the same as stairs within a house, except that extra measures must be taken to avoid trapped moisture, especially on exposed end grain.

Stair Stringers. A basic stair consists of stair stringers (sometimes called stair carriages) and treads. Additional parts include balusters and side cap rails and, on occasion, risers. Stringers are the supporting members of a stair. They are used in pairs spaced no more than 3 feet apart, and usually are made of 2 × 10s or 2 × 12s. Stringers must be well secured to the framing of the deck. They are normally supported by a ledger or by the extension of a joist or beam.

A 2 × 3 or 2 × 4 ledger nailed to the bottom of an edge framing member with 12d nails supports the stringer shown on the left in the illustration. Toenailing or small metal clips are used to secure the stringer to the ledger. Stair stringers also can be bolted to the ends of joists or beams when they are spaced no more than about 3 feet apart (right). Use at least two ½-inch galvanized bolts to fasten the stringer to the beam or joist.

The bottoms of the stair stringers should be anchored to a solid base and be isolated from any source of possible moisture. This can be done by anchoring metal angles to a concrete base. The angles should be thick enough to raise the stringer off the concrete, which should be sloped for drainage. Another method is to anchor a treated wood member in the concrete or in the ground.

Tread and Riser Size. The relation of the tread width ("run") to the riser height is important in determining the number of steps required, and the total length or run of the stairway. For ease of

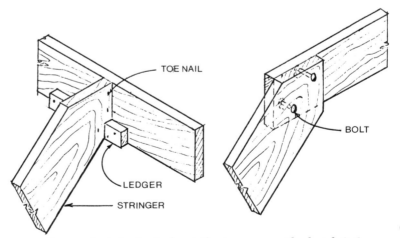

To attach stairs to decks at the top, use method at left for beams at right angles and method at right for parallel beams.

ascent, the rise of each step multiplied by the tread width should equal 72 to 75. If the riser is 8 inches (considered maximum for stairs), for example, the tread would be 9 inches ($8 \times 9 = 72$). Or if the riser is 7½ inches, the tread should be at most 10 inches ($7.5 \times 10 = 75$). The number of risers and treads can be determined when the total height of the stair is known. Divide the total rise in inches by 7½ (each riser), and select the nearest whole number. Thus, if the total rise is 100 inches, the number of risers would be 13, and the total run would be about 120 inches.

Tread Support. For tread support, bolt 2×4 ledgers or cleats to the outside of the stair stringers, extended the width of the plank treads. The ledgers can be sloped back slightly so that rain will drain off the treads. Nail 2×10- or 2×12-inch treads to the ledgers with three 12d nails or 3-inch wood screws at each stringer. Always place plank treads with the bark side up to prevent cupping and retention of rain-water. Treads also can be made of two 2×6 planks, but the span must be limited to 42 inches for less-dense woods.

Stair Railings. On moderate- to full-height stairs with one or both sides unprotected, a railing is advisable. Railings for stairs are constructed in much the same way as railings for the deck, and for the sake of appearance should have the same design. Railings usually are made of posts fastened to stair stringers with top and intermediate rails. Appearance is important, but safety and utility must be considered first. When stair railings are used, tread supports are bolted to the inside of the stringers.

The Outdoor Kitchen 9

If you like to live and work outdoors, you'll almost certainly enjoy cooking and eating there. Outdoor cooking, or barbecuing (they may or may not be the same), has become a suburban ritual, as much as a part of commuter living as the freeways, buses, or rapid transit.

Tracing the word "barbecue" takes us back to the Spanish *barbacoa,* which in turn came from an Indian phrase that referred to a rough framework of green wood that supported meat to be broiled over an open flame. More correctly, the Indian word referred to the technique that is used today for a New England style clambake. This involves digging a pit, preferably on the beach in the sand, and lining it with large stones. In most of the northern United States and Canada today, however, a barbecue simply means anything cooked out of doors—on a portable grill, hibachi, or outdoor fireplace.

In planning your backyard, you don't have to take such history into consideration. Assuming you have decided to provide for some degree of outdoor cooking, the question you have to take into consideration is will a portable unit—hibachi, circular grill, or propane gas —be adequate, or would you prefer a permanent installation?

The answer to that question involves asking some others. How often do you cook out? Only on that first warm day of summer, when the spirit moves you? Once or twice more? If so, there's little point in building a permanent structure. Even if you do cook outdoors a lot, you may not have a favorite spot for barbecuing. Consider the weather, too. If you live in a cold and rainy climate, you may find yourself "cooking out" inside the garage—door open—or under some other shelter. But if you own and often use a portable grill and find that it stays pretty much in the same spot or if you really enjoy barbecuing and find yourself cooking out, even in bad weather on the back porch or in the garage, you should consider a permanent barbecue.

What type of barbecue would you like? Gas-fired units are very popular now for a number of reasons, one of which is their convenience. Just light a match (some don't even require that), and they start right up. Another reason is their variety; gas units can be either portable (using liquefied petroleum gas such as propane) or permanent, using a permanent natural gas line. With their ceramic coals, you'll never have to buy charcoal or starter fluid.

There are numerous brands and types of gas-fired barbecues, some quite large and elaborate. Some have attached cutting boards, spits, and other accessories. All have hoods which can be lowered to convert the unit from open-flame to smoke-and-bake cooking. For the more-than-occasional-but-not-quite-dedicated barbecuer, a gas-fired unit is probably the ideal choice.

In truth, though, you won't be considered a true barbecue *aficionado* unless you have a built-in barbecue. Efficient as a gas-fired unit is, it is just not the same as having a real smoke-billowing fireplace of brick, stone, or other masonry out back.

If you decide on a masonry fireplace, then the choice narrows down to brick, stone, concrete block, or sometimes, a combination of 2 or 3 of them. The advantages and disadvantages of each are discussed at the end of this chapter.

There is a great range of choice in size and complexity, from a simple mortarless fireplace to a complete outdoor kitchen with a fireplace, a revolving spit, elevating grills and grates, draft and clean-out doors, ovens, hoods—you name it. On these pages are designs for all tastes and budgets. Think about what you'll really use, and select accordingly. If you're building an elaborate fireplace, remember that revolving spits, for example, need electricity, so the location of your barbecue may be important.

LOCATING YOUR BARBECUE

A simple barbecue which will be used only on nice days can be located anywhere, but even if you don't use a barbecue that often, it should be as conveniently placed as possible. If you like to eat outdoors but don't have a permanent barbecue yet, the ideal location is probably near your dining spot, which is probably as close to the kitchen as possible. Unless you plan on a barbecue that is so complete you won't need your regular kitchen, common sense mandates that the kitchen be within reasonable walking range. There may be a gorgeous dining spot at the back corner of your property, but you won't use it quite so often if you have to lug the food a hundred yards. The kitchen will remain your primary work and clean-up area, so accessibility is an important requisite.

If you are starting from scratch, the barbecue may well become the centerpiece of your backyard. Its nearby dining area will be a natural spot for family and friends to gather. The patio and pool, if you plan on them, may also be located close at hand. The entire complex should not be too far from the kitchen.

If you already have a patio, the natural spot for a new barbecue may be next to or within it. But also consider the locations of swimming pools, garden houses, "Florida rooms" or gazebos. You should put the barbecue where the family naturally gathers.

If you're entirely renovating your yard, consider whether there is an ugly spot or a shunned area that is little used. You may want to clean it all up and make it a new focal point. This is especially true where there are trees or bushes that can form a natural windbreak and provide shade and privacy. But beware of low branches that can catch fire. And use a high chimney on any barbecue placed among trees or located next to the house, garage, or any other outbuilding.

For your barbecue, take advantage of the protection already available, such as the side of a house or garage, fences, hedges, and so on. Sometimes a barbecue can be built right into a brick or stone wall, where it may look natural and unobtrusive.

In sunny areas some protection from the sun is advisable. This may mean putting the barbecue under the patio roof or devising a separate small roof or sun screen. Or use the side of the house or garage as a sun shield. The opposite tactics may be advisable in the north, but even there the sun can be very hot during the summer months.

Where winds are strong and a nuisance, some type of windbreak may be necessary. But don't consider the wind as only an enemy. On the contrary, a fresh breeze is a fire's best friend. Face your barbecue, if possible, toward the gentler breezes. When winds are more aggressive, a side exposure may be more prudent.

Don't forget about utilities. A permanent gas barbecue will need a permanent gas line, unless you use bottled gas. Don't locate the unit where you will have to snake the gas line around obstructions to get to the barbecue. Even modest barbecues will benefit from an electric line. Not only are they a must for motor-driven spits and skewers, but it is a great help to have some light available in case you want to barbecue after dark. If you use an electric fire starter, be sure that the circuit can handle the high wattage (see Chapter 12).

If you're planning an elaborate unit with a sink, you will need at least a cold-water line. While you're at it, you might as well put in hot-water plumbing for easier clean-up. You will also need drains and a connection to a sewer or drainage bed. As you can see, the more complicated the unit, the more problems you may run into. Be sure to check building codes for set-back regulations, and inquire whether permits are required. Fire regulations may apply, and any type of electrical or plumbing improvement will surely be covered by some sort of code.

LAYING THE FOUNDATION

Whether your barbecue is made of brick or something else, you'll need a strong foundation to support its weight. Brick itself is heavy, and when combined with mortar weighs about 120 pounds a cubic foot. Any brick wall should bear on concrete footings at least twice as wide as the brick itself. The thickness of the concrete will depend on the size of the fireplace, the type of soil on which you're building, the local climate, and whether you use reinforcing wire, which is usually advisable. Such poor weight-bearing soils as loose sand or loam will necessitate a thicker slab. So will severe freezing conditions. In the prolonged freezing areas of most of Canada and the northern United States, you should go below the frost line—at least 16 inches down—to prevent winter damage to your barbecue. In the southern United States or other frost-free areas, you may not need a concrete base at all if your soil is firm. A few inches of gravel or cinders may suffice. But if there is any chance at all of below-freezing temperatures, don't take a chance. Install a concrete base of at least 4 inches.

When planning, determine the perimeter dimensions of the bottom row of brick or other material, then add at least 2 inches all around. If the ground is level and the surrounding soil compact, you

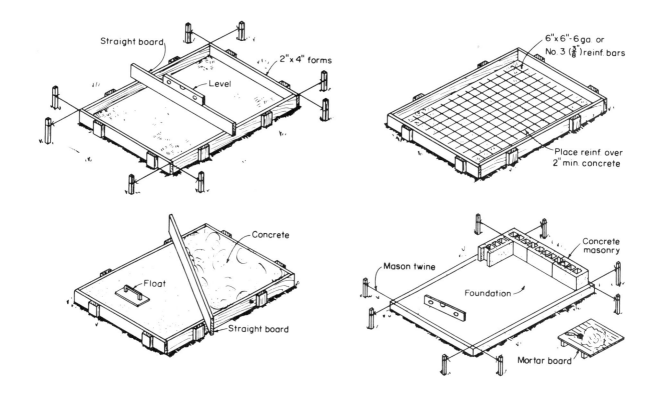

Straight board

2" x 4" forms

Level

6"x 6"-6 ga. or
No. 3 (⅜") reinf. bars

Place reinf. over
2" min. concrete

Concrete

Float

Straight board

Concrete
masonry

Mason twine

Foundation

Mortar board

may be able to lay the concrete without forms. When forms are used, excavate another 2 inches all around to allow for the 2 × 4 forms.

Lay out the area, then mark it with a string. If you set the string a little above the soil line and use a line level, you can use the same string to determine the correct depth of your excavation. Just add the height above the soil line to the depth of the intended excavation and measure down. If you want a 12-inch-deep foundation, for example, set the string 2 inches above the existing soil line and dig down to 14 inches below the string.

For small slabs, dry ready-mixed products such as Sakrete simplify the job greatly. (The same holds true for mortar and other cement mixes.) If you prefer to mix your own cement, the proportions are 1 part Portland cement to 3 parts sand and 4 parts gravel. (See Chapter 11 for more details on concrete work.)

When the foundation has cured, draw a chalk outline of the barbecue 2 inches in from all the edges of the foundation. Now you are ready for bricklaying.

DO-IT-YOURSELF BRICKWORK

One look at the soaring arches of a brick cathedral should convince you that you're not going to learn all about bricklaying in a day—or a year. But you can easily learn the basics and do the simple projects in this book. Just don't attempt anything too complicated until you've fully mastered the fundamentals.

Types of Brick

There are many more varieties of brick than the homeowner would think possible and almost as many sizes. Some of the better-known types are Norman brick (2¾ × 3¾ × 12 inches) and Roman brick (1½ × 3¾ × 12 inches), but the kind most often used by the homeowner is common or standard brick, which measures 2¼ × 3¾ × 8 inches. The projects discussed here assume the use of common brick of this size. Always measure brick yourself before planning your layout, however; sizes and terminology may vary from area to area.

Brick may be either solid or cored (several holes in the center section). The holes make the brick cheaper and lighter without the loss of any strength, but the coring should not exceed 25 percent of the volume of the brick.

Natural fired brick comes in a variety of reds, buffs, and creams, depending on the type of clay and the processing. Glazes, of course, can produce almost any color imaginable. All brick for exterior use should be labeled "SW grade" (check with your dealer).

Tools

The indispensable bricklayer's tool is the trowel. Even if your project is very small, get a high-quality trowel that you can handle easily and that will stand up under hard use. (A professional-grade trowel can even cut brick.) A 10-inch length is best for most people.

In addition to the trowel, you will need:

- A broad-bladed brick chisel ("set" or "bolster")

- A hammer (a brick hammer, and a "mash" or ball-peen type)
- A good level, the longer the better (mason's is best)
- A folding rule
- A length of tough string
- A pointing tool (you can substitute a length of ⅝-inch copper pipe, bent into an S-shape)

You also should have a square-end short-handled shovel for mixing mortar, and a container in which to mix it. A wheelbarrow will serve as well as anything, and can be moved along with you as you work. A mortar board, which can be just a scrap piece of plywood or other clean surface, may be used instead.

Layouts and Materials

When planning any brick project, be sure to account for the mortar (unless, of course, you are making something like a mortarless barbecue or patio). You can do this by establishing an approximate size, converting feet into inches and dividing each dimension by the size of the brick plus ⅜ inch for each mortar joint. If you're left with anything other than a whole or half brick, it is best to adjust your plan so that bricks won't have to be cut.

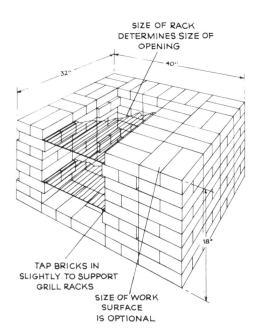

A mortarless brick barbecue.
Racks are available at specialty dealers, or
can be custom-ordered to fit. (BIA)

Actually, there is no need to go through all of these elaborate calculations before ordering brick unless you must fit the brick exactly into a certain area. With most fireplaces, walls, patios, and so on, size is flexible. Use rough dimensions when ordering your brick and make a dry run with the first row to establish the precise finished length. After that, you can plan your project so that each row is composed of whole or half bricks. If you find out later that you're a little bit off, you should be able to stretch or shrink the mortar joints just a trifle, but don't deviate more than ⅛ inch either way. Joints should be no less than ¼ inch and no more than ½ inch. You'll have to cut brick if you find you're off too much.

When ordering, figure roughly 7 bricks per square foot of wall layout and 4½ bricks per square foot of flat installation like a patio. The accompanying chart gives the actual numbers, but add 5 to 10 percent to these figures for waste. Brick can be bought at all masonry and most building-supply dealers.

Mortar

Brick mortar consists of Portland cement, lime, sand, and water. You can buy it premixed, with Type M your best bet for outdoor use. If you want to mix your own, the proportions are 1 part Portland cement, ½ part hydrated lime, and 4 parts clean sand.

Begin by thoroughly blending the cement, lime, and sand with your shovel. Then scoop out a hollow in the middle of the mixture and slowly add water until it is the consistency of soft mud. Unlike concrete and most other cement mixes, mortar is better mixed with too much water rather than too little, since the brick will absorb much of the moisture.

Estimating Brick and Mortar
(Single-tier Walls)

Brick Size	Brick per 100 sq. ft.		Cubic feet of Mortar per 1,000 Bricks	
	⅜" Joint	½" Joint	⅜" Joint	½" Joint
3⅝ × 2¼ × 7⅝	675		8.1	
3¾ × 2¼ × 8	655	616	8.8	11.7

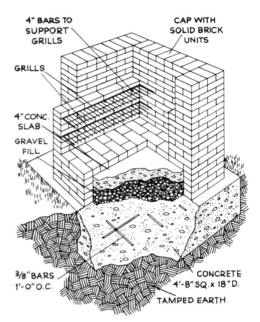

Construction of a mainly double-wythe barbecue. (BIA)

Make sure there are no dry spots in the batch, and mix only as much mortar as you can use in 30 minutes to an hour. To prevent too rapid drying, wet the brick with a garden hose about an hour before using it. The surface of the brick will then be dry when laying so that the mortar will not slip off, but the interior will still be wet and will help avoid premature mortar stiffening. It also is helpful to dampen the foundation before laying the first course.

Brick patterns are called "bond" and can be made in many different ways. The most common and easiest to lay is running bond, in which each brick is placed exactly halfway over the tops of the 2 bricks below it (half on each side of the joint). No matter which bond you choose, remember to lay out the first course in a dry run.

The width of the structure depends on the project, of course. A high wall should be at least 2 bricks thick (2 tiers, or wythes), but there is no need to use more than a single width for a simple project like a small barbecue. A bigger barbecue may consist of 2 or more tiers. If so, follow directions on pages 201–30.

How to Begin

Begin laying brick at a corner and build it up three or four rows high, dovetailed with the adjacent wall (if any) at right angles. Use

A professional bricklayer uses a mason's line, which you can buy if you wish. The same purpose, however, can be served with a regular line and a nail stuck in wet mortar. (Sakrete)

Scrape off the excess mortar with the pointed end of the trowel and return it to the mortar board to mix with the remaining mortar.
(Louisville Cement)

the level and square frequently to keep things in true. When you have built up a corner, go on to the next, lining it up with the first by using a straightedge or line level.

Bricklaying is easy, as long as you take your time. Take a slice of mortar on your trowel and lay it along the foundation about ½ inch thick, and long enough for 2 or 3 bricks (later you can stretch to 4 or 5). Furrow the mortar a bit with the point of the trowel, making sure the bed extends the width of a brick. Lay the first corner brick carefully and firmly into the mortar bed, then butter one end of the next brick and set it next to the first. Some mortar should be squeezed out of these shoved joints. Trim off the excess mortar and return it to the mortar board, butter the next brick, set it against the previous one, and continue. With the first few joints, you should measure the mortar, but soon you'll learn to judge the placement by eye.

When at least two corners are in place, push a nail into the soft mortar between the first two courses (rows) in each corner and run a line between the nails. The line should be almost—but not quite—touching the front and top of what will become the first course. Use this string as a guide for placing the rest of the bricks in the first row. Each brick should be individually lined up at the same distance from the line. After the first course is laid, move the string up to the row above and repeat for each course.

If you've made your dry run correctly, the closure brick—the last one—should fit perfectly. When laying this brick, butter *both* ends of the brick as well as the flanking bricks on either side. Lower this brick carefully into the gap, taking care not to knock off the mortar. Tap it into position.

As long as the mortar has not set, any brick that is set too high can be tapped down into position, but a low brick can't be tapped up. Pull up the brick, scrape off the old mortar, lay down more mortar, and try again.

Keep working on the bricks between corners until you reach the level of the highest course set at the corners, then resume laying corners (depending on height) for 3 or 4 more courses. Go back to the in-betweens, then the corners, and so on, until you reach the top.

Once You're Under Way

As you move along, don't forget to keep checking for plumb, level, and alignment. If you find your wall is bulging, dipping, or otherwise running out of true, don't attempt to tap bricks into place once the mortar sets up. Take out the misaligned brick (and those above it, if necessary), scrape off the old mortar and add new, then reset. Any tampering with the mortar once it starts to harden is sure to cause cracks or hollows in the joint, which will weaken the entire structure and invite leakage.

Sometimes, in spite of good planning, you will find you have to

A pointing tool compacts the mortar and creates a tight, neat, waterproof joint. (Louisville Cement)

cut a brick. In that case, put the brick on a solid surface, preferably tamped-down sand. With the brick chisel and hammer, tap a line all around the brick with the bevel facing in. Then give the bevel a sharp blow. The brick should break clean. (Professional bricklayers can cut brick with the edge of a trowel or the chisel-back of a hammer, but don't try to do this.) Use the back of the brick hammer to chip away rough edges or protrusions.

As each course is completed, run your ⅝-inch pipe or pointing tool across the joints before the mortar has hardened to produce a smooth and uniform appearance. Other tools may be used, but the concave joints produced by the pipe are the best for producing a watertight seal. While tooling (or pointing), you also can fill in the holes left by your line nails and any other imperfections with dabs of mortar.

If you are building a barbecue with grates set into the mortar, be sure to put them in place while the mortar is still wet. When laying the fire bed, pitch it slightly toward the front to allow for drainage (¼ to ⅜ inch).

When mortaring the top course of the brick, try to achieve a smooth surface without concave or beveled joints. A smooth top is much easier to use later. You may prefer to cover the top course with a layer of concrete, ceramic tile, stone, or other material, but a smooth brick finish will do just as well. If connecting bolts are used, be sure to insert them into the mortar joints when laying the top course. Pitch the top row slightly away from the fire so that water will drain away.

Firebrick, which is designed to withstand intense heat and is always used for indoor fireplaces, is not necessary outdoors because there is usually plenty of air circulating to keep the temperature of the brick from becoming as hot as it would in an enclosed area. Furthermore, firebrick is brittle and can be damaged by cold winter weather. For most outdoor fireplaces use regular brick or a cast-iron fireplace, which is installed following the manufacturer's instructions.

If you do use firebrick outdoors, lay it so that the wider surface faces the fire. Use special fireclay-cement mortar, or substitute fireclay for lime in your own mix. Butter firebrick lightly, allowing only $\frac{1}{16}$ to $\frac{1}{4}$ inch between bricks. Firebrick must be cut more carefully, too. Make shallow guide cuts on all four sides before giving the sharp final blow. And don't dampen firebrick. It should be laid as dry as possible.

Finishing Touches

Like all cement compounds, mortar should be allowed to mature for at least two days. Hot, dry weather will accelerate hydration, which should take place slowly. In such weather, give the mortar an occasional watering while it matures. And be gentle to your new barbecue for a few weeks until the mortar is good and strong. Restrain your enthusiasm for at least 2 weeks before firing it.

Meanwhile, clean up any mortar stains with damp burlap. If this doesn't work because the stains have set, remove them with a solution of muriatic acid diluted with 10 parts of water. Wear gloves and goggles when using this solution, and rinse off any acid that lands on you immediately and thoroughly with cold water. Wet down the brick with water and scrub on the acid solution with a stiff brush. After 10 to 15 minutes wipe the brick off again with damp burlap.

After the mortar has completely cured, which should take at least a week, you may want to coat the brickwork with a colorless masonry sealer. This provides a transparent, water-repellent surface that prevents crumbling mortar for many years.

WORKING WITH STONE

Building stone makes an elegant barbecue, which may or may not fit in well with your overall design. Basically, there are 2 kinds of stone —round, flinty-hard stones used in rubble masonry, and softer, stratified stones used for ashlar stonework. Granite, basalt, and similar round stones are very difficult to work with, but are much more resistant to erosion and temperature extremes. Shale, sandstone, bluestone, and other types of wallstone are brittle and relatively easy to cut into shape. They cannot be used next to fire, however, because they will chip, crack, and sometimes explode. Nor does this type of material hold up well to extreme cold.

A round-stone fireplace often can be built with field stone found on your property. If you have a strong back and an eye for pleasing effect, a rubble fireplace is quicker and certainly less expensive than buying ashlar stone. Working with boulders, however, is not at all simple. It is very difficult to work out an attractive pattern, and the work becomes much more difficult as you progress. The higher the fireplace, the heavier the rocks seem. Another problem is that the round stones are almost impervious to water and therefore do not bond with mortar as well or as quickly as do more porous materials.

In many ways, though, a rubble barbecue is easy to build. No firebrick or other material, except for mortar, is needed. Just keep piling up the stones and mortar until you've reached the height and design that please you.

Using Stratified Stone

There are 2 basic ways to build a fireplace with stratified ashlar rock. One is to build a center of firebrick or hard-burned common brick. This is your true firepit, and the stone is then laid around it more as decoration than anything else. A truly artistic barbecue can be built with random uncut wallstone, but this can be expensive because of the quantity of stone that must be used. Juggling the large stones into the right pattern can also be a problem.

Perhaps the best way for the inexperienced stoneworker to proceed is to use cheap and easily laid concrete block as a core, and then lay a brick center and stone veneer. Lay the cinder or concrete block wall first, and use firebrick or hard-burned brick to line the wall and floor of the firebox. Use quarry-cut stone as a veneer. This is easy to work because it comes cut in thin pieces of uniform thickness.

Since you use only a thin veneer of stone in this method, you also should use metal ties to bind the stone and the block. The ties are nailed into the block so that they will later line up with the mortar between the bricks to form a solid bond. Mortar will cover the ties. (See above for details of mortaring.)

CONCRETE BLOCK BARBECUES

Concrete block is lighter than it looks because of its hollowed-out cores, yet it maintains most of the strength and durability of poured concrete. Since block doesn't hold up well to intense heat, most block fireplaces are lined with either firebrick or hard-burned common brick. You also can install a manufactured firebox. A cast-iron firebox is particularly well suited to concrete block, and can be used with stone or brick, too.

The principal drawback of a block barbecue is the rather unappealing appearance of its surface. This can be improved, however, by a sand coat of cement stucco, made of 1 part cement to 3 parts and enough water to make a slightly runny consistency, or by one of the new mortars that can be applied to the face of the block after it is set in place. These mortars act as finish coats in addition to bonding the block without conventional mortar. Cinder block also comes with any of several different decorative facings, most of which are more attractive than standard building block. Instructions for working with block are given on pages 210–15.

PIT BARBECUES

A pit barbecue is probably the purest descendant of the old-time *barbacoa.* It is, in its simplest form, just a hole dug into the ground in which a fire is lit—a firepit, if you will. But it can be much more elaborate, if desired.

The firepit is usually round, placed near the center of the patio, and lined with rocks, bricks, or other fire-resistant material. It can be fitted with a grate or simply filled with sand to a level a few inches below the surface. The food is then cooked in the open as over a campfire. A firepit makes an inexpensive, easy-to-build barbecue, but bending down over it all the time can be difficult. Other disadvantages are exposure to breezes and clean-out problems.

A cozy deck with benches surrounds this firepit made of concrete block touched off with mitered 2 × 6s. (Western Wood Products Association)

An attractive design for a firepit is shown here. The firepit is the center of an outdoor conversation pit, sunk below the main deck, much like an indoor conversation pit. Note that the pit is surrounded by a deck of 2 × 4s set on end and by benches also made of 2 × 4s on end, nailed to 2 × 4 crosspieces supported by 4 × 4 posts. This is a ground-level deck with the 4 × 4s made of woods suitable for ground contact sunk into the ground.

The firepit shown is made of 40 solid concrete blocks 4 × 4 × 16, surrounded by four pieces of 2 × 6 mitered at the ends and attached with carriage bolts. Note that the pit can be converted to a table by constructing a cover. The photograph shows details of deck and bench construction.

Whether you design your firepit as an offshoot of a larger deck or as a free-standing barbecue, keep the pit a good distance from the house itself as a safety measure.

USING YOUR BARBECUE

One of the first things a barbecuer should learn, but often doesn't, is how to build a good charcoal fire in a portable grill. A chimney can be an enormous help. You can buy one at outdoor stores or make one yourself out of an old bottomless pail or similarly tapered metal object. The secret is in getting a draft to pull the flames up. Position your chimney so that air can enter beneath it and escape from the top. If you don't have a chimney, you can hand pile the charcoal briquets into a pyramid shape. Soak with starter fluid, or use presoaked briquets, which are becoming increasingly popular. An electric fire starter is handy, too; even nicer is a built-in gas firer.

Leave the fire alone until all the coals are glowing from top to bottom. When they're white-hot, it's time to spread them out (just lift up the chimney) and start cooking.

Other handy accessories are a roasting spit if you have outdoor electricity, long skewers, a spatula, a fork, cooking tongs, a basting brush, and wire cages for steaks, ribs, or hamburgers. Make sure all have sturdy, long handles. A spray bottle is also very convenient to squelch flare-ups. For items such as cut-up chicken parts, a rotating "tumble" cage makes for more evenly distributed heat.

CARE AND MAINTENANCE

Purists may be horrified, but it's sound practice *not* to clean the grill and other metal parts of the barbecue after cooking. The cooking grease is actually good protection from the elements and will help inhibit rust. The grease will burn off the next time you use the barbecue and will feed the flames at the same time. You can scrape off any excess grease with a wire brush if it doesn't burn off.

If you're using brick or porous stone for your barbecue, protect it during the winter with a good masonry sealer. Apply the sealer every year or so to avoid water damage. And each spring, break the unit in the way you would a new one. Wait until it dries out, then cure it slowly with a small fire kept burning for a few hours.

When using any kind of metal barbecue, portable or permanent, remember that fire gradually eats iron away. Spread foil over the bottom of any metal grill when using charcoal, and insulate portable grills with gravel, sand or other material, taking care not to cover air holes.

Walls and Fences 10

Robert Frost's line, "Good fences make good neighbors," from *Mending Wall,* is often quoted by people who believe in erecting walls. If you read the poem completely, however, you get a much better sense of what Frost was driving at:

> *Something there is that doesn't love a wall*
> *That sends the frozen-ground-swell under it*
> *And spills the upper boulders in the sun. . . .*
>
> *Before I built a wall I'd ask to know*
> *What I was walling in or walling out*

In other words, although it is true that good fences often *do* make good neighbors—especially where there are dogs and children—it is something of an affront to erect a barrier between you and your neighbor if there is no good reason for it. All too often, people flee the city for green, open spaces, and then begin exurban existence by automatically putting up a chain-link or stockade fence around their property.

WHAT'S GOOD ABOUT WALLS AND FENCES

Several legitimate reasons do exist for erecting walls and fences, and it's worth examining them to see how they fit into the backyard scheme.

This city home is built very close to the street, with a useless, skinny front yard. A courtyard fence made of fir 1 × 8s with 1 × 2 battens solves problems of privacy, wandering children, and stray animals. The recess by the gate allows a 3-foot shrub bed, alleviating the fortress look.
(Western Wood Products Association)

Definition of Property. A wall or fence establishes once and for all the limits of property. Surveys tend to confuse, with their indecipherable symbols and abbreviations (50.5, for example, means 50½ feet). The stakes driven in by the original developers rot, get overgrown, or are just plain lost. If there is a vacant lot next to a built-up one, neighbors tend to "squat," often in all innocence. (If no one is using the land, why not plant a few tomatoes?) Later on, when the rightful owner tries to reclaim his property, the squatters become resentful.

Privacy. A good fence or wall often provides needed privacy. Especially in densely built areas where there is little room between houses, residents feel naked in the view of their neighbors' eyes. Everyone has the right to moments of quiet, and sometimes the only way to have them is to build a tall solid fence. If you are patient, a better alternative might be trees or shrubs, but these can take years to grow mature enough for the purpose.

Safety. Children, dogs, and swimming pools usually require a closed-in area. A fence keeps your own children and animals in and the neighbors' out. Most municipalities have laws requiring that a pool be surrounded by a fence fitted with a self-closing gate. Even if the law or the insurance company doesn't require this, common sense dictates that at least in-ground pools be fenced and secured.

Shelter. With intelligent planning, walls and fences can be built to divert harsh winds, invite cooling breezes, and provide shade where desired. Also, offensive sights such as the garbage area, compost heap, work area, or woodpile can be put out of sight.

Background. Fences and walls, if tastefully selected and installed, can be used for attractive backdrops for such plantings as flowers, rose beds, shrubbery, and the like.

Dividers. When play areas run into dining areas or restful regions run into active ones, a lacy screen fence or wall can serve as a subtle divider. Space dividers can be used in several other ways, as illustrated in some of the photographs in these pages.

WHAT AND WHERE TO FENCE

Don't think that just because you have a good reason for putting up a wall or fence, you should automatically put it around the perimeter of your property. For example, wouldn't it be better, especially if

An inviting backyard corner is created by the high fence, trellis, and benches. Because of the placement of the fence, the protected area is partly shade and partly sunny. The fence keeps out harsh winds and prying eyes. Western red cedar is the main ingredient of the shelter.
(Western Wood Products Association)

your lot is large, to confine the dog to one part of the property? Do you need privacy *all* around the house, or would it be better just to wall in that section along the driveway where the neighbor's house is close?

A friend of ours loved to sit in his backyard and stare out at the sloping land that spread behind his house and his neighbors'. The view included at least a dozen other backyards and provided a lovely communal setting. Then one neighbor, for reasons still not fathomed

The screen wall around this patio makes it more private, yet allows breezes and sun to filter through. (Western Wood Products Association)

by the others, decided to fence in his backyard. Since it was at the center of the aforementioned vista, it absolutely ruined the view. (The fence builder erected his fence with a gate leading to his next-door neighbor's yard, where he liked to use the swimming pool. Needless to say, the gate remained unused, since the pool-owning neighbor thereafter refused to allow the fence builder onto his property.) Soon another fence arose, then another, until the communal setting was completely obliterated.

The point of this anecdote is that when you decide that a wall or fence is what you want, it is not a bad idea to first discuss it with your neighbors. Some may be delighted to have you keep your dog out of their yard. Others may object, but might be made to understand if you explain your reasons. Perhaps you should request suggestions as to type and design. If you have a really cooperative neighbor and the fence will benefit both of you, perhaps you can arrange to share costs and/or labor.

Unless you live in an extremely dense area where the lots are very small, it is often considered bad manners—and is sometimes illegal —to fence in your front yard. Also, be aware that an unwritten, and often written, law is that the so-called ugly side of the fence should face in. (An exception would be where there is a highway, railroad, or similar "neighbor" on the other side of the fence.) If you can pick out fencing that is good-looking on both sides, by all means do so.

TYPES OF WALLS AND FENCES

A fence or wall can take as many different forms as the functions it can serve. It can be a solid wall, open framework, louvers, latticework, or any combination. It can be made of boards, pickets, panels (wood or fiber glass), brick, stone, or block, in a variety of shapes and patterns. And yes, it even can be chain link, which is appropriate at times.

If you want fencing that is attractive as well as utilitarian, study the walls and fences shown on these pages. Most of them require building from scratch.

It's often possible to buy sectional fence. This is fencing material put together into prebuilt sections, usually 8 feet long, which require simply nailing to posts. If you check out their prices, however, you'll find that any good-looking sectional fencing is quite expensive; gates are extra; and you still have to put in the posts, which is the hardest part. Since decent-looking sectional fence is expensive, most people settle for stockade fence, which creates barriers and privacy but is not very good-looking. The less attractive side that faces in can be downright ugly.

Now, back to chain link. In my opinion, a front yard surrounded on all sides by industrial-looking chain link does not add to the beauty of a home. Chain link does have its good side, though. It can be put up quickly and rather cheaply by contractors. (Construction does not lend itself to easy do-it-yourselfing.) Recently developed vinyl-covered chain link blends in well with the landscape, so that if in a wooded or shrubby area you install chain link covered with brown vinyl, the fencing will tend to disappear—or at least lose its fortress look. Conversely, if you merely want to fence around a built-in pool to conform to local regulations, chain link at least allows a relatively unobstructed view from the pool area.

On the other hand, although you might not want to miss the view, you may prefer that the whole neighborhood not be observing your yard. This is the chief disadvantage of chain link; it sets up barriers without providing privacy. The only way to achieve a degree of privacy with chain link is to purchase wood, aluminum, or plastic strips to thread between the links. The cost of this is surprisingly high, if a contractor does the work. Each strip must be hand threaded, raising labor costs. Your best bet, if you want this type of fence, is to have a contractor put up the fence, and then thread the privacy strips yourself. Be forewarned that it is a tedious job.

Fence and wall design is largely a subjective matter. One of the designs shown on these pages may fit your purposes exactly as is. If so, use it. You may prefer to adapt a plan to your own tastes and budget. Remember the long run, though. Wood that is susceptible to insect and weather damage requires laborious preparation (pages 136–38). If you intend to stain or paint the wood, frequent renovation is necessary—not an easy job. If you can afford it, use redwood, red cedar, or pressure-treated wood to cut down on future maintenance.

Also remember that the contour of the land will influence your choice. Masonry walls require footings and a reasonably level surface. The contour of the land can make a big difference. Note, for example, the privacy fence shown here, and see how the difficult problems were solved. In a situation like this, the fence *must* be custom-built. No sectional fencing could be adapted to such diverse slopes.

Location, too, will affect your choice. For example, you won't want to cut off the patio's pleasant view with a solid wall or fence.

Steep grades make fencing difficult. Note how the problem is solved with this fence. (Western Wood Products Association)

This sturdy redwood retaining wall was designed to protect the tree and its roots after the land in front was leveled off. The purpose and height of a retaining wall are important considerations in determining the materials used. (California Redwood Association)

Nor will you want to cut off cooling breezes, or hide any of the other desirable features of the landscape. Be careful, also, when building next to a driveway, to allow adequate room for easy access to the car on both sides.

TERRACING

Thus far we have been discussing the garden wall, really just another term for a masonry fence. Walls also are used, however, for terracing property and altering the contours of the landscape. This type of wall, if low and used only to raise a flower bed or edge the driveway, for example, is easy to make and poses no construction problems.

The handsome stone retaining wall at the right coordinates nicely with the irregular stone patio at the left. Pools must, of course, be perfectly level, often requiring a retaining wall. Tall evergreens in background and a concrete walk around the pool make a nice setting for this pool; also note the pagoda lamps along the wall for nighttime light. (Olympic Pool Company)

When the alterations to the landscape involve more than just a few inches or a foot, however, it is quite another story. Now we are talking about *retaining* walls, whose purpose is to hold back earth. Unlike a garden wall, only one side of the wall is open, while the other is covered to the top with soil.

The purpose of a retaining wall is to separate living or planting areas from the rest of the lot. This may be necessary because of steeply sloping land or because of a need for a level area to hold a swimming pool, garden, patio, deck, or similar structure. Retaining walls also are built to protect trees and shrubs when the natural contours are disturbed, or serve simply to prevent erosion on hilly ground. Although a steep grade can be a disadvantage, proper planning and the use of terraces can make such a building plot much more interesting than a flat, level one. The construction of retaining walls is discussed later in this chapter.

SETTING FENCE POSTS

If you have decided upon a boundary fence, make sure you know where your property lines are and familiarize yourself with all of the local building and other applicable codes before laying out the perimeter. You will need your survey to make certain of the property line. Look for stakes, monuments, or other objects defining the boundaries. If there is chance of error, it is a good idea to hire a surveyor to put in markers or monuments.

When you are satisfied that the boundaries are in order, outline the fence with stakes driven into the ground at the corners. Most ordinances allow you to build a fence within an inch of the property line, but make sure of this and remember that the law refers to the *outside* of the fence, which can be several inches beyond the post.

With the corner stakes in place, string line tautly between each stake. Determine the siting of the posts, which usually are 8 feet apart, but remember to allow for gates and other anomalies. Using a long tape, if you have one, mark off the location of each post by driving a temporary stake into the ground. Leave the string in place during post erection as a guideline for keeping the fence straight.

You will need a posthole digger to excavate for the fence posts. They are available at most rental agencies, but the clam-digger type usually used is not expensive to buy. If you have a lot of holes to dig, you may find it cheaper to buy than rent. Some soils, such as hard clay, are better suited for an auger type digger. If you can rent a power auger, the job will go a lot faster. These do not work well in rocky soils, however. Some lumber and fence dealers let you use a free posthole digger for a limited period of time. On bedrock, you can use concrete piers like those used for decks (pages 155–57).

Posts should be set into the ground approximately ⅓ of their total length, or half as deep as the post is high. A 4-foot-high post, for example, should be 6 feet long, with 2 feet buried underground. The

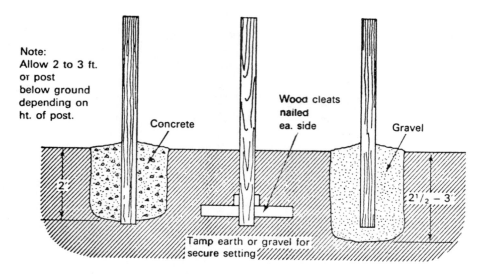

Ways to achieve solid fence posts.

hole should actually be dug about 4 inches deeper (in our example, 2 feet 4 inches). The extra 4 inches should be filled with gravel for better drainage.

It goes without saying that fence posts should be the best grade of wood available, for they are very prone to rot. Assuming you have the right type of lumber, you can use any of the methods illustrated here to backfill the post. Posts used to support gates should be stronger than the others. Either use 6 × 6s instead of 4 × 4s, or set these posts in concrete and bury them a foot lower in the ground than the others. Also take extra care in setting the corner posts.

All posts should be plumbed with a spirit level. Set corner posts first. Then string a line across the tops of these to establish the height of the intermediate posts. Depending on the type of post used, the intermediate posts can be brought up to proper height at the time of setting or the tops can be cut off later with a portable saw.

Because of the many varieties of fences, it is difficult to give exact instructions for further construction. In general, though, rails are strung between posts at the top and near the bottom. These can be butted, dadoed, notched, or cut in any way shown in the drawing. Blocks are the easiest to use but may not look very attractive. Use only hot-dipped galvanized nails for fence construction, 16d for nominal 2-inch stock and 8d for 1-inch.

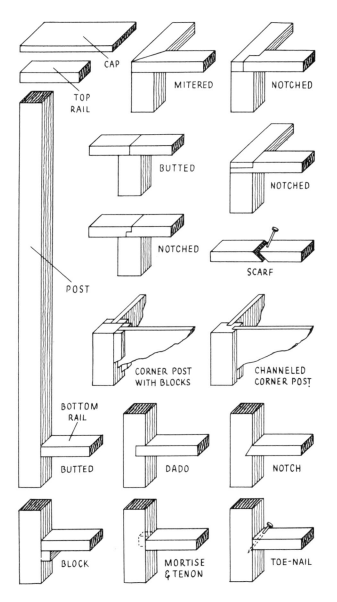

CAP

TOP RAIL

MITERED

NOTCHED

BUTTED

NOTCHED

POST

NOTCHED

SCARF

CORNER POST WITH BLOCKS

CHANNELED CORNER POST

BOTTOM RAIL

BUTTED

DADO

NOTCH

BLOCK

MORTISE & TENON

TOE-NAIL

Make sure that fence posts are plumb, by using a spirit level. Posts should be brought into position with the line to the height you have chosen. (L. Donald Meyers)

Fence joinery, or ways in which the rails are attached to the posts. (California Redwood Association)

GATES

It is especially important to design and build gates carefully because they take a lot of abuse. Gate posts should be a little bigger and set about a foot deeper than the other posts and should be embedded in concrete.

Be sure to build the gate frame at strict right angles, either square or rectangular in shape. After nailing the outside frame together with 16d nails, lay a piece of 2 × 4 diagonally between the furthest two corners. Trace the contours of the corners with a pencil. Saw along these marks and nail the board into the corners to form a brace. Then nail the exterior fence boards onto both top and bottom frame pieces as well as the brace. Additional cross-bracing may be necessary for extra-wide or heavy gates. Avoid, if possible, very wide gates, such as those needed across a driveway. If you must have gates that

When building a gate, nail and square the perimeter boards, then set them on top of the cross-brace, marking so that the brace can be sawed to fit into the corners. (L. Donald Meyers)

wide, construct 2 gates, with a latch and sliding vertical metal brace in the center. The brace should rest in a hollow in the concrete or blacktop, and is then raised to allow the gates to swing open.

Any gate should be wide enough to accommodate anticipated traffic, yet not so wide that it prevents convenient opening and closing. Three feet is a typical width for a garden gate, with a ½-inch clearance allowed between the gate and latchpost so it will swing clear. Be sure that the gate does not swing uphill, or into some impediment like a tree.

The design of the gate should be inviting, especially if it is the first greeting to visitors. The pattern of the fence is usually repeated in the gate, but can be varied to create a more dramatic effect. The posts can be higher than the others, or the gate can be recessed, lowered, or made higher than the rest of the fence. Hinges, latches, and other hardware should be sturdy and attached with heavy, non-corroding screws.

WALLS

As handsome and durable as well-built wood fences are, they cannot compete with masonry walls for longevity. Stone and brick are, if not forever like a diamond, almost as durable as one.

A free-standing garden wall is used, as is a fence, to define zones, add an accent or background, provide privacy, or mark off property lines. A garden wall need be no stronger than (but certainly no weaker than) a wood fence. Unlike the retaining walls discussed later, there is no pressure from earth or water to worry about. If a brick or stone garden wall is built properly, it should last a long time —much longer than its builder.

Low brick walls, or higher walls away from stress, can be built of 1 wythe, as described on pages 176–77. Most high walls, and those on boundaries, should consist of 2 wythes or be built with concrete block backup.

To achieve the strength required for a 2-wythe wall, the 2 tiers must be tightly bonded. There are several ways to do this. Metal ties can be inserted in the grout and the 2 wythes erected simultaneously, with the ties between them. Concrete block also can be used for the walk, with brick as a veneer; again, use metal ties. Another, trickier method, usually employing reinforcing bars on longer bricks, is the building of a cavity wall, where space is left between wythes and grout (watered-down mortar) is poured in between. (See pages 216–17 later in this chapter.)

The most satisfactory double-wythe wall, in my opinion, is one which interlocks the bricks themselves. The resulting bond between

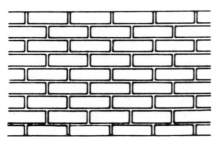

Running bond. It consists of all "stretchers" (that is, brick laid lengthwise along the wall). Running bond is frequently used in veneered walls and in interior walls.

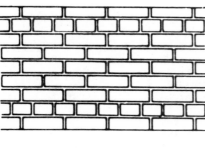

Common bond. A variation of running bond, it has a course of "headers" (brick laid with the short end along the face of the wall) at regular intervals. These header courses may appear every fifth, sixth, or seventh course.

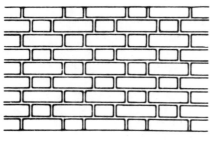

Flemish bond. A handsome bond often used in Colonial American buildings, each course of which is made up of alternate stretchers and headers, with the headers in alternate courses centered over the stretchers above and below.

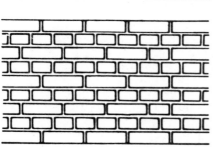

English bond. Composed of alternate courses of headers and stretchers, with headers centered on the stretchers and joints between stretchers in all courses lined up vertically.

the two wythes is solid. Any number of different and interesting patterns can be used. In American or common bond, for example, 5 stretcher courses (laid the long way) are laid, then 1 header course is laid across the 2 wythes. Flemish bond alternates stretchers and headers in each course, and English and Dutch bonds use stretcher courses followed by header courses in different patterns.

No matter what pattern or bond you use, there should be a minimum of one header course for every seven stretcher courses. Only the most widely used bonds are discussed here, and you may want to discuss other patterns and specific instructions for laying them with your masonry dealer. Also ask your brick dealer about the ties needed for other types of walls and how they should be used.

If you want to use concrete backerblock, see the instructions later in this chapter for retaining walls. Garden walls do not need the weep holes or the strength of block retaining walls. Walls less than 4 feet high need no reinforcement at all, but walls from 4 to 6 feet in height should have ½-inch reinforcing rods set in the footings at 4-foot intervals. The rods need extend only into the first 2 feet of wall aboveground, and the footings themselves need no reinforcing bars. Fill the holes in the block around the reinforcing bars with mortar.

While plain concrete block makes a rather uninteresting wall, there are many decorative blocks which make a concrete wall an exciting option in many circumstances. See pages 210–15 later in this chapter for detailed instructions on installing concrete block.

Stone Walls

If you travel the back roads of New England or along the Hudson River, or even in the hills of Pennsylvania, you can find examples of old, still intact stone walls, of the type described by Robert Frost in the beginning of this chapter, that seem to serve little or no purpose. Sometimes they are found deep in the woods, where it seems highly unlikely that any farming ever took place.

The only possible explanation for such walls is that they were put there by early settlers to define the boundaries of their land. These are not fancy walls. Where they coexist with farming or grazing land, they served another simple purpose. They "stored" the rocks which had to be removed from the land for farming. There were no fancy patterns or mortared joints. Every time a rock was found, it went into the wall. Surprisingly, some of these early fences can be charming— and still useful.

The stone used in this type of wall is called rubble. It consists mostly of boulders. Where natural ashlar stone was available, however, you may find walls built of that instead. In any case, the walls are rough and rustic. If your landscape lends itself to this type of wall, you may find that a modern version is just the right thing.

Today most stone walls will be built of ashlar stone, with or without mortar, and often with concrete backerblock. Walls less than 2 feet can be built in any of these ways. For a garden wall over 2 feet, use mortar (the same mix as for brick), and try to fill joints as best you can. For a large project, which most walls will be, it is highly doubtful that you will be able to afford precut stone for a solid stone wall. You probably will buy the stone by the ton, using some of the pieces as is and cutting others as explained on pages 219–20 later in this chapter. With or without mortar, stone garden walls are built in a manner similar to that for stone retaining walls, as discussed below.

The principal differences will be that you will want your garden wall to be plumb, not sloped backward, and you will want to create an attractive appearance on both front and back sides. Concrete footings should also be used for walls over 2 feet. Unless the wall is quite low, you should use mortar for safety and durability. And do not try to build any wall over 4 feet. Anything higher can be difficult, dangerous, and prohibitively expensive.

Higher walls can be built with concrete block as the main ingredient for strength and stability and ashlar stone as a decorative surface. As with barbecues built in the same manner (pages 182–83), metal ties are inserted between masonry joints to hold the mortared stone to the block. See pages 210–15 for complete instructions on laying block.

Concrete Walls

Concrete is a convenient material for use in slabs, and in that use it is easy for the do-it-yourselfer. In walls, however, concrete requires much more elaborate and professional forming. There are certain situations where its use is justified for a retaining wall. It hardly seems worthwhile to use concrete for making a garden wall. A concrete wall is not especially pretty, nor does it blend in well with most landscapes. Parging (using a decorative mortar coating) can improve the look of concrete. Try to use concrete only for retaining walls. Never build a concrete wall higher than 4 feet by yourself. If you need a concrete wall higher than that, consult a professional. Special directions for concrete retaining walls are discussed later in this chapter.

"Natural" and Other Walls

Shrubs and trees makes excellent natural walls or fences, but they can take a long time before they are big enough to do much good. If time is no problem, there are plenty of thick-growing shrubs which can be used to eventually provide a dense, private cover.

The most commonly used shrubs for hedges is privet, which grows fast and high. Bayberry is often used for the same purpose, as are countless other types. The trouble with these fast-growing hedges is that they need frequent trimming.

If an almost impermeable security fence is what you'd like, try Washington or cockspur hawthorn. It is a small tree that grows very thick and has long thorns. Planted 4 feet apart in zigzag fashion, a mature hedge is as imposing as a solid wall and yet features white flowers in spring and red berries for birds in the fall. Other deciduous "living fences" can be made of viburnum, which is slower growing, or of tall trees such as poplar and hedge maple. Some landscapers advise a mix, alternating specimens for a little variety and different stages of growth.

When privacy is important year-round, evergreen shrubs are the best choice even though they are mostly slow-growing. Hetzi juniper is one favorite because it is relatively fast-growing, and it becomes very dense and thick if kept well-trimmed. Japanese yews *(Taxus)* probably make the best-looking hedges, but they are slow-growing, and it is not easy to keep them trimmed to a hedge shape. They tend to keep growing in their original pyramidal, round, or "cap" shape. Hemlock is also used for hedges, although it is not as dense as some of the others. Arborvitae are also popular, but they tend to grow too big and tall as the years progress, and they try to resume their original tree shape if not kept rigidly trimmed.

Planning a Retaining Wall

It is essential in planning a retaining wall to have a clear understanding of its purpose. Is it primarily decorative, or does it have a vital job to do? The choice of materials and design depends upon a proper balance of utility and appearance, which in turn depends upon the specific problem and your personal preferences. A railroad

A retaining wall can be used to hold back earth and create a flat area for a terraced garden or can serve many other purposes. (Toro)

embankment, for example, may be shored up securely with precast concrete cribs, but these are hardly suitable for your backyard. A single-tier brick wall may look very nice for a low planting area, but will not hold up under any severe pressure.

No retaining wall should exceed 4 feet in height unless greater height is absolutely necessitated by a severe slope and you have no other option. It is easier, safer, and esthetically more pleasing to break up a slope into several terraces instead of building a single huge wall. Whenever possible, for example, build three 2-foot-high walls rather than one 6-foot-high monolith.

Your job is less difficult when the soil is loose and sandy with no pre-existing drainage problems. Earth alone exerts a tremendous pressure on the retaining wall. If the soil is mucky or clayey, it will retain a lot of water, which will exert even more pressure and create a serious problem. Even loose soil should have a backfill of 6 to 12 inches of sand or gravel behind a small wall. Large walls with heavy soils require weep holes (see below) and/or a drainage system to deflect water pressure around the wall.

To avoid serious drainage problems, use dry construction (without mortar) of ashlar stone. It will leave enough room for the water to seep through, which such impermeable materials as concrete or other masonry won't do. Railroad-tie walls will also allow some seepage, and can be used without drains or weep holes as long as they are not too high and the soil is not too heavy.

If you *must* build a wall higher than 4 feet, it is much better to seek professional help than to do it yourself. Such walls can be built by the use of "dead men" inserted into the soil and attached to the top of the wall, or by a complicated type of concrete forming. These walls, however, are potentially dangerous and sometimes are forbidden by local codes. Even if you decide to try them yourself, get competent advice on the design and workmanship before proceeding. I will not attempt such advice here.

Another factor to be taken into consideration when planning is the possibility of extraordinary weight at the top of the wall. If the earth behind the wall slopes sharply upward, or if a house, driveway, or other structure is immediately above, increase all the dimensions given here by 25 percent (at least) to provide extra strength. Where the wall is being built to contain a swimming pool, the strength factor must be augmented by 50 percent. As a matter of fact, if you are putting in a pool that requires a retaining wall, let the contractor build both the wall and the pool. Any mistakes here will be just too costly and dangerous.

Concrete Retaining Walls

A low concrete wall is built in much the same manner as is a home foundation. Footings are built twice as wide as the wall is thick, and as deep as the wall is wide. A 6-inch wall, for example, requires a footing 12 inches wide and 6 inches deep. Although it is not essential for a low wall, it is wise to key the footing by placing an oiled 2 × 4 down the center of the footing, about halfway into the concrete, when it has started to firm up. When the concrete has set, remove the board. The key, or slot left by the board, is a further precaution against the wall's shifting on the footing, since the concrete of the wall will become "keyed" inside this slot.

Forms for the wall are built of ¾-inch exterior plywood or wide 2-inch lumber, as shown in the illustration. The forms are braced and staked as shown with pieces of 1 × 2 joining the forms on each side. In addition, every 2½ feet, pieces of 1 × 2 should be nailed between each side of the wall. Now take # 10 or # 12 wire and run it between the studs on each side of the wall near the pieces of 1 × 2. Twist the wire until it is drawn as tightly as possible against the 1 × 2 spacers. This will prevent the heavy concrete from bulging against the forms. As the concrete is poured, remove the 1 × 2s, but leave the wire in place, cutting off the ends as the concrete is cured.

The extent of bracing and the size of the lumber depend on the height of the wall. Walls 2 feet or under do not need extensive shoring, but the higher you go, the heavier the bracing and lumber dimensions must be. One- or 2-inch lumber or ¾-inch plywood will suffice for most do-it-yourself walls. Six-inch-thick concrete should be wide enough for walls up to 2 feet, but an inch or 2 of thickness should be added for every additional foot of height, depending on the pressure that will be exerted. If you go higher than 4 feet, which is not recommended, you may have to get into 4 × 4 bracing, tapered walls, step forming, and other complications. Avoid it if you can.

Even a small wall requires a lot of concrete, so it usually is simpler and not terribly expensive to have the concrete trucked to the site in a cement mixer. Unfortunately, many retaining walls are built in inaccessible sites, where it is difficult even to wheelbarrow the concrete. If so, the best solution is to rent a portable mixer. Use the same proportions as for other concrete (pages 235–36).

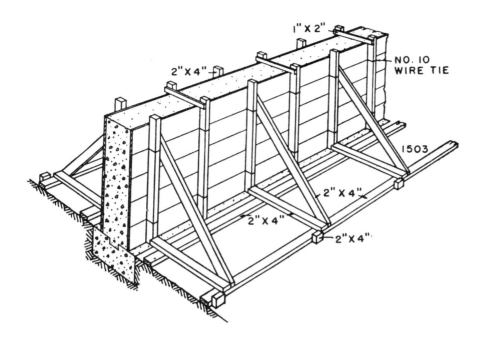

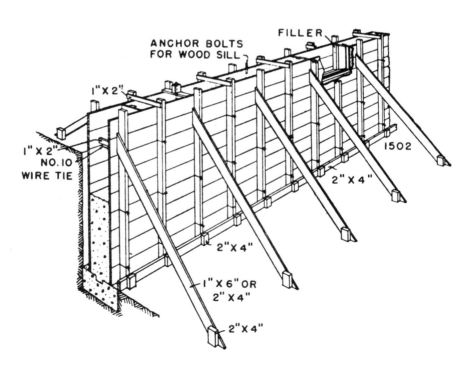

The concrete forming for a free-standing wall (above) and for a basement or retaining wall (below).

Before placing the concrete, be sure to oil the forms and wet the surrounding earth. If the wall is a small one, a single pour should be sufficient; larger walls may require several pours. If the placing extends over several days, key each pour where you left off with an oiled 2 × 4 as you did for the footings (above), so that the next section will be securely tied to the last.

The only part of the wall that really needs finishing is the top, and rough-floating usually suffices. After the last pour has set for a day or 2 (longer for high walls), remove the forms. Cure by soaking with water for a few days, then backfill. Since the bare concrete is not particularly attractive, you may want to add a slush coat or aggregate mix to the front.

If you plan to top the wall with stone or some other type of coping, be sure to insert the bolts, rods, or proper connecting devices into the top of the concrete before it sets. Wood benches or other wood coping can be added any time within the first few weeks or so, while the concrete is still comparatively soft, by hammering in helical concrete nails with a sledge or mash hammer.

Working with Concrete Block

The overwhelming advantage of concrete block is that it is quite easy to lay up once you get the hang of it. In the time it takes to build the forms for a concrete wall, an experienced mason would have a block wall finished.

Block also has some disadvantages. It is probably, by itself, the least attractive of building materials. It also lacks the strength of poured concrete and some other materials because of potential weakness at the mortar joints.

Although there are many types of concrete and cinder block (slightly lighter and more porous) on the market, by far the most familiar type is the nominal 8 × 8 × 16-inch block with 3 or 2 holes, or cores. When planning your concrete block wall, though, you should be aware of at least some of the other sizes and shapes available. Special corner blocks, 8 × 8 × 8-inch, and 4 × 8 × 16-inch half or partition blocks, as well as numerous other specialty shapes and sizes are available. In addition, there are topping block, stone-faced, slush, and numerous varieties of decorative screen block and masonry shapes, only some of which are illustrated here. The best bet is to visit a nearby large masonry dealer and see for yourself what is available.

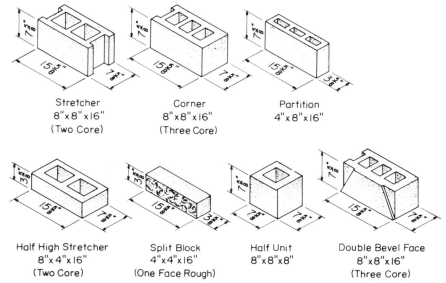

Stretcher
8"x8"x16"
(Two Core)

Corner
8"x8"x16"
(Three Core)

Partition
4"x8"x16"

Half High Stretcher
8"x4"x16"
(Two Core)

Split Block
4"x4"x16"
(One Face Rough)

Half Unit
8"x8"x8"

Double Bevel Face
8"x8"x16"
(Three Core)

Some of the many types of concrete block, with their nominal and actual sizes. (Portland Cement Association)

Block sizes are always nominal, so that a standard $8 \times 8 \times 16$ block actually will be $7\frac{5}{8} \times 7\frac{5}{8} \times 15\frac{5}{8}$. Mortar joints are designed to be ⅜-inch, so each block is a "mortar-joint" less than the nominal size. If you use the recommended ⅜-inch mortar joint in your construction, then the blocks will measure 8 inches on center lengthwise and 4 inches high. Unless your wall will be crammed into a certain confined space, it is wise to plan concrete block projects in units of 8 inches (or 4 inches, at least) to simplify construction.

Premixed mortar is easy to use and widely available, and beginners are advised to buy it. If you prefer to mix your own, get bags of masonry cement (Portland cement and lime). Follow instructions on the bag for best results; usually they call for one bag to 3 parts clean sand, plus just enough water to make the mix workable. Strive for a mud-like consistency, with either premix or mix made from scratch.

Starting Out. Lay down footings as described for other types of walls, keying them as described above for best results. As always, the first course is the most important. Carefully mark off the dimensions and make a dry run with unmortared block to see how it works out. Allow ⅜ inch between each block for mortar. If it appears that cutting of block or other problems may ensue, change the length if possible.

Wet the footing and the surrounding earth, if any. *Never* wet the block itself. When laying the first course, lay down a "full bed" of mortar, covering the entire horizontal surface where the block is to be laid. In the beginning, don't put down at one time any more mortar than will cover the length of 2 or 3 blocks. Furrow the full mortar bed so that the face shells (front and back) of the block get the bulk of the mortar.

You may not realize it at first, but the core holes of each block are narrower on one end than the other. Lay the block with the narrower cores on top, so that they can hold more mortar. Set the corner block in place first, checking carefully for plumb, level, and alignment. Then butter the next block, allowing about ⅜ inch for mortar, and align it next to the corner block. There should be plenty of mortar on both "ears" of the stretcher block. If you have used enough mortar, it should ooze out of the joint; cut it off with the trowel. Return this mortar to the mortar board.

Lay down a full mortar bed, enough to accommodate 2 or 3 blocks, to set the first row on top of the footing. (Portland Cement Association)

Spread mortar on the "ears" of succeeding blocks, and shove them next to the preceding ones. (Portland Cement Association)

Set the block firmly, so that mortar squeezes out below and between the blocks. (Portland Cement Association)

A "story pole" is marked off in increments of 8 inches and is used to make sure that proper height and mortar line are being maintained. (Portland Cement Association)

As with bricklaying, build up the corners first, using a line from one corner to the other. After the first course, succeeding courses should be mortared only on their faces or shells, not on the entire bed. Vertical buttering is the same as before. Check each block with a spirit level for correct placement. A "story pole," marked off in increments of 8 inches, can be used to check the height of the courses.

If the wall is to be straight, with no adjacent walls, the entire bottom row can be laid first. Use full-bed mortar for the entire first course. When working in from the corners, use the mason's line to maintain alignment between the 2 corners, and use face-shell mortar after the first course. Each succeeding course should alternate exactly with the course below, so that the mortar joints will bisect the blocks above and below. In other words, common or running bond is used for standard concrete masonry. Decorative block usually is laid with straight vertical joints.

Assuming all else has been completed to perfection (or close to it), the last "closure" block in each row should fit without too much difficulty. Measure first, though, to make sure that the space remaining is 16⅜ inches, counting mortar joints, on both sides. You can fudge by maybe ⅛ inch or so, but if necessary, cut off parts of the ears of the closure block with a brick chisel to make it fit.

Watch your mortar as you work along. Keep throwing the squeezed-out mortar from the joints back onto the mortar board. If the mortar gets a little stiff, add a little more water, then mix again thoroughly. In a few hours, the mix will get too rigid for such mixing, and you will have to throw out what is left and start a new batch.

Keep tooling the joints as you move along, making a concave or V shape as you do with brick. This not only makes for a neat joint, but compresses the mortar to make it more waterproof. If you notice that a block is out of alignment, or if you happen to knock it awry somehow, don't try to set it back into place. You will destroy the integrity of the mortar. The only thing you can do is knock down that part of the wall and start over from there.

If you are using the block as backup for brick, stone, or whatever, don't forget to insert ties periodically as required. The type and spacing of ties will depend on the material being used. Check with your masonry dealer.

For the top row, use special cap or topper block, or insert metal attachments into mortar in the cores for a lintel, coping, or whatever type of finishing row you have decided upon. You can build the backerblock wall separately, and then add whatever facing you want afterward, or, in the case of brick or precut stone, you can put both up together.

In most block retaining walls 4 feet or under, reinforcing bars will not be needed. If, as mentioned earlier, additional stress is placed on the wall by a driveway, pool, or the like, reinforcing bars (re-bars) may be needed. Check with your masonry dealer, and see page 216 regarding the proper installation of re-bars, if needed. In all probability, block retaining walls over 4 feet high will need reinforcement, but I recommend that you see a contractor if you must have a wall higher than 4 feet.

If you are using wood or other material for the cap, insert an attachment device into the core of the block, filling the rest of the core with mortar.
(Portland Cement Association)

Brick Retaining Walls

Brick is probably the most elegant material for retaining walls, but it is also the weakest. Since it has even more mortar joints than block, it has commensurately less strength. A small decorative wall of up to 3 or 4 courses can be put up in a single wythe. Anything higher will require either a double wythe or concrete backerblock.

A brick veneer retaining wall with concrete backerblock is put up in the same way as is the garden wall described on pages 201–3. If you keep the height below 4 feet, however—as you should—there should be no need for reinforcing bars. Check with your masonry dealer to be sure, especially if your wall will receive special stresses, as mentioned above.

An all-brick retaining wall is very handsome, but it is not a project for beginners. It takes a higher degree of workmanship than do most brick projects, and in no case should it exceed 3 feet in height.

Vertical reinforcing bars should be placed every 42½ inches and be propped in place with brick scraps before the footings are poured. Wire the vertical re-bars to the bottom re-bars of the footings (all ⅜ inch diameter), then pour the footings. The top row of re-bars is inserted into the concrete as the footings are poured.

Study the drawing carefully before deciding to build this type of

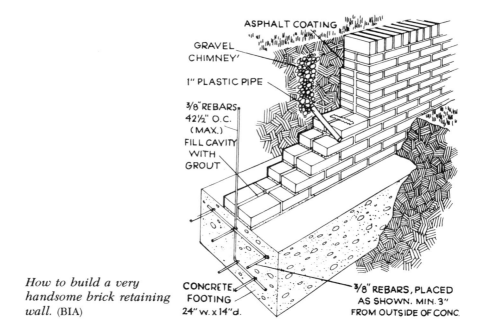

ASPHALT COATING
GRAVEL CHIMNEY
1" PLASTIC PIPE
3/8" REBARS 42½" O.C. (MAX.)
FILL CAVITY WITH GROUT
CONCRETE FOOTING 24" w. x 14"d.
3/8" REBARS, PLACED AS SHOWN. MIN. 3" FROM OUTSIDE OF CONC.

How to build a very handsome brick retaining wall. (BIA)

wall, and refer to it when ordering materials and while in the process of construction. Note that the 2 wythes are laid on each side of the re-bars and that metal ties are used to hold the wythes together. The re-bars should not extend the entire height of the wall. Note in the diagram that the space between the wythes is slightly smaller in the last 3 courses of brick.

When you get to the last course using re-bars, pour grout (watered-down mortar) into the cavity. For the last few courses, treat as a standard double-wythe wall, using mortar between wythes. Make sure that the front of the brick lines up with the bottom courses (the back will not be seen). The top course can be a header course (laid flat) or a rowlock course as shown (laid on edge).

Use 1-inch plastic pipe and French drains as discussed below for drainage. When the wall is complete, brush asphalt coating on the back or earth side to make it watertight. See pages 174–81 for further directions on basic bricklaying.

Drainage and Weep Holes

All solid walls over 2 feet high should have some sort of drainage system to prevent water buildup from cracking or breaking down the wall. This can consist of gravel backfill with drain tiles at the bottom of the wall, as discussed in Chapter 5, or of weep holes. Depending on the type of material, weep holes can be simply chinks between stones or bricks, or any type of hole that lets the water escape from behind the wall. The French drain is an excellent drain for a solid wall; it is shown in the illustration for the brick retaining wall. A 1-inch section of PVC or plastic pipe is inserted at an angle as shown, leading down from the earth in back of the wall to the front of the wall. A gravel chimney leads from the top level of the ground down to the drainpipe to provide a route for the water from the top level to the bottom. These drains should be inserted about every 4 feet along the wall. The same method can be used for any solid wall. The block, brick, or stone must be chipped away around the drains as you lay the masonry, to allow passage for the pipe.

Working with Stone

Stone has been mentioned at various places throughout this book, and we have noted that there are two kinds—rubble or boulder type, such as granite, limestone, and basalt—and ashlar or stratified rock, such as sandstone, bluestone (which comes in a number of colors), shale hardpan, or slate. Most retaining walls are put up dry, but you can use mortar if you desire. Mortar is usually used only when you want your wall to be completely vertical.

When you want to build only a small, surface-covering wall to prevent minor erosion, you can simply lay rubble stone or boulders against the sloping surface. The spaces between the stones will allow sufficient drainage, and the great natural weight should keep the stones in place without much movement from frost or heaving. Larger rubble walls are built in a pyramid shape, with or without mortar. Start with the larger stones on the bottom, about 6 to 12 inches below grade, and lay them on a bed of sand 2 to 4 inches thick.

If you want the front of the wall to be plumb or vertical, you will have difficulty with rounded boulders. Look for the more squarish rubble stones or use ashlar stone. Check with your stone dealer to see what is available. (In some areas, such as New England, you may find all the stone you want simply lying around on the roadside, in abandoned quarries, on a willing farmer's land, and so on.)

Use the largest, heaviest stones at the bottom of any type of stone wall to act as footings. Also save the better looking, more level stones for the top row or coping. If you are incorporating steps, be sure to save the widest stones for these.

Ashlar stone is laid horizontally, and comes in naturally clean, level lines. Because of the great natural weight of stone and its abrasive surfaces, it can be laid up dry and will hold up to surprisingly severe stresses. If the wall is slanted back as described below, there is no need to use thick stone. Any course in a wall up to 4 feet high can be just 5 or 6 inches from front to back, if it is tied in tightly enough to the stones around it.

The main drawback of stone is the great difficulty of cutting it. The nice, neat precut stones you buy at the dealer have been sawn with special blades and are very expensive. Unless you use precut stone as a veneer with backerblock, you usually would not use precut stone in a retaining wall. If you buy your stone by the ton from the stone dealer, he will most likely deliver it in a heap on a dump truck. This will break up some of the stone for you, but you will have to cut the rest yourself.

Building a dry ashlar stone wall is more of an art than a science. It is difficult to plan anything more than the overall design and dimensions. Each piece is different and must be fitted in as you go along. The best method is to pick out pieces that are already the desired size and shape, and use them as is. The rest must be cut with a cold chisel and a mash hammer. Score the rock along the desired line, at least on one side. Thick, stubborn pieces may have to be scored on both sides. Keep whacking away along the line with the mash hammer, and eventually the stone will break. It may not be as neat as you'd like, but it will probably do well enough.

Another virtue of using this type of stone is that perfectly straight lines *aren't* required. Try to use pieces with at least one reasonably straight edge for the front of the wall, but don't worry about small imperfections on individual pieces as long as the overall look is straight (or curved, if you wish). The back edge of each piece can be as jagged as possible. In fact, the more jagged it is, the better bond it provides with the earth behind it. To enhance this effect, turn a piece lengthwise, or sideways into the earth about every 2 feet.

Try to choose pieces that will lock tightly against each other, with plenty of friction. Shim any loose spots with small pieces of stone. For corners, such as stairwells, choose large square or triangular pieces. Your stone will probably arrive in varying thicknesses, so keep the levels uniform as much as possible by using two rows of thin stone alternating with thicker ones.

Cutting stone is a physically difficult job. First, score a straight line, then whack repeatedly along the line with a cold chisel and mash hammer. (L. Donald Meyers)

Rows are kept reasonably level by checking with a long straight 2 × 4 and a spirit level. (L. Donald Meyers)

Gaps and uneven stones are tolerable as long as the row is generally on an even plane. Check this periodically with a long 2 × 4 and a spirit level. It is important, though, to stagger joints and any open spaces from one row to another. Make sure that, in addition to lapping joints, each stone has good contact with the stones above and below. Shim if necessary.

Taper your wall backward 2 inches for every foot in height. For taller walls, tip the stones slightly backward into the earth. Since the wall is tapered backward, you should backfill every 6 inches or so as you progress. Use either gravel or loose sand, which should be packed behind the wall and wetted down for stability.

If you are adding steps, remember that each step must have its own individual footing and foundation. Placing the steps will take a good bit of trial and error. The most important part of the job is

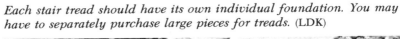

Each stair tread should have its own individual foundation. You may have to separately purchase large pieces for treads. (LDK)

keeping the corners strong. Keep adjusting and shimming if there is the slightest wobble. If you have no pieces large enough to serve as stairs, you may have to purchase these separately and have them cut at the stone dealer's. But wait and see what you can salvage out of the first load before you do this.

A mortared stone wall is put up in a fashion similar to the method for a dry one, except that there is no need to taper the wall backward. Here again, you must depend more on art than science. Neat, measured mortar joints are out of the question. Just try to fit the stone as best you can, and use mortar where there are gaps and joints. As with any other solid wall, drainage will have to be provided by one of the methods indicated above.

Wood Retaining Walls

As previously noted, most woods are unsuitable for contact with earth. For many years, retaining walls made of used railroad ties were popular, because the ties were pressure-treated with creosote and railroad tracks were being torn up all over the country as trains were replaced by air travel. Ties were plentiful and cheap.

Today true pressure-treated ties are scarce and pretty expensive, but they still make excellent retaining walls. Do not use creosote-*coated* ties. They won't last much longer than will regular wood. Real, used railroad ties, even though they may look in rather bad shape, are one of the best materials for retaining walls. The brown color of these ties, if not used to excess, has a rustic look which blends rather well with the landscape. An increasingly used alternative is pressure-treated lumber, such as Wolmanized ties. These are just as durable as railroad ties, although the greenish color may require staining.

Ties are tricky, as far as looks are concerned, no matter what type you use. Used low and tastefully, they are usually quite attractive. In walls that are too high or too massive, though, ties tend to look forbidding and unnatural.

Construction of a tie wall is relatively easy, although ties are heavy, and 2 people—two *strong* people—will be needed to move them. Walls up to 2 feet high can be toenailed using large galvanized 20d to 40d nails. Any larger project demands super-long spikes (up to 12 inches), which are really pointed rods rather than nails. Drill through the top ties and whack the spikes in the rest of the way with a sledgehammer. In some cases, galvanized bolts and nuts or lag screws may be easier to use, depending on the installation. (See Chapter 8 on deck construction.)

Depending on the height and the amount of pressure exerted on the wall, it is good practice to turn every other tie lengthwise into the hill. This is mandatory for walls over 4 feet, but you shouldn't be building them that high anyway. It may also be advisable for walls of over 3 feet, as mentioned above, depending on circumstances. Consult your dealer for advice, or use your own judgment. You can saw the ties in half, or even into thirds for smaller walls, to tie back into the hill. Another alternative is to install dead men, as previously discussed.

A low tie wall such as this can be simply constructed by toenailing the ties to each other, using large galvanized spikes from 20d to 40d. (LDK)

A boundary fence need not be hostile. Most neighbors, in fact, would be pleased to have this lovely split-rail fence, covered with roses, between the 2 properties. (Jackson & Perkins)

Rot-resistant lumber such as redwood or pressurized lumber can be used in a more conventional manner to build a retaining wall. In this method, 4 × 4 posts are inserted into the ground a distance equal to their exposed height (for a 3-foot wall, for example, use a 6-foot piece of 4 × 4). Pieces of 2 × 6 or 2 × 8 are nailed to the backs of the 4 × 4s, which are placed on 4-foot centers. A cap 2 × 6 (or wider, if you want to use it for a seat) is placed at the top, which also helps shed water.

For walls from 2 to 4 feet, the 4 × 4s should be placed every 3 feet, and some sort of drainage should be provided, as previously described. If you must go above 4 feet, dead men will be necessary, and the post size should be increased to 6 × 6. Dead men should be used every 8 to 10 feet.

PLANTINGS

Fences and walls can radically alter both the shape and looks of your landscape. In most cases, the walls should be an esthetic improvement. Well-designed terracing can make a dull hillside into a landscape architect's dream.

On the other hand, poorly designed or executed walls can be a real eyesore. Walls and fences, in almost every case, should be combined with creative plantings. Walls and fences that were built out of pure necessity, for example, and were never intended to be pleasing in themselves (such as chain link, stockade, or a high retaining wall), should be disguised as completely and quickly as possible by some of the quick-growing plants. Low plantings, preferably evergreens, enhance most walls, and are a must for any wood retaining wall higher than a foot or 2 (don't plant too close to any creosote tie however). Shrubs and flowers of all types break the monotony of a fence. Climbing roses or wisteria can literally blot out a picket or similar fence if you want them to. Kept properly trimmed, climbing bushes can nicely set off many fences.

For fences or walls that are very long, consider breaking them up with clumps of trees, trellises, a built-in nook or barbecue, or a similar structural change that will create a little interest and relieve the sameness. Alternate the types of shrubs you plant along such a wall, and try to plan for blooms at various times of the year.

11 Walks and Driveways

Though they are an essential part of any residential landscape, walks and driveways need not *look* utilitarian. Without diverging from their purpose as traffic directors, these elements usually can be designed so that they will detract as little as possible from the landscaping of your home and its setting.

There are situations, of course, where it is simply impossible to hide the intrusive look of a straight, plain concrete driveway. A driveway, let us always remember, must primarily serve the purpose of getting vehicles from the street to the garage or parking area. Similarly, a walkway is intended to provide a surface for getting human beings from the garage to the house or from the house to the street.

In urban areas, you often have little choice about design and construction of public walkways which pass the front of your property near the street. The municipality you live in most likely has strict rules concerning the size, shape, and content of such sidewalks. If you don't build them according to the rules, you will get into trouble with the city. The same often applies to at least that part of your driveway which extends from the street to your actual property line, which may be a lot further back than you think it is.

Except for the part of your land which is subject to an easement owned by the municipality, you probably can build any kind of walk and driveway you want, of any material and any design you fancy.

As far as driveways are concerned, the most practical material is concrete. It holds up best, is reasonably priced (although blacktop is

An exposed aggregate walk. (Portland Cement Association)

cheaper), and does the job it is supposed to do—provide a solid, long-lasting surface for cars—better than does anything else. In fact, if you live on a typical suburban plot, where most of the houses have a relatively short stretch from the garage to the street, you probably shouldn't even consider anything except plain concrete. Any other surface might stand out conspicuously in a fairly conservative neighborhood.

On the other hand, if your home is somewhat private or the neighborhood tends toward individualism, you might consider other surfaces. While concrete is still the material of choice, consider the appeal of exposed aggregate or other fancier types of concrete. In a rural area, blacktop may look and work fine. Even gravel or plain dirt may suffice, especially if there is a long stretch to the road. At the

Brick walks and flower bed edgings are much more affordable than brick driveways because they can be set in sand or mortar. (BIA)

Precast concrete rounds, with beach pebbles as fill, make a distinctive informal walk. (Portland Cement Association)

opposite extreme are brick or stone driveways. Because of their weight, brick and stone drives must be laid in mortar on a concrete slab—nice-looking but expensive.

Walk design follows similar criteria. In the suburbs, particularly in so-called developments, there often is a short walkway from the driveway to the entrance. This, too, is generally of plain concrete and is poured at the same time as the driveway. More rural and private settings deserve more creative design, and farm-style homes may have dirt paths instead of walks.

But there the similarities end. For one thing, walks do not have to bear the same weight as does a driveway. Whereas brick in sand would never hold up under the impact of a delivery truck, it is fine for the walk from the delivery truck. And in the backyard, walkways need not be so utilitarian. For carting groceries from the car to the house, the shortest, briefest walk is best; and that means a straight line. Through the garden, however, a haphazard, meandering tour is more restful and pleasurable. The choice of materials for this type of walk is almost unlimited, from fancy concrete to dirt or gravel.

In private settings, walks can be built of flagstone, brick, concrete rounds, wood, or anything else. They can be formal, informal, or somewhere in between. The idea is to suit the walkway to its setting. In a formal garden, a formal walk such as flagstones or bricks set in concrete or sand may be the best. When the setting is informal, a few random pieces of stone, wood, precast concrete, blacktop, gravel, or plain dirt may suffice. For the construction of some of these types of walks, see Chapter 7; they are built in the same way that patios of the same material are built.

PLANNING

The Portland Cement Association recommends a maximum grade of only 14 percent (1¾ inches per foot) for a driveway. If you're planning a grade steeper than that, try to use switchbacks, running the drive in a few gentler curves to reduce the steepness. Of course, you have to work with what you have, so this may not be possible. Give your major attention to the most critical stage, the point at which a

a) Contact of vehicle undercarrige with driveway

b) Contact of vehicle rear bumper with street

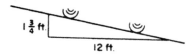

1¾ ft.

12 ft.

c) Maximum grade should not exceed 14 percent (1¾ in. per ft.)

The critical point in a driveway grade is where the vehicle enters from the street. The bottom illustration shows the proper grade for driveways; the other drawings show what happens when grade is incorrect. (Portland Cement Association)

Pressurized wood runs down the center of a courtyard shared by several houses and makes a good-looking informal entry to each of the homes.
(Koppers)

vehicle approaches the driveway from the street, as shown in the drawing. As you can see, at that point, when the rear wheels are in the gutter, too steep a grade can cause the bumper or underside of the car to scrape the ground.

You face one of the worst conditions for driveway building when your home is below street grade. The driveway then acts as conduit for rain and runoff, resulting in a flooded garage, and perhaps worse. If your driveway *must* run downhill, be sure that you allow some method of drainage away from the garage and house. In extreme cases, a catch basin or dry well should be built in front of the garage. If this must be built into the driveway itself, a metal grate can be used over the dry well, made of heavy-duty steel so that cars can be driven over it.

DIMENSIONS

With a single garage or carport, the driveway should be at least 10 feet wide; 14 feet is better. Today's small cars may get by with a little less, but the drive should be no narrower than the width of the car plus 3 feet. In planning, remember that someday you may want to sell the house and a prospective buyer may like larger cars, so wider may be better.

Two-car garages require a driveway 16 to 24 feet in width, at least near the garage. Short driveways should be at least 16 feet wide all the way. Longer driveways can be gradually narrowed to 10 to 14 feet near the street. Concrete drives should be at least 4 inches thick, with 5 to 6 inches recommended if heavy vehicles such as oil trucks will be using it. If indicated, allow for back-up space and parking.

Walks in the front of your home should be 3 to 4 feet wide. Private walkways in the rear or on the side of the house can be as narrow as 2 feet. Public sidewalks in front of your house will probably be governed by regulations. In no case should they be narrower than 4 feet, with 5 feet better yet. If you live close to a school, church, shopping area, or other places that create heavy traffic along the sidewalk, 8 feet may be required.

If you have a choice, don't build a sidewalk next to the curb. Studies have shown that pedestrians and bicyclists are much less prone to accidents when the sidewalks are at least 7 feet from the curb. Public concrete walks should be at least 4 inches thick; a 5-to-6-inch thickness often is mandated by law if there is a lot of traffic.

Lightly used private walks can be as thin as 2 inches, but cracking is probable so thin walks should be used only for out-of-the-way areas.

DRAINAGE

Most homes are built at least slightly above street level, so drainage is not usually a problem because all the runoff goes right into the street. In any case, there should be a slope of at least ¼ inch per foot in the direction of the nearest drain. Where the slope is not toward the street, it is also helpful to use a crown (see below) or cross-slope to help divert the runoff more gradually along the sides of the driveway.

Walks made of brick or stone in sand or made of other permeable materials provide built-in drainage. When concrete or blacktop is used, drainage can be a problem, although not as serious as it is for larger driveways. Sidewalks should have a ¼-inch-per-foot slope toward the most convenient drainage, which usually is the street. Walks should not slope toward the house or other buildings. Where there is no convenient drain, the best solution usually is to "crown" the sidewalk, or build it with a slight slope from the center to the edges. Water is then diverted harmlessly all along the edges of the walkway.

In all cases, remember that flat impermeable areas, especially

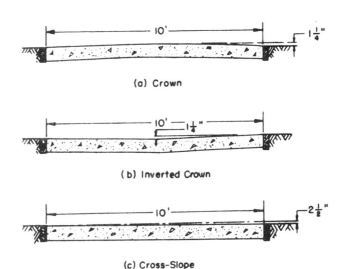

Several ways to provide driveway drainage. A regular crown (top) is the best. (Portland Cement Association)

(a) Crown

(b) Inverted Crown

(c) Cross-Slope

driveways, serve as conduits during a heavy rain. Therefore be sure that water is directed away from the house, garage, or other areas subject to damage and erosion. If runoff is unavoidable, build a dry well of sufficient capacity to capture it.

WORKING WITH CONCRETE

The type of concrete work discussed in this chapter is the easiest for the do-it-yourselfer. Basically, driveways and walkways—indeed, any flat concrete work—involves making a slab, or, simply laying flat concrete.

Except for a few minor differences in formwork, all slabs are constructed alike. What is important in making a concrete slab is good planning, form building, and finishing, all of which can be easily learned. Also important is a strong back, which, obviously, can't be learned. Pouring and placing concrete is tough work. Those with bad backs, weak hearts, or other disabilities must either get a strong helper or avoid this work. As a matter of fact, a strong helper—or 2 or 3—is almost a must when the concrete truck arrives.

What Is "Concrete"?

There is no such thing as a *cement* walk or drive. Cement is only one element of concrete. Concrete is a mixture of water, aggregate, and Portland cement with the cement comprising only 7 to 14 percent of the total concrete. The Portland cement serves precisely the same purpose as other cements. Just as rubber cement holds paper together, so Portland cement holds the concrete mix together. It acts as a binder for the main element—aggregate. Aggregate, the main ingredient of concrete, gives the mix its strength. It is mainly stone of some sort—crushed rock, pebbles, gravel, sand, slag, or often several of these mixed together, with the smaller parts, such as sand, filling in between the larger parts. The sizes of the aggregate particles should be varied, though larger jobs generally call for larger sized particles. Unlike the cement and water, the aggregate is chemically inert and plays no part in the process that takes place when those elements are mixed. When set, the concrete mix will be 66 to 78 percent aggregate by volume.

Portland cement is a fine, soft, gray-green powder made from limestone and other materials such as clay, shale, or slag from blast furnaces. It was named Portland when it first came into use over a century ago, because it resembled Portland stone, a widely used building material in England.

Portland cement usually comes in 94-pound bags and must be accurately mixed. Aggregate should always be ordered from a reliable building-supply dealer, since any organic foreign matter will prevent the cement paste from binding the aggregate properly. For small jobs, premixed concrete such as Sakrete is available in bags from manufacturers. If you are planning a large job like a driveway, it is best to order "ready mix" from a supplier; look in the Yellow Pages under "Concrete—Ready Mixed." The required amount of concrete is discussed on pages 244–45. If you are mixing your own, see table below.

Grade Preparation and Formwork

Working with concrete is very much like baking a cake. You have to mix the ingredients in the right proportions, and you need a proper pan. If the mix isn't right, the cake won't rise or the concrete won't last. You can't bake a sponge-cake on a cookie sheet and you can't pour concrete without the right form.

Proportions by Weight to Make 1 Cubic Foot of Concrete

Maximum-size Coarse Aggregate, in.	Air-entrained Concrete				Concrete Without Air			
	Cement, lb.	Sand, lb.	Coarse Aggregate, lb.*	Water, lb.	Cement, lb.	Sand, lb.	Coarse aggregate, lb.*	Water, lb.
⅜	29	53	46	10	29	59	46	11
½	27	46	55	10	27	53	55	11
¾	25	42	65	10	25	47	65	10
1	24	39	70	9	24	45	70	10
1½	23	38	75	9	23	43	75	9

*If crushed stone is used, decrease coarse aggregate by 3 lb. and increase sand by 3 lb.
Metric conversion: 1 lb. = 0.454 kg.   10 lb. = 4.54 kg.
1 in. = 25 mm.   1 cu. ft. = 0.028 m³.

Guide for Ordering Ready-mixed Concrete

Exposure	Coarse aggregate, nominal maximum size, in.	Portland cement, minimum lb. per cu. yd.	Water, maximum lb. per cu. yd.	Air entrainment, % by volume
Severe	1½	510	230	5 to 7
Many freeze-thaw	1	564	254	6 to 8
cycles per year;	¾	586	264	6½ to 8½
deicer chemicals	½	640	288	7 to 9
used	⅜	660	300	7½ to 9½
Moderate	1½	470	235	4 to 6
Few freeze-thaw	1	520	260	5 to 7
cycles per year;	¾	540	270	6 to 8
deicer chemicals	½	590	295	6½ to 8½
not used	⅜	610	305	7 to 9
Mild	1½	470	*	†
No freeze-thaw	1	520	*	†
cycles per year;	¾	540	*	†
deicer chemicals	½	590	*	†
not used	⅜	610	*	†

Slump: 5-in. maximum for hand methods of strikeoff and consolidation.
   3-in. maximum for mechanical strikeoff and consolidation.
*Amount of water limited by compressive strength needed for service.
†2% to 3% to improve cohesiveness and reduce bleeding.

Soil Preparation

Other than poor mixing, the most frequent error in concrete work is poor soil preparation. Slabs will settle, crack, and fall apart in poorly prepared or compacted soil. The subgrade should be free of all such organic matter as sod, grass roots, and soft and mucky ground. Dig out all poor soil. If some spots are very hard and others very soft, the concrete will surely crack from settling in the softer areas. Break up these areas and disperse the soil to provide uniform support for the concrete.

On the other hand, do not routinely remove the soil under your slab area and replace it with fill. If the soil is already reasonably uniform and free of vegetable matter, it is better left alone. Nature has already done your compacting for you. Most sandy soils merely need tamping on the top portion disturbed by your spade.

If the soil is soft and organic, it should be dug out to a depth of 4 to 6 inches below the concrete bed (or about 8 to 12 inches in all, depending on the thickness of your slab). Fills should be made in 4-inch sections, compacted, and followed by another layer. The fill should be extended at least a foot in all directions around the slab to prevent undercutting during heavy rains.

Common fill materials are sand, gravel, crushed stone, or blast-furnace slag. Sand usually is preferred because you can level it more easily. You can also use leftover soil from high spots as long as it is similar to the rest of your subgrade.

All fill material must be tamped down and compacted.
(Portland Cement Association)

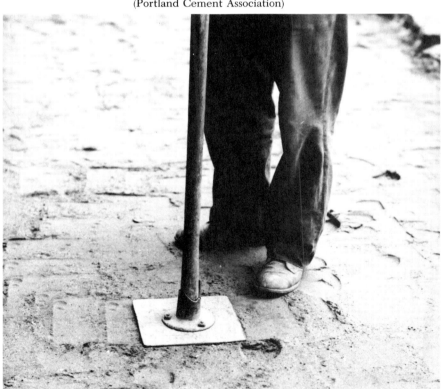

After the fill material has been graded, it must be compacted. Use a hand tamper for small jobs. For large jobs, use a roller or vibratory compactor. You should be able to rent these machines at a local supplier. Before you lay the concrete, you should dampen the subgrade with a garden hose. Otherwise, the ground will absorb the water from the concrete. Do not leave standing water, however, or any sort of muddy spot.

Setting Forms

Professional masons often use steel stakes and forms, but wooden forms are perfectly acceptable. Nominal 2-inch lumber is used in most form-building, although 1-inch boards and thin plywood usually are used for making curves.

In most slabs it is important to establish the proper grade. Small jobs and complex slopes are sometimes best determined with your own eye, but for any larger slabs you'll have to use a line level.

Drive stakes in at the corners of the slab and about every 8 feet between the corners. Run a line from one corner to the next, and

Construction details for a concrete driveway. (Portland Cement Association)

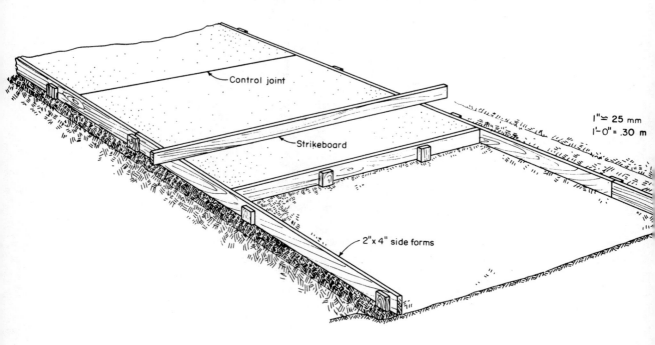

Control joint

Strikeboard

2"x 4" side forms

1" ≃ 25 mm
1'-0" = .30 m

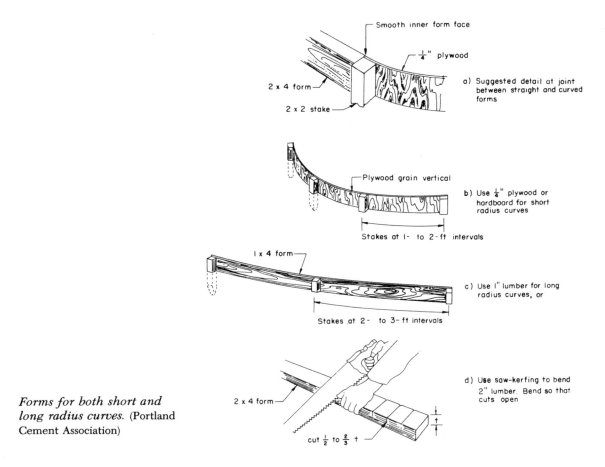

Forms for both short and long radius curves. (Portland Cement Association)

a) Suggested detail at joint between straight and curved forms

b) Use $\frac{1}{4}$" plywood or hardboard for short radius curves

c) Use 1" lumber for long radius curves, or

d) Use saw-kerfing to bend 2" lumber. Bend so that cuts open

Smooth inner form face

$\frac{1}{4}$" plywood

2 x 4 form

2 x 2 stake

Plywood grain vertical

Stakes at 1- to 2-ft intervals

1 x 4 form

Stakes at 2- to 3-ft intervals

2 x 4 form

cut $\frac{1}{2}$ to $\frac{2}{3}$ t

place the line level in the center. If the distance is a long one, place the level between the intermediate stakes, repeating the procedure as you go along. The line must be very taut. When the line is level, make a mark, and then measure down to where the top of the form should be. If the grade, for example, is ¼ inch per running foot and the distance between stakes is 8 feet, the drop should be 2 inches for that 8-foot distance. Mark the stake 2 inches below the top of the line. That is where the top of the form should be.

The sizes of the forms and stakes depend on how deep the excavation is and how much concrete pressure will be exerted. For most sidewalks, patios, and other slabs, 2 × 4s are best. Thicker slabs will take 2 × 6 forms.

One-inch lumber or ¼-inch exterior plywood is used for curves. One-inch lumber can also be used for straight runs, but it requires more staking to prevent bulging. For most slabs, 2 × 2 staking is

If there is any doubt that the forms will hold the weight of the concrete, a stake can be braced by driving another beside it at an angle. Nail the 2 stakes together. (Portland Cement Association)

Stakes are driven into the forms so that they can be removed afterward. Hold the form with your foot while nailing. It is best to use double-headed nails, as shown, for easier removal. (Portland Cement Association)

sufficient. Stakes should be driven every 4 feet for 2-inch formwork and every 2 to 3 feet for 1-inch lumber. On gentle curves, regular spacing is sufficient, but stakes must be driven every 1 to 2 feet on short-radius curves.

For ease in placing and finishing concrete, drive all stakes slightly below the tops of the forms. Wood stakes can be sawn off flush, if that is easier. Drive all stakes straight and true to insure plumb. If there is any doubt that the stake will hold, you can brace it by driving another stake diagonally and nailing the 2 together.

Nail all stakes *into* the forms by holding the form boards with your foot. Otherwise, removal of the forms would be very awkward. Since nailing the stakes can be difficult, especially when using thinner lumber, set temporary stakes inside the forms to hold them, then remove them after everything is nailed up. Double-headed nails are recommended for all formwork, since they are removed easily and cleanly.

When making curves with plywood, the outside plies should be vertical to permit easy bending. For a shorter radius, make saw kerfs (notches) on the insides of forms and bend them so that the cuts are closed. One-inch lumber is your best bet for medium curves.

You can, if you wish, use redwood or other rot-resistant lumber for forms and dividers and leave the wood in place after the concrete has hardened. Although this design is usually used for patios, there is no reason why it can't be done for walks and drives too.

Permanent forms should be carefully mitered at the corners and neatly butted at the joints. Masking tape should be applied to the top of the wood to protect it from abrasion and concrete staining. In such decorative forming, stakes must either be removed or—better—cut off 2 inches below the surface of the concrete. Galvanized nails should be driven through alternating sides of dividing strips at 16-inch intervals before pouring the concrete. The same should be done for the forms, except that all nails should face in. These nails anchor the wood permanently to the concrete.

After all the forms are in place, backfill under the outside to prevent the concrete from escaping. Install isolation joints or decorative strips at intersections, such as where the patio meets the house, where the driveway meets the walk, around poles, and so on. Use premolded fiber joint material, available at concrete dealers. The joint material should be flush with, or ¼ inch below, the concrete surface.

As a final check before pouring concrete, inspect all forms for

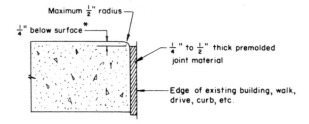

Cross-section and detail of an isolation joint. (Portland Cement Association)

plumb and trueness to grade. Make sure the proper slopes allow for drainage. Dampen the subgrade and forms to prevent theft of water from the mix. If you plan to remove the stakes, apply motor oil to the forms to make removal easier.

The Proper Mix

It is vital that the concrete ingredients be mixed in the right proportions. Too much or too little of any one ingredient will cause cracking, dusting, chipping, or some other imperfection. For larger jobs, it is best to order ready mix from a local concrete service. The "cement" truck will not only bring a perfect mix, but will save many hours of back-breaking work.

For very small jobs, a bag of premixed cement and aggregate will solve the same problems. Just add water as directed on the package, and place the mix.

Most do-it-yourself jobs, however, fall somewhere in between large and very small. Sometimes, too, the area is inaccessible. For these jobs, you can probably mix your own concrete. You can work up a good concrete mix by following 2 simple rules. First, always buy clean ingredients from a building-supply dealer. Second, use the proper proportions. For each 94-pound bag of cement, add: 215 pounds of sand, 295 pounds of coarse aggregate, and 5 gallons of water.

A regular bathroom scale is accurate enough for weighing the materials. Use large buckets to hold the material, but be sure to weigh the bucket first and deduct its weight from the weight of the material. Don't put any more in the bucket than you can handle. Put the sand and aggregate into 3 or 4 buckets of equal weight. Once you get the right weight established, mark a line on the bucket for each ingredient and reuse.

A simpler but less accurate guide is volume. Use 1 part Portland cement to 2¼ parts sand and 3 parts coarse aggregate. Add 5 gallons of water for each bag. Each 1-bag formula should yield about ⅙ cubic yard of concrete. Whether you mix your own or order concrete, it is wise to add an air-entraining agent. This chemical causes minute, well-distributed bubbles to develop, reducing damage from frost and salt. Air entrainment is especially important in cold climates.

Since the right mix is essential, the best method is the formula given in the table. These proportions are based on wet sand, which usually is the type available. Test the degree of wetness by squeezing the sand into a ball with your hand. If it is properly wet, it will form into a ball but leave no noticeable moisture in your palm. If the sand is too wet, it will ball up but also will leave noticeable moisture in your hand. Sand that is only damp or too dry will fall apart when squeezed. For very wet sand, increase the sand quantity in the table by 1 pound, and decrease the water by 1 pound. Reverse the procedure for sand that is too dry. (Add 1 pound of water and deduct 1 pound of sand.)

Properly wet sand will form a ball when squeezed but will leave no noticeable moisture in your hand. (Portland Cement Association)

It is wise to make a test batch of concrete first. Float the test batch as directed on page 245 to see if it sets right, with sufficient mortar to fill all voids. If it seems too wet, add 5 to 10 percent more sand and aggregate. If it is too stiff, add more water and cement (never add water alone). Also check sand and aggregate content, and make adjustments as necessary. Keep track of what you add and subtract, and retain the changes for subsequent batches.

Ordering Materials

Most home concrete projects require a 4-inch thickness. To determine how much concrete is needed, calculate the volume of your project (length × width × depth) in cubic yards. The easiest way is to calculate the area in square feet, then multiply by ⅓ (the 4-inch depth is ⅓ foot). If the area is 10 feet by 30 feet, for example, you have 300 square feet in area. Divide by ⅓ to get 100 cubic feet of volume. Since there are 27 cubic feet in a cubic yard, divide the result by 27 and you have the cubic yards needed (about 4 yards, in this example). The following chart will help you:

Estimating Cubic Yards of Concrete for Slabs*

	Area in Square Feet (Width × Length)					
	10	*25*	*50*	*100*	*200*	*300*
Thickness (IN.)						
4	0.12	0.31	0.62	1.23	2.47	3.70
5	0.15	0.39	0.77	1.54	3.09	4.63
6	0.19	0.46	0.93	1.85	3.70	5.56

*Does not allow for losses due to uneven subgrade, spillage, and the like. Add 5–10 percent for such contingencies.

For a 6 × 20-foot walk, for example, multiply the length and width to get 120 square feet. Using the chart, you will see that you need 1.23 cubic yards for the first 100 square feet, and 0.31 cubic yards for the remaining 25 square feet (the nearest amount to 20); your sum is 1.54 cubic yards. Since your total reflects a 125-foot area instead of the actual 120, you might possibly get away with exactly 1.5 cubic yards of concrete, but this assumes that you have graded and measured exactly and that you won't waste a drop of concrete.

It is much better to have a little more than you may need. If mixing concrete yourself, figure on using 5 to 10 percent more than your calculated amount. For ready mix, get the smallest additional amount that the supplier will sell you (probably 2 yards).

A ready-mix dealer can give you a more precise mix than you can achieve yourself, so you may as well take advantage of it. When ordering, specify at least 6 sacks of cement per cubic yard and 5 to 6 percent air entrainment. Ask for coarse gravel aggregate with 1- to 1½-inch maximum, and request not more than a 4-inch "slump" (a measurement of the workability). Tell the supplier you want the 28-day compressive strength to be 3,500 pounds per square inch (a measure of durability).

It is best to order ready-mix a day ahead. Be sure to tell the dealer exactly when and where to deliver it. When mixing your own concrete, get all the materials ahead of time in the proportions mentioned earlier.

Placing the Mix

Before the concrete is placed, wet the surrounding earth and the forms with a garden hose. Have a wheelbarrow handy for both delivered and homemade mix. If there is much wheelbarrowing to be done, add 1 more person to the 2 or 3 extra hands recommended earlier.

Place the concrete in the forms to the full depth, spading along the sides to complete filling. Try to load the concrete as close as possible to its final position without too much dragging and spading. This will not only save your strength but will prevent overworking of the mix. Use a square-end short-handled shovel and/or a concrete rake for this. You should be able to rent all the tools mentioned here.

Do not pour too large a portion of your slab at one time. The mix should be placed and floated as quickly as possible. After placing, strike off the surface with a 2 × 4 straightedge, working it in a sawlike motion across the top of the form boards. This screeding will smooth the surface while cutting off the concrete to the proper height. Go over the concrete twice in this manner to take out any bumps or to fill in low spots. Tilt the straightedge slightly in the direction of travel to get a better cutting effect.

Immediately after striking off, rough-float the surface to smooth it and remove irregularities. Use a small wood hand float for close work, and a large wood or steel bull float for larger areas. The darby

After the concrete is placed, strike off the surface with a 2 × 4 straightedge, using the forms as a guide. (L. Donald Meyers)

is an excellent all-around tool that can be used as a straightedge as well as a float. The bull float is tilted slightly away from you as you push it forward, then flattened as it is pulled back. The darby is held flat against the surface of the slab and worked from side to side.

Do not overdo any of the preceding motions. The overworking of concrete causes excessive water and fine particles to rise to the surface, rendering the surface more prone to flaking and chipping.

Finishing

If you use air-entrained concrete—as you should—finishing can usually follow immediately after floating. However, check the surface before finishing, particularly when the weather is cool and humid. Make sure that there is no water sheen on the surface, and

When the concrete has been placed and struck, rough-float the surface with a wood float. Hand-floating is shown here. (Portland Cement Association)

A darby can be used both for striking and floating. (Portland Cement Association)

The first step in finishing is to cut the concrete away from the forms with a pointed trowel.

An edging tool is run between the form and the concrete to give a smoother appearance. (Portland Cement Association)

Control joints are made with a grooving tool, which cuts to a depth of ⅕ to ¼ of the total concrete depth. (Portland Cement Association)

test stiffening with your foot. The indentation from your shoe should be no more than ½ inch before you proceed. You can help insure that the surface is dry enough by cutting away the concrete from the forms before finishing. Work a pointed trowel along the forms to a depth of about an inch.

The first finishing step is edging, which should take place as soon as the surface is stiff enough to hold the shape of the edging tool. Run the edger between the form and the concrete, holding the body of the tool flat on the concrete surface except for the leading edge, which is tilted up slightly.

Control joints are desirable if the slab extends more than 10 feet in any direction. These joints help control large cracks. They are made with a groover, which is similar to an edger except that it separates concrete from concrete, rather than concrete from the form. The tool should cut to a depth of ⅕ to ¼ of the slab thickness. A portable circular saw can be equipped with a masonry-cutting blade to serve as a groover.

Finish floating is done with a wood hand float. This procedure eliminates any remaining imperfections—such as the marks from the edger and groover—and produces a smoother surface, with large aggregates embedded and mortar consolidated at the top for further finish operations. If you want a rough surface, as for a nonskid surface, finish floating can be the final step.

Although the slightly rough surface created by floating is safer for walking, many people prefer the smooth finish created by troweling. For this purpose, rectangular steel-bladed trowels are used. At least two passes are necessary. The final troweling should produce a ringing sound as the blade traverses the hardened surface.

Hydration

The chemical reaction between water and cement is called hydration. This process must continue for several days or a week after the concrete is placed in order for the concrete to attain maximum durability. Hydration stops if too much water is lost by evaporation or if the temperature falls below 50 degrees Fahrenheit.

Curing is an essential step and is designed to hold water in the concrete for the right length of time. To stop evaporation, several curing methods are used, the best of which is simply keeping the surface moist. To do this, wash out some burlap bags with a hose to remove any foreign matter that can cause discoloration. Place the bags on top of the concrete and wet them down, keeping them at least wet during the entire curing period. Don't worry about the concrete's being too wet. Water won't hurt it.

You also can keep the surface wet by running a sprinkler or soaking hose continuously over the surface. For small jobs, try ponding, or building dikes around the edges of the job, which keep a pool of water on the slab.

An easier but less effective way to cure concrete is to spread sheet plastic or waterproof paper over the entire surface. These materials form a moisture barrier and thus prevent evaporation. To do a proper job, however, the plastic or paper must be thoroughly sealed at joints, and anchored firmly on all sides. The material must be laid perfectly flat to avoid discoloration.

Curing time can be as little as three days, but at least five days are recommended in warm weather, and seven in cold weather. During very hot, dry weather, hydration may occur very rapidly, and precautions should be taken to prevent excess evaporation while working. Be sure to wet the area thoroughly before placing, and work as rapidly as possible. Try to work in some sort of shade; avoid the hot hours of late morning and early afternoon. The cooler hours will be kinder to your body as well as to the concrete.

Decorative Finishes

Many people are perfectly content with regular concrete. There are, however, a variety of specialized concrete applications which have more eye appeal than plain concrete.

Coloring. If you have ever tried to paint concrete, you know that all too soon the paint wears or starts flaking off. Those who like colored concrete are well advised to pay the extra cost of having color worked into the concrete itself. If you simply want a nice white look instead of the usual concrete gray, order white Portland cement instead of regular. It costs a little more, but not that much, and there are no special directions to be followed.

Other colors require the addition of a pigment, and this is done in several ways. A coloring agent (a mineral oxide made especially for concrete) is added to the mix before it is poured. This can be done with ready mix or with batches made from scratch. Coloring agents are available from most of the same sources that provide cement. The agents should not exceed 10 percent of the cement by weight.

Guide for Mixed-in Concrete Colors

Color Desired	Materials to Use
White	White Portland cement, white sand
Brown	Burnt umber, or brown oxide of iron (yellow oxide of iron will modify color)
Buff	Yellow ocher, yellow oxide of iron
Gray	Normal Portland cement
Green	Chromium oxide (yellow oxide of iron will shade)
Pink	Red oxide of iron (small amount)
Rose	Red oxide of iron
Cream	Yellow oxide of iron

For true colors, white Portland cement and white or light-colored aggregates should be used.
Not more than 9 lb. (4 kg.) of pigment should be used for each bag of cement.
Directions of the pigment manufacturer should be followed.

To save money on pigment, you can pour the concrete in 2 courses, using the coloring agent only in the top course. If you do this, however, be sure to leave the surface of the first course very rough to provide good tooth, or purchase, for the second. The top course need be only ½ to 1 inch thick.

If you prefer to use the quicker but more costly 1-course method, make sure either to soak the ground thoroughly the night before or to put down a moisture barrier like plastic sheeting *under* the slab. If you don't, some pigment may escape with the water and cause uneven coloring.

You can also color the concrete with dry shake compounds, applied by hand to the surface just before final floating. Two applications are necessary, and the surface must be floated, edged, and grooved after each of them.

Exposed Aggregate. This popular terrazzo-like finish takes extra time, effort, and money, but the investment is worthwhile. The result is antiskid and highly durable, as well as very attractive. For best results, use colorful, rounded pebbles of equal size. Adjust your usual concrete formula to provide a stiffer mix with more and larger aggregates.

First, place this concrete mix in the usual manner, without the stones. Level it off at ⅜ to ½ inch below the top of the forms to allow for the extra aggregate. Screed and float in the usual way, then spread your rounded stones evenly over the surface with your shovel. Fill in the bare spots by hand until the surface is completely covered with aggregate. If the first few stones sink to the bottom, wait a half hour or so until the mix gets a little stiffer.

When you have a good, even stone cover, tap it into the surface of the concrete with a 2 × 4, darby, or wood hand float, working the stones down into the concrete until they are entirely covered again by cement paste. The surface will look almost as it did before.

Wait for an hour or two until the weight of a man on kneeboards does not leave an indentation. Then brush the surface lightly with a stiff nylon-bristle broom to remove the excess mortar.

The final and most difficult job is hard-brooming the surface while washing the stones with a fine spray. Either have a helper for this, or alternately spray and broom. But brush hard enough to dislodge as much cement film as you can. Ideally, you should see only the pretty, colorful stones. If the surface is too dull, give it a bath with muriatic acid. (Your supplier may be able to rent you a combination spray-broom which will do both jobs at one time.)

Tap the stones into the concrete with a darby, hand float or piece of 2 × 4. (Portland Cement Association)

Go over the entire area with a hand float, pressing the stone in so that the surface looks like a normal slab after floating. (Portland Cement Association)

Brush and spray the surface alternately to dislodge as much cement film as you can and expose the aggregate. A combination spray-broom can be rented from some dealers. (Portland Cement Association)

Brooming is an effective way to create a surface texture which is attractive and also helps prevent skidding. (Portland Cement Association)

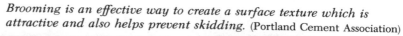

Textured and Novelty Finishes. The only limitation when finishing concrete is lack of imagination. Almost any pattern is acceptable as long as you can figure out a way to apply it.

A textured finish is one in which the regular floated or troweled surface is altered in some way. The most common and easiest pattern is a broom finish. Simply work a stiff-bristle broom back and forth over a newly floated surface. Either a straight or wavy pattern provides a good-looking, skid-resistant surface. An attractive swirl finish is produced by making semicircles with a hand float or trowel. To produce a uniform pattern, use your entire arm and keep your wrist rigid.

For another textured surface, scatter rock salt over the top of the slab after hand floating or troweling. Press the salt into the surface so that it is almost invisible. After the concrete has hardened, wash and brush to dissolve the salt and leave a pitted surface.

Geometric patterns can be pressed into the concrete surface using a variety of tools or instruments. A piece of curved copper pipe, for example, can be used to produce a random flagstone pattern. Make the scored lines, which look like recessed joints, after bullfloating and while the mix is still plastic. Run the pipe through again after hand floating and clean the joints of burrs with a fine broom and a soft-bristled paintbrush. You can use empty cans of varied sizes to create circles, or rent stamp-like devices to create brick and other patterns.

PRECAST CONCRETE

Precast concrete is available in a variety of applications, from an entire set of steps to small squares or circles. Precast slabs for patios or sidewalks are very handy, but are too heavy for hand work and require a vacuum lifting device.

Precast rounds come in regular, exposed-aggregate, and other patterns. They are ideal for informal patios, garden walks, and other uses. Blocks can be used in formal as well as rustic settings. For proper installation, the ground beneath precast blocks should be level, with a flat bed of sand or mortar on top of the subgrade.

As long as traffic isn't too heavy, you can sometimes get an excellent result by casting sections of concrete in place yourself. A flagstone-like walk can be built by carefully digging out sections of

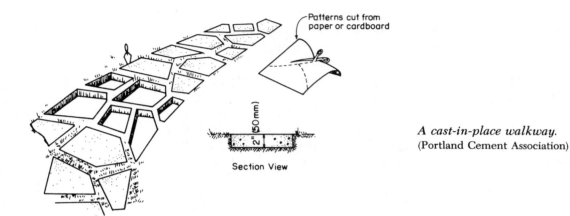

A cast-in-place walkway.
(Portland Cement Association)

ground, pouring sand beds up to 2 inches below the surface, and pouring concrete into the holes. Patterns help eliminate guesswork.

OTHER TYPES OF WALKS

As discussed previously, walkways can be made of brick, stone, or slate laid in sand or concrete just as you would for patios. Wood blocks laid on edge or long slats can also be used for walks. For walks that are not in frequent use, wood chips or bark, pebbles, gravel, or asphalt can be employed.

If you do use loose materials such as bark or pebbles, they should be confined so that they don't spill over into the flower bed, the grass, or other areas where you don't want them. Use wood 2 × 4s or 2 × 6s on each side of a walk of this type, or switch to other materials when spillover could be a nuisance.

Be careful, too, when using any type of pebble or gravel, to choose stones that are smooth and rounded. Sharp edges can be difficult to walk on—especially if you or other members of your family like to walk barefoot. Unless you have a particular yen for this type of walkway, it is best to use solid materials. Wood chips, bark, pebbles, and similar materials are better suited for mulch or for dressing up plantings than for walks.

If you use any type of wood as a surface or divider, be sure that it is specified for outdoor use. Chemically treated wood should be marked as suitable for ground contact. Other types of wood that can be used are all-heart redwood or red cedar, or cypress.

REPAIRS AND PATCHING

If a section of driveway or sidewalk is heaved and broken by tree roots, the best cure is to break it up with a sledgehammer, remove the concrete, and chop off the root. A tree with roots that big and powerful will be mature enough to survive the surgery. Afterward, you can simply replace the sidewalk section. Save the broken pieces and use them as fill.

If the problem is flaking or other surface deterioration, you can probably do a quick and easy job with vinyl patching cement. This type of patch can be feathered at the edges and will not wear off like some other cement compounds. Chip out the bad areas and apply the vinyl patch with a steel trowel. Use sparingly and quickly. It's expensive and dries fast.

When only certain areas are damaged or if there is a large crack that should be filled, the deteriorated parts should be cut out with a cold chisel. Undercut the crack or edge so that the crack is narrower at the surface than underneath. Ordinary concrete, with finer aggregates, can be used for patching, or premixed non-vinyl patch, available at the hardware store, can be used. The undercut edges should hold the patch in the same way that your tooth holds a filling.

If the original concrete job was a poor one, resulting in overall deterioration, patching is too mild a word for what has to be done. The only remedy is to cover the whole surface. You can't do this with regular concrete unless you break up all the old concrete and start anew.

Although the remedy isn't cheap, it is much less expensive and space-saving than completely starting over or putting a new slab over the old one. A topping such as a silicone material can be laid down over the entire surface in a thickness of only ⅛ inch.

Blacktop will deteriorate, too, especially if you fail to provide a sealant every 2 or 3 years. When it gets badly cracked, about all you can do is dig it out and put in new asphalt. If just part of the driveway has broken down, however, cold patch can be purchased in bulk at asphalt plants, or bags of premix can be bought at most building-supply houses. Cold patch is not as effective as the real thing, which should be applied hot and compacted by a roller. (That is why I don't encourage the homeowner to use blacktop.)

You can, however, make a decent cold patch, which will stand out brightly at first but should blend in better with age and a few sealings. All loose material should be removed to a depth of 2 inches or more.

You can use fill if the hole is deeper than that. Really deep holes can be filled with almost anything, but the fill shouldn't extend any higher than 4 inches below the surface. Use a 2-inch gravel fill between the junk and the blacktop. The finer the grade, the better.

The preliminary work can be done anytime, but wait for a hot sunny day to lay the blacktop. The warmer the blacktop, the easier it is to work. Pour the blacktop so that the patch projects about ½ inch above the surface. Pack it down hard and thoroughly with an iron tamper. For very small jobs, a shovel or rake may suffice.

Not only *can* you drive over the patch right away, you *should* drive over it a couple of times, back and forth in as many directions as possible. Drive smoothly and avoid skidding or accelerating quickly. The car's tires will act as rollers and help compact the material.

Outdoor Wiring and Lighting 12

Outdoor wiring and lighting are perhaps the most neglected aspects of landscape planning. It is only when you realize that there is nowhere to plug in the electric fire starter or that the party must be called, or at least move inside, because of darkness, that the importance of exterior electricity is realized.

Outdoor lighting not only is convenient but adds to safety and security. Properly located outlets can provide power for electric lawnmowers, hedge clippers, and other outdoor equipment. Your outdoor kitchen and living areas will be greatly enhanced by electricity for barbecue starters, revolving spits, blenders, and other appliances. Radios, television sets, video games (if you like), and other power-driven conveniences and luxuries can transform your outdoors into true 24-hour living space. Even more important, lights can obliterate the dark recesses around your home that invite burglars or can illuminate dim steps and walks that are common sites of nighttime accidents.

If you are fortunate enough to have recreational areas outdoors such as a swimming pool, tennis court, horseshoe pit, or basketball hoop, there is no need to use them only during daylight hours. Proper lighting can give you many more hours of fun from these facilities.

The intelligent use of outdoor lighting also can greatly enhance the beauty of a house at night. Spotlights can highlight an inviting doorway or a handsome tree; "bonnets" and similar lights allow night-time enjoyment of a flower garden or of other outdoor features.

No burglars can lurk in the shadows of this home, because there aren't any, thanks to intelligent lighting. Also note the ornamental tree lit from below. (General Electric)

EQUIPMENT

There are several ways to approach outdoor wiring and lighting. If you will need only a few lights to highlight some feature of the landscape or point the way down a pathway or the steps, modern low-voltage lighting may be the best choice. It is safe and easy to work with. Once the transformer is installed to the standard-voltage line, anyone can work on the circuit on the low-voltage side of the transformer with perfect safety and with no fear of code violations. Low-voltage lighting is explored at greater length at the end of this chapter.

Here is an imaginative use of equipment not originally designed for outdoor lighting. The swivel spotlights, meant for indoor use, were converted to 12-voltage lighting with a transformer. They are mounted in a protected location in the soffit. A Japanese lantern was wired to accommodate a 12-volt bulb, which casts a warm, flame-like glow through the amber glass. (General Electric)

What Lights to Use Where

In general, lighting should fit the task at hand. Low-voltage lighting, for example, can serve nicely for pointing out walkways and providing understated illumination of a favorite low-growing flower bed. If you want to play outdoor sports at night, high-wattage floodlights or high-intensity lights should be used.

Where the bulb and wiring are completely enclosed or there is an overhang which protects the fixture from the elements, standard incandescent or fluorescent lamps may be used. When the fixture is unprotected from the rain or snow, use projector (PAR) lamps in suitable outdoor fixtures. Colored lights are available in both standard and PAR types for special effects. Portable fixtures, spiked into the ground, may be useful if you wish to vary the locations for different seasons—daffodils in spring, for example, or roses in June.

For most uses, the lower wattages should be tried first. If they don't give enough light, try the next higher wattage. Electricity costs money, and understatement is esthetically more pleasing than overdoing it, especially for lighting landscaping features.

Use	Type of Fixture	Wattage
WALKS AND STEPS	Mushroom, bonnet, pagoda; recessed, if wall available.	25–60
PATIOS AND DECKS	Same as above, plus spotlights or brackets on house.	40–150
OUTDOOR KITCHEN	At least two PAR fixtures on poles or in trees, 12–20 ft. above ground, 20 ft. away.	150–200
SPORTS AND GAMES	PAR floods mounted on house, trees, or poles, at least 16 ft. above ground; high-intensity.	150 and up
FLOWER BEDS	Mushroom, bonnet, pagoda. PAR floods for wide area.	25–40 standard 75–150 PAR
TREES	PAR spot and floodlamps, at least 2 for highlighting, mounted high; for background, mount or spike into ground.	150–200
SCULPTURE	PAR flood or spot placed above and left of viewer; additional light for "modeling" if desired.	75–150
SECURITY	Brackets under eaves; PAR floods and spots in open. Illuminate doors and low windows to discourage burglars.	100–150

At the opposite extreme are areas where you need large amounts of light for extended periods. An example might be tennis courts which are in frequent use at night or a house whose perimeter is lighted at all times for security. If this is the case, high-intensity lighting, using sodium or halide lamps, is more efficient and less costly in the long run. You'll have to see an electrical contractor if you believe high-intensity lighting may be best for you.

Most of us probably fall into the middle category. We not only need some low lighting for safety's sake along our walkways, but we'd also like some higher wattage and a few outlets for appliances.

High-intensity Discharge Lamps
Recommendations for Type and Amount of Lighting

Type of Lighting	No. of Foot-candles	Type of Lamp and Ratings
SECURITY	0.2	High-pressure sodium, 50–200 watts; low-pressure sodium, 35–180 watts
GENERAL (*driveways, walks, etc.*)	1.0	High-pressure sodium, 100–400 watts; low-pressure sodium, 180 watts; metal halide, 250–400 watts for best color
ACTIVITY AREAS (*recreation, sports, etc.*)	3.0	High-pressure sodium, 200–400 watts; metal halide, 250–400 watts for best color; low-pressure sodium, 180 watts

Note: Mounting height should be 20–25 feet, with shielding for a 45-degree cutoff. Mercury lights are omitted here because of their lower efficiency. Do not interchange incandescent and mercury lamps unless mercury lamps have built-in ballasts designed for that purpose. Both types of lamps are likely to be damaged or destroyed if connected to improper circuits.

Source: Adapted from data by the Illuminating Engineering Society

Special Equipment

Outdoor work is a completely new ball game as far as electrical equipment is concerned. Water is the traditional enemy of electrical equipment, and any exterior installation needs protection not only from the wet but from corrosion, frost, animals, and other outdoor hazards.

Consequently, each electrical cable and device has to be specially designed to withstand the elements. Obviously, cable must be buried deep enough to ward off the spades of landscapers and the claws of dogs in search of bones. Not so obvious, perhaps, is the fact that it may have to be buried deep enough to ward off the effects of frost—heaving of the earth, for example. The types of cable best suited for underground use and the depths at which they must be buried are specified by the National Electrical Code (NEC). I highly recommend that you also check your local code for this information, as the requirements vary according to the specifics of the intended use of the installation.

Since 1975, every exterior installation has had to be protected with a special safety switch—a ground-fault interrupter—that gives an extra measure of safety in case of a short or other circuit failure. It was always an excellent idea to provide this additional safety device, and no one should try to circumvent the code in this respect. Technically called a ground-fault *circuit* interrupter (GFCI), this device is usually referred to without the word "circuit," and GFI is the more common abbreviation. It is what its name implies: a supersensitive circuit breaker or fuse that shuts down the circuit in about ¼₀th the time that a standard breaker would take. Only 0.005 of an

Fixtures must be specialized for outdoor use, unless they are away from the weather under the eaves. Shown here are some of the various weatherproof fixtures. These can be mounted on walls, risers, or adjacent buildings. They are often used in stairways with enclosed walls. Top to bottom: a portable unit for projector (PAR) lamps; a similar unit, with deep metal shield; a mercury adjustable floodlight on enclosed ballast; a floodlight with cover lens; an enclosed "handy" floodlight, with a cover glass that allows the use of regular household bulbs up to 300 watts; a flush-mounted fixture for projector lamps (housings are available for use with 150–500 watt PAR lamps or mercury lamps); a mushroom unit and, below, a bonnet, both used for general landscape lighting; a fancier version of the last 2, flower-shaped for gardens and steps; a recessed unit with lens or louver control. (General Electric)

Outdoor fixtures must be specifically designated for such use. Left to right are a receptacle outlet with snap-up cover, exterior switch plate, and special outdoor box. Gasket between box and cover helps keep water from getting to wires.

amp over the standard amperage trips the GFI, thus insuring that a shock caused by a defect in the system will last only a tiny fraction of a second and that serious injury or death will be prevented.

All fixtures and devices used outdoors must be specifically designed for such use. Lights must have waterproof sockets, outlets must be protected by waterproof covers, and all boxes must be of weatherproof aluminum or steel (known as T or PF boxes). Switches and receptacles are the same as those used indoors, but waterproof covers and gaskets protect the wires inside from the elements. Cable must be specifically designed for outdoor use. Either nonmetallic type UF cable, which is encased in tough plastic, must be used, or the wires must be run through rigid conduit (sometimes both are advisable, as discussed below). All aboveground wiring must be shielded in conduit, even if type UF cable is used.

Local codes can be even more restrictive than the NEC with regard to outdoor wiring, and the NEC is quite restrictive in itself. This is as it should be, because of the many hazards of outdoor installations.

Nevertheless, the basic technique and overall circuit theory are the same as for indoor work. The same general methods and principles apply, and if you are somewhat familiar with electrical work, you should be able to adapt them to outdoor work. The differences will be explained here as we progress. If you know very little or nothing about electrical wiring, it is suggested that you hire a licensed electrician—or get some practice first indoors.

PLANNING

The theory of circuit planning is the same as that for indoor work. If you have an underutilized circuit and do not plan on a high-wattage load outdoors, you can tap into the existing circuit. A 20-amp circuit extension is generally advised, however. Otherwise, start a new circuit from the entrance panel (20-amp, with # 12 wire).

Before you even begin the technical planning, some careful thinking about function and esthetics must be done. First, take a critical look at your property. Functional needs include such things as safe steps and walkways, visible entrances, and well-lighted recreation areas. Esthetic considerations include comfortable lighting in lounging areas, highlighted landscape features, and avoiding the parking-lot look.

Judicious use of outdoor lighting means combining the practical with the esthetic. In this backyard, 2 75-watt blue-white reflector lamps light the patio from above, while the up-lighting into large trees forms a canopy of light which is reflected into the area. (General Electric)

There must be a judicious balance between practical and esthetic considerations. Yes, you want an entrance walkway that can be traversed safely, but you don't need to bathe the entire area in eye-straining glare. You want a patio where you can entertain, but it doesn't have to be lit up like a baseball stadium.

To many people, outdoor lighting means a series of spotlights making the area as bright as day. This *is* a good idea for play areas, such as tennis or basketball courts, or perhaps for the parking area. It is not wise for other installations.

Steps and walkways, for example, are more suited for intermittent mushroom or pagoda lights. If the pathway is straight, perhaps lights at the beginning and end are enough. Add others at curves and corners. There should be enough light on steps so that no one trips over them but not so much that it is blinding. That is all that is necessary. If there are walls alongside, recessed lights are adequate and attractive. Otherwise, rely on the bonnet type of light.

Patios and decks serve a multitude of purposes. If you like sitting outdoors on warm summer nights, install mushroom or pagoda lights on the perimeter, with plenty of outlets for portable lights, radio, television, or barbecue spits. For parties, add spotlights. Even better, fit overhead lights with a dimmer control. That way you have full control over how much illumination you want. After all, with too much artificial light, you can't see the moon and the stars.

Bring out your creative best by highlighting trees, shrubs, and other landscape features. Use your imagination to conjure up special patterns, textures, and colors. One secret here is to place the lights so that they are themselves unobtrusive.

Regardless of where and how you place your outdoor lights, do all that you can to keep them in the background. Avoid glare at all costs. If you light your entrance walk in such a way that the lights shine in your guests' faces, it is just as bad as, or worse than, having no lights at all.

DOING THE WORK

Once your plans are carefully drawn up, it's time to get to work. No matter how you slice it, outdoor electrical work is expensive. Every device that is suited for the outdoors costs more than its interior counterpart because of the need for weatherproofing. Even if you use low-voltage lights, the initial cost for the transformer is relatively high, although additions to the system cost less.

The first step is to bring the current outdoors. You may be able to tap into an existing outdoor light, such as one located on the porch. In most cases, this will involve using an exterior box extender because there will probably not be enough room in your present box for an additional set of wires, and since most of these lights are placed high, you probably will have to run conduit all the way down to the ground, which is both unattractive and expensive.

The most common way to bring the current outside is to either tap into an underutilized circuit inside, or run a new circuit from the entrance panel. In either case, you must somehow get the cable through the exterior wall or foundation. (See page 272 for running cable through masonry.)

The most desirable way to begin is to install a switch inside the house near the outside door. If this is too difficult—and it often is—you might run conduit to the exterior, again near the door, and install an outside switch. In any event, the GFI must be placed on the line somewhere before the first outside device.

The GFI

Depending on the routing, an exterior or interior GFI may be used. For example, a new circuit may be run from the entrance panel to the basement or garage, where you can install a receptacle-type interior GFI. (This also provides a needed outlet in the garage.) The cable can then be run directly from the GFI through the header joists directly above the sill plate. Use a ⅞-inch spade bit to drill through the header, and insert a small piece of ½-inch rigid conduit in the hole to lead outside from the GFI. Type UF cable can be inserted through the conduit to an elbow on the other end, where it can run through more conduit up to the exterior switch.

On the incoming line or feed side of the GFI, a white wire is attached to the white wire of standard Type NM cable (nonmetallic sheathed cable, popularly called Romex). The black wires are similarly attached with solderless connectors (wire nuts). The corresponding wires on the outgoing load side of the GFI are attached to Type UF wiring. Use solderless connectors throughout.

When the wires to the GFI are attached properly, they are inserted into the box and covered with the special plate that comes with it. When the cable is attached to the entrance panel, the GFI becomes operational. If anything is wrong in the wiring on the line side, the GFI trips, shutting off the current on the load side of the circuit, as well as in the integral outlet, if any. The GFI may be reset, if there is only a temporary surge, by pressing the button so marked. If there is a short or other serious flaw, the GFI will keep tripping. (When that happens, shut off the current to the entire circuit and check for such defects as loose or crossed wires. Better yet, call in a licensed electrician.) There is also a test button to make sure the GFI is working properly.

Conduit

As mentioned above, all exposed outside work must be enclosed in conduit. Rigid metal or PVC plastic conduit is permitted by the NEC, but local codes also should be consulted. For the work described, the simplest method is to extend rigid metal conduit from the boxes into the ground and use bare Type UF cable underground for horizontal runs between the boxes.

When deciding which type of underground wiring to use, you must balance several factors. The easiest material to work with is bare Type UF cable, but this must be buried below the frost line and at least 2 feet below the surface. If the ground is rocky, full of hard clay, or has a high water table, conduit may be a better choice. Rigid metal conduit need be buried only 6 inches below the surface, while PVC conduit should be buried a foot below the surface. (Thin-wall EMT is not recommended for underground use.) Rigid metal costs quite a bit more than the other types and is very difficult to bend. The PVC conduit bends more easily but is more difficult to put together, requiring special connectors. (Rigid metal is prethreaded.) All types of conduit require that Type TW or UF wiring be pulled through after the conduit is laid.

It is impossible for anyone to say which method will work best for you. You must consider weather, type of soil, cost, and so on.

Type UF cable should be installed as flat and as straight as possible in the bottom of the trench. Where it is brought up to the boxes, lengths of rigid metal should be used, with plastic bushings on the ends to avoid cutting the cable on the sharp end threads.

Exterior Boxes

Although many local codes forbid it, the NEC allows exterior T or PF boxes to be placed underground as long as they are not under sidewalks, driveways, or other obstructions, and as long as they are

The bottom of this exterior box has 2 "screw-outs." Wires enter through one hole, and a support pipe is screwed into the other. Cable proceeds to next box through hole in back.

Weathertight connections are a must. Use a wrench to tighten the nut and plastic bushing over the wires. (L. Donald Meyers)

easily identifiable and accessible. Instead of "knockouts," which are supplied on interior boxes and which are punched or pressed out to allow entry of the cable, exterior boxes have "screw-outs," which are turned on with a screwdriver. You can use 2-foot lengths of ½-inch pipe in one hole for stability and insert the cable into the other knockout with special exterior connectors. These fittings have plastic bushings that are squeezed into the cable inside the conduit fittings to make a weathertight connection and keep the cable from slipping or getting damaged by the metal.

A word of caution for those using exterior cable connectors. Always put the cable inside the plastic bushing before attaching the other parts. Otherwise, you will have a very difficult time squeezing the cable through. Even then, it isn't easy assembling these fittings. You may have to use a lubricant and sometimes a hammer to get all the parts together. They are supposed to be tight, and they are. Use a wrench to screw the assembled fittings to the box.

Completed assembly shows solid watertight cover and gasket over box, lamp screwed into top of box with rigid conduit.
(L. Donald Meyers)

Outside boxes are attached to walls, railroad ties, or whatever you want by nailing or screwing through one of the punch-out screw holes in the back of the box. You will have to punch out the back of the box to get completely through. Rigid conduit actually holds the box in place, so don't worry about a little looseness when you attach the boxes. The conduit is secured with conduit straps. You can install boxes without actually attaching them to anything because the conduit will hold the box up. Where conduit does not extend far enough into the ground to give stability, drop a concrete block around the box and fill the hole in the block with gravel.

Recessed Fixtures

To install a recessed fixture in a retaining wall, stairway, or elsewhere, make a fixture-sized opening in the wall. Use a cold chisel for concrete, brick, or other hard material. If the wall is thick, bore a ⅞-inch hole through to the back of the wall with a masonry bit or star drill. Install an outdoor box at the back of the wall, and connect the two with a nipple. Run the wires from the fixture to the box through the nipple and caulk any opening with mortar. Boxes can be recessed into concrete blocks or other masonry using similar techniques. Before drilling completely into a concrete block, make a test hole to make sure that you hit a hollow part of the block. Adjust the hole if necessary so that it fits into one of the cores instead of a solid section. Avoid the top row of a block foundation, because it is usually solid. (The same applies for bringing cable through a foundation.)

LOW-VOLTAGE OUTDOOR LIGHTING

Low-voltage outdoor lighting has most of the advantages of standard outdoor lighting and is quickly and easily installed with minimum risk. Like low-voltage indoor wiring, it operates from a transformer that steps down the voltage to a hazard-free 12 volts. The lighting is not as powerful as standard outdoor illumination, nor can receptacles for outdoor equipment be installed. For decorative or walkway lighting, however, it is an excellent choice.

The expensive part of the installation is the transformer, which usually is sold as part of a kit with 6 or so integrated lights. Some kits also contain a timer built into the transformer unit so that the lights can be turned off and on automatically. Once you have the transformer, you can add other lights at minimal cost.

The transformer must be UL-listed for outdoor use. It is installed on the line side in the same way as is any other outdoor fixture. Regular cable or conduit must be used up to the transformer, which is installed in the same way as is an indoor transformer. On the load, or outgoing side, however, there are no restrictions as to where and how the wiring must be installed.

Follow manufacturer's instructions for running the wiring, installing lights, and so on. Most lights can be installed anywhere by spiking them into the ground. Wiring can usually be buried slightly underground or laid on top of the ground, if desired. To avoid damage, however, it is best to run the wire alongside a solid structure, such as a sidewalk, fence, or retaining wall. If wire is not included in the kit, check the instructions to make sure you use the correct size and type of cable.

Index

.